DREAM CATCHER

Based on a true story

TOM SPINKS

DREAM CATCHER

A Story of Friendship, Family, and Football

Melinda Folse

with

Kimberly Spinks Burleson
and
Teri Spinks Netterville

THE FOLSE GROUP

Dream Catcher: A Story of Friendship, Family, and Football

ISBN: 978-0-9826960-4-0

The Folse Group LLC
Fort Worth, TX
www.folsegroup.com

Printed in the United States of America

Back cover photos courtesy of Spinks family
Cover design by Richard McQuillar
Book design by Caroline Petty

"I believe that imagination is stronger than knowledge. That myth is more potent than history. That dreams are more powerful than facts. That hope always triumphs over experience. That laughter is the only cure for grief. And I believe that love is stronger than death."

— Robert Fulgham
All I Really Need

FOREWORD: BRADSHAW TO SPINKS

Written by Terry Bradshaw on January 27, 1988 on the occasion of Tommy Spinks' induction into the Louisiana Tech University Hall of Fame.

I remember the first time I met Tommy; he had just transferred to Oak Terrace Junior High School from Alexandria. He was extremely warm, friendly, but more importantly, he was funny. He had the silliest laugh. And, he always squinched his nose when he laughed.

The other thing that stuck out in my mind the most was that he was a natural shortstop. He had the greatest hand-eye coordination I had ever seen. He was a natural athlete. But he had one major drawback. He was slow.

We both attended Woodlawn High School and Tommy had beaten me out for the junior varsity quarterback spot. He was a better ball handler, a better runner, and even a better passer, especially on the sprint outs, and all the players liked him. He was fun to be around.

Going into our senior year, I went to Lee Hedges and told him what a great pair of hands Tommy had. Now, I figure if I can convince Hedges to make Spinks a wide receiver, then that leaves only me to quarterback. I thought that this was a proper and fair thing to do since I was only concerned about winning.

Now, Spinks becomes an all-state wide receiver. He also becomes Mr. Woodlawn High School. But above all his accomplishments, he was my best friend. We were pals.

We used to throw the football up and down the field at Woodlawn pretending that every pass was the most important pass in the game. Up and down the field we would go until we were exhausted.

I always felt that no one was as dedicated to the love of football as much as I was. Tommy was my equal. He made me great in high school. He made me greater in college. And of this writing, he was the best receiver I have had including pro football.

He had the best hands and moves, and a heart bigger than his big ole' ugly smile. I learned how to play quarterback by throwing passes to you, Tommy. I developed all my skills in our backyards in Southwood and on the football field at Louisiana Tech.

I am so proud of you for finally being recognized for what you really are – the greatest receiver that Louisiana Tech has ever had. One thing really puzzles me though. How in the world can someone so ugly get into the Tech Hall of Fame?

Congratulations,
Your Buddy,
Terry

PROLOGUE

It's another hot, Louisiana Fourth of July, and it couldn't be more beautiful. I can smell the burgers on the grill, and I can hear the voices of little girls in the pool yelling "Marco . . . Polo!"

Most of the boys, stair-stepped in ages, big and small, are running around in the spacious front yard playing football under the tall pine trees. This is where I love to be, sitting on the marble bench under the oak tree, watching the kids play ball with as much heart and passion as my best friend and I did back when we were kids.

I see my oldest daughter, Kimberly, now making her way toward me with a tall glass of sweet tea in hand. She sits down beside me and together we watch the children playing football on the expansive green lawn.

Kimberly turns to me now, an earnest curiosity in her eyes. "Dad," she asks, "Did you always dream of being in the NFL?"

I thought for a moment. "No," I said. "It was Terry who had that dream. I just caught it. Dreams are contagious, Baby. You have to live your life having many dreams — and following each one of them."

My attention is diverted back to the football game on the lawn with my grandchildren. How big they have grown. Watching my oldest grandson throw a perfect spiral pass to his younger cousin, my mind whisks back to that summer of '62 . . .

CHAPTER 1

The spiky leaves of the holly hedge tickled my nose as I strained to get just enough taller to see what was going on — but not so tall as to be detected. Just about every afternoon when I rode by this one particular yard after school the thick hedge, clipped even with the top of the chain link fence, kept me from being able to see inside the yard.

Day after day as I rode by on my bike during my afternoon exploration of my new neighborhood, I heard sounds in this yard that intrigued me beyond measure. Someone on the other side of the dense green barrier was talking, sometimes yelling, and often, calling out numbers. Then there would be a sound of shuffling steps, followed by a thud and a rattle — and sometimes a metallic crash. I couldn't tell how many people were back there, or what they were doing, but this mystery had developed a magnetic pull on both my imagination *and* my bicycle. I couldn't resist riding past this house any time I got the chance.

• • •

I attacked the hill that wound upwards from the end of our driveway, pouring my frustrated rage into every push of the pedals. From the first afternoon since we arrived in Shreveport, my daily bike ride under the guise of "exploring the neighborhood" had offered opportunity for some much-needed privacy as I struggled to cope with all that was happening. Each day as I rode, I replayed, again and again, the chain of events that had ruined my life.

"Son," my father had said through the telephone receiver in that fateful call from the Annual Methodist Conference, "Your Daddy has just been assigned to Summer Grove Methodist

Church in Shreveport, and the Bishop says I have to be there in two weeks." Without allowing any time for protest, he had continued, "Now, I'm gonna need for you to help your mama start getting things packed up and ready." He paused, as if realizing that the shock had set in to render me speechless. "I'm really sorry, son," he said, his tone softening a bit, "but you'll need to let your baseball coach know right away that you're leaving so he can have some time to shuffle the boys around." He cleared his throat in a weak attempt to cover the catch in his voice. "I love you, son, and I will see you tomorrow."

With those four sentences, my dad had destroyed my 13-year-old world and what I held dearest — playing baseball in the Dixie Youth Baseball Program. The unfairness of it all twisted in my gut and fueled my furious pedaling through the Southern Hills neighborhood of Shreveport I was now supposed to call home.

You see, I was a *star* in the baseball town of Alexandria, Louisiana. I was more than a legend in my own mind. Last year I pitched three no-hitters and five one-hitters in eight games. I hit 11 home runs in the whole 18-game season. Already this summer, just two games into the season, I had already hit three home runs. In my own mind, I was just about ready for the New York Yankees, and being the first kid drafted into the renowned Dixie Youth Baseball Program seemed like a solid first step.

How could my own father — my own flesh and blood — just end it all? He obviously missed the magnitude of the mistake he was making. How could he possibly make HIS job THE priority in our family, putting my baseball future at stake? How could he be so selfish?

I pedaled even faster as the road flattened out, as if more sweat could disguise the tears that now flowed along with my angry words. "How could the Bishop do that?" I cried aloud, letting the wind whisk away the words I couldn't say anywhere else. My rant gained momentum as I attacked each rolling hill, standing on the pedals on the steeper ones to stomp emphasis into each angry word. *I bet the Bishop never even played baseball. I bet he's just a great big sissy. Or a bookworm. He probably doesn't even know what a jock strap is for.* Not that I knew that yet, either, but that was beside the point.

Most days, my angry bike ride calmed me down. Today, however, felt different. The more I railed at the memory of that fateful afternoon and the awful days that followed when we all said our hasty goodbyes to Alexandria, the more worked up I got. So I just kept riding, way beyond where I usually went, looking for new hills to attack, new streets to explore, and new alleys rough enough to help me ride out my anger. And beyond the anger and grief lurked the clutch of fear that I would never, ever find friends like my Alexandria teammates — or the stardom that baseball would surely have lain at my feet.

I turned another corner and saw nothing familiar, but I kept riding anyway as my mother's words echoed in my head. "This is a really important appointment for your dad," Mom had tried to reason with me. "You and your sisters will have some adjustments to make, but the most important thing to remember is how proud we all are of Dad."

My dad, you see, was a beloved Methodist preacher in our little town. He had done his job — and done it well — by building up the membership of Trinity Methodist Church on Chester Street. In our world, Dad's success in Alexandria meant it was time for him to move on to a bigger church in a larger community. "That's just the way it works," Mom had explained.

Coasting a bit now, I looked around, trying to get my directional bearings as I let my mind go back to my last and greatest appeal to Mom. If Dad would listen to anyone, it was my mother. Plunking down that big 12 x 12 scrapbook she kept onto our kitchen table, I had summoned my most desperate and earnest plea.

"Mom?" I had said, fighting back real tears that no self-respecting baseball star should ever have to admit to, "Please. Do something to stop this from happening. What about baseball? What about *my* future?"

Taking the next downhill fast, I leaned into the curve, remembering each page of Mom's scrapbook in vivid detail. She had started that scrapbook when I started playing baseball, and even in just these few years it was packed with the newspaper clippings and photos she had gathered, pasted, and labeled — all about ME. If that wasn't proof of my potential for Major League

Baseball, I don't know what was. As I had tried hard to point out to my mother, staying in Alexandria — where my path to the bigs had already begun — was a moral obligation. Alexandria needed me. Every hometown needs its heroes to stick around, right? But even my most valiant and reasonable arguments held no quarter, even with Mom.

The wind whistled in my ears as the long downhill began to wind into a new street. I closed my eyes for a moment and let the wind wash over me, remembering as I did the tinge of sadness in my mother's eyes just before she dashed my last hope with the tight hug that told me it was over. We were moving to Shreveport. My life, as I knew it, had ended.

I rode on in numbed silence as acceptance started to settle in. With no idea how long I had been riding, or where in the heck I was, I realized I must be pretty far from home. The tears had long since mingled with sweat and dried into defeat, leaving a bitter taste in my mouth I was pretty sure would be permanent.

I looked all around me, unable to see the sun behind the tall pine trees that blocked the horizon and made each street undistinguishable from the next. I took a deep, tentative breath as a new issue surfaced. *Which way is home?* I kept riding, slower and more deliberate now, scanning the street signs at each intersection for something familiar.

As much as I hated to admit it, it was beautiful here in the hilly and picturesque Southern Hills area of Shreveport, Louisiana. The sound and the smell of the pine trees swaying in the afternoon breeze added their own small comfort, and I breathed it all in as I chose the direction that felt right and pedaled past street after street of enormous landscaped yards I couldn't help but admire.

Everything here, it seemed, was bigger. And while the people we'd met so far seemed warm and friendly enough — exuding much of the same southern charm we had loved in Alexandria — it still seemed impossible to me that this town could ever feel like home. And just because it wasn't the wasteland I imagined, that didn't mean I liked it.

I rounded the curve and suddenly realized that not only was I nearing my street, but also that I was approaching from a new angle a brick house that was about a block from ours. What had captured my attention about this house every single day was the strange sounds coming from its backyard. Approaching the house from this new direction, I could actually see into the backyard.

I stopped my bike in a place where I could sit and watch the gangly, blonde-haired boy I could now see playing in this backyard. While at first it looked like he was alone, what he was saying and doing made it seem like there were several other kids back there with him. Mesmerized, I began to piece together in my mind the sounds I had heard coming from that yard with what I was now seeing.

I positioned my bike a little further behind the tree where I was certain he could not see me, and in a full-on trance I watched this kid throw a football, first at a swing set, then a tree, then through the tire swing hanging from the tree. His next targets included a pigeon coop and then several different pieces of lawn furniture. The lawn furniture that skittered and collapsed when the ball found its mark explained the clatters and crashes. Each of his targets looked to be stationed at specific distances and angles in his backyard.

Then the kid started talking, but I couldn't make out what he was saying. I peered around the tree. Who was he talking to? I still couldn't see anyone else back there, but he was talking right out loud to someone. Laying down my bike at the curb, but still behind the tree, I inched closer to see if I could hear what he was saying.

Taking advantage of that same thick hedge surrounding the yard that had hidden me earlier on the other side, I was able to get close enough to realize that this kid was narrating a football game — apparently a big one — taking place inside his imagination. In his play-by-play commentary that sounded quite real to me, he was the star quarterback, and the objects he had placed in the yard were his receivers.

My attention was riveted as he took the imaginary snap, jogged back a few steps, positioning the ball in his right hand. He looked left, then right, as if trying to find his open receiver.

"Third and eight, Bradshaw fades back, he sees his man downfield and fires." He drilled a perfect spiral pass into the waiting arms of the lawn chair next to the fence. "COMPLETE!" he hollered as the lawn chair collapsed around the ball and clattered to the ground.

The commentary went on as the kid leaned down to pick up another football that was lying at his feet. "Man, is this kid great!" he said, adjusting the timbre but not the volume of his voice, just like they did on TV. "Can he do it again? It's first and ten, folks, but there are only seven seconds on the clock. Bradshaw takes the snap and fades back, dodging right. No one open. He moves left. Still, no one open. His receivers are all covered up with no time left on the clock. Wait! There's a man deep in the end zone! Bradshaw fires!"

I watched as the ball pounded onto the slide at the end of the swing set at the far end of the yard.

"COMPLETE!!" The kid's impression of an ecstatic announcer was spot-on.

Then the kid turned, cupped his hands to his mouth and hollered toward the sky to emulate the breathy, hollow roar of a stadium full of ecstatic fans.

Then, returning to his commentator voice, the kid continued his press box narration, "The crowd goes wild! Bradshaw has done it again!"

• • •

Every day for the next week or so, about the same time every afternoon, I returned to my hiding place behind the tree to watch this kid. And on most days he'd be out there — winning imaginary games by completing spectacular passes — and beating up lawn furniture with amazing speed and accuracy in what to my eyes seemed to be perfect passes. This goofy kid intrigued me not only with his love of throwing that football, but also the dedication and consistency of his daily solo practice.

Then one afternoon, to my surprise and terror, this kid starts jogging straight toward me. My heart pounded as my thoughts raced. *Has he seen me?* He wasn't looking at me. *Maybe he's taking an imaginary victory lap.*

The kid turned and opened the gate leading out of his yard. My heart was double-timing now to keep up with my panicked thoughts. *He's discovered me spying on him and now he's going to come over here and give me the "what for."* My panic continued to escalate with every step he took toward me.

The kid stopped right in front of me and stuck out his hand. "Hi, my name is Terry Bradshaw," he said, "You wanna throw some?"

CHAPTER 2

Do I wanna throw . . . what? I thought, but didn't dare say to this kid, who was much taller up close than he had looked from my hiding spot. *Do I look like someone who wants to catch something that has been destroying lawn furniture, swing sets and pigeon coops?*

With all the cool I could muster, I said, "No thank you, I just moved here and I play baseball, not football." I paused, sizing up the situation . . . and my escape route. I could probably make it to my bicycle before he caught me if I timed it right. Not only am I a quick thinker, but I'm also known for my quickness around the bases. So I decided to see if this guy had a sense of humor. "Plus," I added, grinning, "I think your spiral might kill me."

For just a moment he didn't react at all. I glanced at my bike. Then he burst into a laughter so deep and genuine it made me laugh, too. We just stood there laughing as both of us, I'm sure, imagined me walking around, cartoon style, with a hole drilled right through my breadbasket.

Wiping his eyes with the heel of his hand he took a step back, sizing me up.

"It probably won't kill you," he said. Then he grinned. "Especially if you catch it right."

I pondered this for a moment. I wasn't sure how many ways there were to catch a football. *Don't you just catch the thing however you can?* I thought, but didn't dare ask. Football, in my mind, was a sport that didn't require nearly as much finesse as baseball.

Intruding on my thoughts, Terry said, "I haven't seen you around before. Are you new?"

"Yeah," I said, looking down at my shoes and stubbing one toe in the dirt. *Is it that obvious?* "We just moved here from Alexandria," I said. "I was in a really great baseball program there and was actually doing pretty well." I decided to go with humility since I had just met this kid. Dad always hated it when I bragged. He called it "tooting my own horn." "Let other people do the bragging on you, son," he always said.

"Well I don't know if we even *have* baseball here," Terry said. "And if we do, nobody plays it. Football is what's king in Shreveport," he added, taking on the air of a local expert. Then he grinned. "Besides," he said, "if you want to get the girls you gotta play football."

Suddenly it looked like I might need to figure out how to become a football player.

Tossing the football back and forth in his hands, Terry continued as self-appointed Shreveport expert, "There is a new high school here in Shreveport called Woodlawn High," he said. "It's only been here two years, and their football team has already won district." The excitement in his voice rose with each factoid. "Those guys get crowds of 15,000 coming to watch their Friday night games."

"Wow," I said. "That's a lot of people." I had never seen that many people at our Alexandria high school baseball games. Maybe this guy was onto something.

"So you know what?" Terry said, still tossing that football back and forth, "I'm not only gonna be the quarterback for the Woodlawn Knights, I'm gonna get recruited to play in college, and then I'm gonna play pro football after college, and then after that I'm gonna be in the Football Hall of Fame."

I didn't know whether to believe these far-fetched future accolades delivered as matters of fact — or to get on my bike and get out of there fast because this guy was crazy. But something in his tone intrigued me beyond his words. After weeks of mourning my shattered life without baseball and Alexandria, I felt something new stirring inside me. "Ok, I'll throw that thing with you," I said, reaching over to grab the football mid-toss. "But you're going to need to take it easy for a few throws 'til I figure some stuff out."

"Deal," he said, heading back toward his backyard.

I followed him through the gate to the yard that would be our first gridiron, striped with an imagination so vivid that I could see the stadium — formerly known as hedges — now surrounding us. In that single moment I knew my life was about to change. This big kid that lived around the corner became my first and best friend in Shreveport. From that moment on we were as inseparable as the football that was almost always being passed between us. We communicated almost exclusively in excited recaps of games we watched, plays we heard about, or dreams of our near and far-off football futures.

For the rest of that summer of '62, Terry and I threw the football every single day in his backyard . . . and when it got too dark to see, we moved under the street lights. Now, when I say "we" threw, what I mean is that Terry stood in one spot and *I* ran all over the yard as he directed my every move.

I wasn't wrong about the velocity of his passes, either. I learned after that first day that I'd better get good at catching those bullet passes pretty darn quick if I was going to survive. I thought of the cartoon character with the hole through his midsection often in those first few days of learning to catch what Terry threw.

Terry's backyard was huge. With his house sitting close to the street, there was lots of room on the gradual slope toward the creek that ran parallel to the house. A wooden fence ran down the north side and a chain-link fence delineated the south side. Right next to the house was the swing set that, before I came along, was Terry's favorite receiver. We moved the swing set, the lawn chair, and the picnic table "receivers" into place, along with the barbecue pit to make space for the new football field formed by our shared imagination.

Between the house and the creek, stretching from one side of the yard to the other, was the biggest obstacle in our stadium, Mr. Bradshaw's garden. Terry's dad spent most of his spare time tending to this, his most prized possession. I'll never forget the delight on his face each evening as he harvested his vegetables and then presented them to his wife for the family's nightly meal.

Mr. Bradshaw was an average-sized man with an immense presence. He was strong and capable, with a "no-nonsense" kind of demeanor that was able to get his boys to do whatever needed to be done with just one look. For him, words were seldom necessary, but when he did speak, there was a gentle gruffness in his voice that made people listen.

Our main challenge with Mr. Bradshaw's garden was that there was only enough space for one person to walk around it. That sometimes didn't work out so well when Terry and I were throwing the ball. As far as I was concerned, that garden and Mr. Bradshaw were one and the same. And, because I was truly afraid of Mr. Bradshaw, I would do anything to avoid stepping one foot in his garden. I became, therefore, the self-appointed protector of his vegetables.

• • •

The screen door on the back of the Bradshaw home creaked open and Mr. Bradshaw stepped onto the back porch. He stood there, arms crossed, watching us run our plays. I glanced at him from time to time to gauge his reaction to some of my most impressive catches. I even thought I saw him smile from time to time. It wasn't the Alexandria Daily Town Talk, but it was good to have some kind of interest coming my way again.

We had progressed, by then, from just throwing the football to actually running pass patterns in which I would run to a designated spot, cut left or right, turn and wait for Terry's torpedo pass to find me. Most of the time I caught it. Sometimes I didn't. One day the week before, we got mixed up on a pattern and Terry's pass took out a couple of tomato plants. We had tried to prop them back up and packed the dirt around them, but a spindly plant was no match for a football with that kind of force behind it. Although Mr. Bradshaw hadn't mentioned this casualty, I couldn't help but wonder if that was why he was standing there.

Terry took the imaginary snap and I ran my pattern — straight down the field, then a cut left toward the sideline before easing downfield, waiting for the pass to find me. Terry's imagination was so vivid that I had actually begun to "see" the field, the other players, and the stadium around us.

While Terry had stopped his verbal play-by-play and commentary, I knew it was still always running in that big goofy head of his. And right then it seemed that the defense was all over him, because it was taking *forever* for him to throw that football. Finally

I saw his arm coming forward and watched the trajectory of the football lofting my way.

And then I realized I was too deep. I was near the back corner of Mr. Bradshaw's garden and that pass was losing altitude. Fast. I sprinted back up the sideline to the front of the garden and dove with everything I had to catch the ball just before it took out the string beans.

As my hands closed around the ball, I heard Mr. Bradshaw's big laugh coming from the porch, followed by clapping. "Thank you, Tommy," he boomed. "The garden and I are so glad you're here."

Terry scowled and didn't say a word, and then grinned and pointed at me as he would for years to come in appreciation for catching a pass pretty much destined for the dirt. So that day I learned two things. One, Mr. Bradshaw was out there to save his garden. And two, for the sake of Mr. Bradshaw's vegetables I would learn to make great catches. I'll always believe that my desperation to stop that deadly spiral from wrecking Mr. Bradshaw's garden taught me to dive for passes and keep my big feet "in bounds" — out of the garden. It was my duty to keep that dang ball from killing the okra, the peppers, and those front-row string beans.

By now Mrs. Bradshaw had joined her husband on the porch — coming out, I suppose, to see what all the commotion was about. She was tall and slender, with dark brunette hair always coiffed into a perfect 1960s beehive. She was stunning — the height of style and poise — and always well dressed and impeccably groomed. I heard her laugh as Mr. Bradshaw most likely told her what just happened. She put her arm around her husband and they stood there, arm in arm, watching us throw the ball.

In addition to her sense of style, her kind heart, and her quick laughter, what impressed me most about Terry's mom was her unflappable belief. The Bradshaws were solid, hard-working people who were also strong disciplinarians and God-fearing Southern Baptists. They scared the holy crap out of me.

You must remember that this was during the early sixties, the "yes-sir" and "yes-ma'am" era when most kids did not have smart mouths. As far as I knew, "talking back" to your parents, or any other adult, for that matter, was not an option. This kind of respect was expected in most families, mine included, and even more so in the Bradshaw home. They didn't even have to ask me a question to get a "sir" or "ma'am" out of me.

"You're such an Eddie Haskell," Terry liked to say, likening me to the infamous *Leave it To Beaver* suck-up.

I didn't care what he thought about how I talked to his parents. I just knew I wanted to stay on their good side.

• • •

Aside from his family and his vegetable garden, what Mr. Bradshaw loved most was fried chicken. It was his very favorite meal, and Mrs. Bradshaw could fry chicken better than just about anyone in this world. Some of the sweetest words to my young ears became, "Tommy, we're having fried chicken tonight. You want to stay for dinner?"

Of all the nights that I put my feet under the Bradshaw dining table, "fried chicken night" was one of my favorites. It was on the first of these "fried chicken nights" at the Bradshaws that I learned the protocol Mrs. Bradshaw insisted upon.

"Tommy," she said in her soft southern drawl, "On chicken night our guest always gets the first choice of meat."

"Wow," I said. "Thank you, Mrs. Bradshaw." And then, remembering what my mother taught me to say, "and thank you for inviting me to dinner."

Terry chortled beside me. "Yes, Mrs. Cleaver," I heard him whisper.

"What's that, son?" Mrs. Bradshaw turned her attention to Terry. "I hope you are complimenting Tommy on his good manners. He just said exactly what you're supposed to say when someone invites you to dinner. Go on, Tommy, choose your favorite piece of chicken."

I felt Mr. Bradshaw looking at me with those eyes that spoke beyond the uttered word. Common sense and a strong survival instinct told me that my days would be numbered if I laid one finger on his piece of white meat.

I hesitated for a moment to think this through. The white meat was obviously off limits. The drumstick was probably best left for Craig, the baby, so Mrs. Bradshaw would probably appreciate my leaving that for him. Gary, the oldest brother, and Terry would eat anything. I chose the wing.

A huge grin crossed Mr. Bradshaw's face. "We're so glad you're here, Tommy," he said.

This was a relief because when he came into the house a little bit earlier holding yesterday's smashed corn stalk in one hand and the broken tomato plant in the other, I had already accepted Mrs. Bradshaw's invitation to stay for dinner — it was too late to back out. After the awkwardness of his sarcastic thanks to Terry and me for helping decide what vegetable would be included in supper tonight, I wasn't sure where I stood.

As hard as I tried to protect them, vegetables sometimes fell to the cause of our spirited practices. And, while these mangled casualties weren't very pretty to look at, they always tasted just fine. That garden taught me to make spectacular catches and also helped feed me for several years.

• • •

"And thank you, God, for Tommy," Mr. Bradshaw said in his deep, gruff voice that always made his words feel important. The Bradshaws prayed before every meal, and when I was with them, they always thanked God for me. This made me feel special — like I was part of their family, and I loved feeling like I was important to them.

Sometimes however, being considered "family" offers up the fuller experience of family — beyond the warm fuzzies. One of these times was the day Novis Bradshaw almost lost her ever-lovin' mind. There was not a doubt in my mind that this was the day Terry and I were going to die.

It was a beautiful Saturday afternoon and we had been out there throwing the football for several hours, working up the appetite growing teenage boys are known for. It was time to lighten the Bradshaw refrigerator's load. We entered the house, the screen door banging closed behind us as we descended upon the kitchen.

Standing in the welcome cool of the open refrigerator, we surveyed our options. I had my eye on some cold cuts and cheese in the back of the refrigerator, and just as I was reaching to free them from behind the leftovers, Terry's mom walked in.

I didn't hear the question Mrs. Bradshaw asked Terry. And, engrossed in retrieving my snack, I didn't really hear his reply. The tone between them, however, made me turn around just in time to see the beginning of Mrs. Bradshaw's unraveling.

Growing up in the South, you learn to recognize the white-hot anger of a Southern woman. There's an eerie smile that shows way too many teeth, pasted onto a face whose eyes didn't quite get the message that the smile was happening below. When I saw this happening on Mrs. Bradshaw's face, I realized in a flash that Terry was as good as dead. Whatever he said to his mom — and most likely the way he said it — had sealed his doom.

Novis Bradshaw wheeled around, grabbing one of Mr. Bradshaw's old cracked belts hanging on a nail beside the door. I realized in an instant what it meant to have a belt hanging in the kitchen. These people were serious about discipline. *What was that knucklehead thinking, mouthing off like that when he knew his mom kept a belt that handy?*

She charged toward Terry, belt raised in her right hand. I was settling in to watch this entertaining scene unfold when I realized I was trapped right between them. My best friend, my good buddy was using ME as a human shield.

By this time Mrs. Bradshaw was so mad she was grabbing both of us. She was going to beat someone with that belt, and it didn't look like she cared which one of us it was.

"Mom!" Terry screamed. "I'm sorry!"

I was just screaming, period.

Terry's mom, undeterred, kept on coming at us like a blitzing linebacker. There was nowhere for us to go. Then I felt a shove from behind as Terry let go of me, pushing me straight toward his mother.

I was no longer a human shield; I was now a human sacrifice. I felt her fingers close around my shirt collar and wondered how in the world this could be happening.

Terry wheeled and sprinted down the hall toward the bathroom. My own survival instinct kicked in then, and somehow I twisted myself free from her grip and sprinted after him into his "safe" room — the bathroom.

Terry locked the door behind us. We stared at each other, panic-stricken, gulping for air, hearts beating through our chests.

When at last I had enough air to speak I glowered at him. "How could you do that?" I demanded. "I almost died out there!"

"What was I supposed to do, Tommy?" he said in a tone somewhere between growl and whine. "You saw her face. She likes you. She would just have hurt you. I'm pretty sure she was gonna *kill* me!"

"So now what, Mr. Brilliant?" I snarled. "We'll just stay in this bathroom for the rest of our lives?"

Then Mrs. Bradshaw's voice was at the door. She spoke in a low, calm monotone, which was much scarier than yelling. "Terry. Honey. You need to open this door right now."

Now, if you've never experienced true, crazy anger, I will tell you a secret. You don't see or hear it. You *feel* it — even through a solid wooden bathroom door.

"Mom, please," Terry begged. "I'm really, *really* sorry. I don't know what I was thinking. I never, *ever* should have talked to you like that and I promise I never will again."

The silence on the other side of the door said it all.

"Mom?" Terry tried again. "You know, *Tommy's* in here with me." He looked at me as an idea dawned. "We're both really, really sorry. We'll do extra chores for a week. No. Two weeks, to prove how sorry we are."

"We?" I said in a hushed voice. I crossed my arms and turned my back on him. I didn't mind doing extra chores for Mrs. Bradshaw, but not to save his sorry hide.

"Terry, open the door right now or you will be in more trouble than you can possibly imagine." Mrs. Bradshaw's voice was still low and slow, sending a chill right through me.

In my own assessment of the situation, every wheedle and whine from Terry only ratcheted up his mother's fury even further.

As if reading my mind, and to my complete horror, Mrs. Novis Bradshaw now turned her attention to me. In that same horrifying monotone, she said "Tommy. Son. I need you to open this door right now."

Terry banged both hands on the counter top. He knew I was incapable of handling this kind of pressure from his mother.

"Don't you do it," he hissed. He knew I was about to cave. "If you open that door I'll never speak to you again. Our football *and* our friendship will be over."

I sat on the closed commode, cupping my face with my hands. "I wanna open the door Mrs. Bradshaw," I yelled through the door, "really I do, but Terry won't let me!"

"Well, honey, would you rather take a beating from Terry — or from me?" There was that Southern sweet and salty that made my blood curdle.

How did I get in this position? I whined to myself. *Why is this happening?*

As if recognizing the need for a new plan that didn't rely on my waning loyalty, Terry raised the bathroom window and knocked out the screen. Without even glancing my direction, he bailed out through the open window.

I was right behind him.

We sprinted toward my house, crossing yards, jumping hedges, dodging kids on bikes, and escalated this drama with no real thought about the reality of the situation. We ran like we were being chased by a pack of wolves, never looking back.

Terry ate dinner with us that night. My mother, not letting on she had talked to Terry's mother, served up the roast beef and mashed potatoes and green beans — and a thick slice of chocolate cake for dessert — as if this was just simple reciprocity for all the great meals I ate at the Bradshaws. After dinner, when it was time for Terry to go home, my parents bid him a cheerful goodbye as he thanked them for dinner and trudged out into the evening air. I really didn't know if I'd ever see him again, but at least *I* was safe at home.

It would be many, many years later when I found out that when Mrs. Bradshaw told this story to Mr. Bradshaw they both had a good laugh over it. Once Terry got home, Mr. Bradshaw just scolded him and assigned extra chores for smarting off to his mom. Mrs. Bradshaw never spoke of the incident again. Neither did we.

There have been times, at different points throughout my life, when I went back to that house on Shady Lane Drive. Propping my arms on that same old wooden fence that, like me, had grown more weathered with time, I gazed into that familiar yard. My nostalgic eyes could still see the area, now overgrown, where that glorious garden once grew. The old swing, pigeon coop, and besieged lawn furniture were long gone. The little creek behind the house was cemented over. But if I stared long enough at that old yard, my mind's eye could always see it all again, just as it was. My mental replay of the antics of those two young boys, throwing the football and dreaming big dreams, even from my adult vantage point, always reminded me how much bigger everything seems — especially our dreams — when we are young.

Growing up, you see, means realizing that some dreams can come true — and some just aren't meant to be. And sometimes just as one dream dies, a new one reveals itself. We can spend our entire life chasing a dream, and we might even catch it. And sometimes we discover that the chase is as important as the dream itself.

CHAPTER 3

The start of school began to loom over the last days of summer just as I was getting comfortable with my new life in Shreveport. I was even starting to enjoy the idea of playing football, based on all I was learning from Terry on our backyard gridiron.

Terry and I were both enrolled in the ninth grade at Oak Terrace Junior High. On the day before school started, Terry's face grew very serious.

"You're going out for football, right?" It was worded as a question, but the tone told me otherwise.

"I don't know yet," I said. I really didn't. As much fun as it was to throw and imagine great plays with Terry, even I knew the difference between a patch of string beans and a bunch of guys bigger than me also trying to catch — or at least stop me from catching — that football.

Terry snorted. "If you don't go out for football, everyone will say you're a sissy — or a weenie," he said.

I looked down at my spindly arms and legs and long, gaunt torso. I ate constantly, but nothing seemed to stick. "I am kind of a weenie, Terry," I said. "I think I might weigh about 115 pounds. I cocked my arm to "make a muscle."

Not much happened.

"See?" I said. "I don't have enough muscle on me to even show up, much less hold my own. "What if all the guys are bigger than me?"

"You're not big, but you're fast," Terry said. "You have to play. You've got good hands and you can catch anything I throw. I need you — and *you* need to play football so we can still be friends. And don't forget what I told you about the girls."

Oh. Right. I'll never know for sure whether it was the promise of girls, Terry's friendship, or continued flattery that wore me down, but I yielded to peer pressure from my buddy and went out for the football team.

• • •

Because I did not know anyone but Terry, and he already had his equipment from the previous spring training, on the first day of school I found myself in the locker room, sitting alone, waiting to be issued my uniform.

I noticed that my hands were a little bit clammy, and even though I tried to deny the anxiety coursing through me, my mind and body seemed to be ganging up on my ego. *Why am I doing this?* The question kept circulating as if swirling around in my head might attract an answer. *How can I get out of here without Terry seeing me quit?*

I still didn't know very much about the game itself beyond throwing and catching. Terry had explained some things to me, but I suspected this information had more to do with him than me. He had no clue how much objective knowledge I was missing — the gaps that remained in what I'd need to know to play the game with real people instead of lawn furniture.

Heck, I didn't even know how to put on the pads and uniform. What was I going to do when they handed that pile of equipment to me? I'm a ninth grader. I couldn't just ask someone how to put the stuff on — then they'd know how stupid I was about football. *Give me a baseball uniform and I'll know what to do*, I silently begged as the equipment manager headed my way with all my gear. Lacking the nerve to do anything else, I accepted the delivery and said, "Thank you."

Then luck smiled on me. Looking down a row of lockers to my left I saw a guy who had just come in and was starting to put on his pads. Watching him out of the corner of my eye and trying not to be obvious, I copied everything he did, in exactly the same order he did it, and somehow I managed to get all my football gear on more or less correctly before I stepped onto my first real football field.

• • •

"What position do you play, son?" The voice behind me came from Coach Bruce, the head ninth grade football coach for Oak Terrace Junior High.

I turned around, expecting to find a huge man, but found instead a guy who was far less intimidating in size than he was in presence. There was an authoritative kindness in his voice that got my attention right away. From that moment on I knew I wanted to listen to whatever he had to say — and to do whatever he said to do.

I looked around the field, hoping to see something that would help me answer his question. Truth be told, I had no idea what most of the positions even were, much less what they did — or which ones I might be good at. Still, I needed to give the coach some kind of answer, so I pointed to a group of boys on the far side of the field and started jogging toward them. I knew better than to stick around and try to answer any further questions about why I wanted to join that group. I had no idea what they were doing or what the position was, but they seemed far enough away that maybe I could blend in.

Standing quietly on the perimeter of this group and trying to learn as much as I could before opening my mouth, I discovered I was going to be a defensive back. *Sounds pretty macho,* I thought to myself. *I might be in the wrong place.*

The coach blew a whistle to let us know practice was beginning, so I just did what everyone else did. Everything was going okay, too, until we started the tackling drills with the offensive backs.

All of the defensive backs were larger than me. Heck, even the manager was larger than me. I tried not to think about this as I stepped to the front of the line to take my turn to try and tackle a back. One of the largest players lined up to run opposite me.

I gulped hard, summoned all my courage, and met him in the hole. My head was up, my back arched, my legs driving for all they were worth. That giant butthole pummeled and dragged me about 15 yards before I was finally able to use my body to trip him.

I just lay there, wondering why in the world I had agreed to this. The next thing I knew, Terry was standing over me, winded from running from across the field to see if I was OK.

"Tommy?" he said, with a concern in his voice I had never heard before.

"Yeah?" I croaked.

"Are you OK?" he asked. This uncharacteristic concern was freaking me out.

"I guess so," I said. I really hadn't checked. I was too occupied with getting dragged and clobbered by the Incredible Hulk. I had just read the new Marvel comic book over the summer about this big green bundle of inhuman anger, and I was pretty sure I had just met him in person. "What are you doing over here?"

"Well I heard you screaming, so I came over here to see if you were OK," he said.

Crap. "I was hoping I was just screaming on the inside," I said, managing a weak grin.

Terry laughed, relieved that my humor had returned. "Nope," he said. "I think everyone within a five mile radius thought you were being murdered."

I sat up, the world still wobbling around me. "I've never been hit by a car before, so I really don't know if I'm OK or not," I said. I tried to focus my eyes on Terry, and to my surprise there were now two of him. "Terry, why am I seeing two of you?"

That was the last thing I remembered before blacking out.

• • •

"Who's that guy?" I whispered to Terry as we walked onto the field for practice on Monday of the second week of school. I was referring, using only my eyes (daring not to point or even turn my head), to the biggest guy on our team. It hadn't taken but a few days for me to realize how much he enjoyed dragging me down the field like a rag doll.

"Oh. Yeah." Terry replied, also careful not to look in the big kid's direction. "His name is Thomas Clickscales. He's the fullback. He just moved here from New Orleans."

"He's big," I said. The obvious never escaped me. During tackling drills I was pretty sure he counted down the line of the defensive backs until he found me, and then got in his line at the same place, just so he could be across from me and we would come up at the same time.

"He calls himself T.C.," Terry said, still keeping his eyes firmly on the ground before us as we walked toward the field.

"Right," I said. "Makes sense. Lots of people like to go by their initials. It's shorter."

Terry looked at me now. "No," he said like I was the dumbest guy on the planet. "It stands for "Top Cat" — and my guess is we'd better believe it. Don't mess with that guy, Tommy."

Like I even *could* mess with that human mountain. I still doubted my decision to try to play football with my scrawny build, but Terry would hear none of it. So my question of the day now had become, *How far will T.C. drag me before I fall off of him and land flat on my face?*

• • •

After practice Terry and I liked to hang out for a while, usually perched on a brick retaining wall that edged the parking lot. We watched the other kids and talked about their cars. I was still trying to get my bearings in this new crowd, and Terry, as always, was happy to help. He knew a little something about everyone and was all too glad to share — along with lots of opinions stated as absolute fact.

I hung on his every word.

"So what's his story?" I asked as Ronnie Brown, a guard on our team set his gear bag down beside a brand new Ford Mustang, the baddest car in the parking lot — and maybe in the world.

"He's a ninth grader," Terry said, squinting his eyes toward Ronnie. "He goes steady with Ann Whalen, one of the cool girls, and she has ole' Ronnie wrapped around her little finger."

"Oh," I said, having no idea what that even meant. But the way Terry said it, it sounded bad.

We watched the steady stream of kids from the school to the parking lot. Some walked on, some headed down to the bike racks, and the lucky ones either had a car or made friends with someone who did. I squinted into the afternoon sun, recognizing, I thought, two more guys from the team. It was hard to tell when they were out of uniform and out of the context of the position they played or the way they moved on the field.

"That's Sam Perry and Paul Morgan, right?" I asked Terry.

He followed my line of sight to the edge of the parking lot. "Yeah," Terry said. Something in his tone — it sounded a little bit like awe — made me pay even more attention. "Paul's cool. He also plays the guitar in a band." It took quite a bit to impress Terry. "He dates an eleventh grader."

Paul, as it turned out, was that handsome kid all the guys wanted to be like — and all the girls wanted to date. Yep, we all wanted to be like Paul, wished we could play in Paul's band, and would have given anything to be as smooth around the ladies. Paul was our hero.

Sitting on that wall with Terry, I learned who was friends with whom, who dated whom, and, above all, which car they drove or piled into. From the early days of that first semester, I wanted to know more about the guys on the team than the position they played. For as long as I can remember I've always been interested in people and curious about their stories; moving to a new town and a new school and a new sport all at the same time sparked that curiosity as never before. And with Terry as my best friend, this information was easy to come by.

"That's Johnny, right?" I said, my eyes following a kid as he walked toward a yellow Model T.

"Yep," Terry said, hopping down from the wall. "C'mon. Let's see if he'll give us a ride home."

I followed Terry, speechless and wide-eyed as he asked Johnny Bean for a ride home.

Johnny looked at me and nodded his recognition. "Sure," he said. "Hop in."

We got to ride home in Johnny's Model T almost every day that year. Johnny was even cooler than his car.

• • •

Over the next few weeks I began to fit in and find my place among the team. Rather than watching and comparing myself to them, I was starting to appreciate their talents and abilities. Russell Evans was a natural-born athlete. That guy could do anything. Warren Jennings and David Prestridge, two of our best linemen, were also best friends. Jimmy Buckner was our star running back. Jimmy was that good-looking kid who was always fun to be around, and man-oh-man, could he run. We'd all go on to be football standouts in high school, but none of us knew that then, of course. We were just enjoying the moment in all the ways our ninth grade minds could grasp it.

As a football team, we were pretty sure we were top notch — top dogs with a giant "Top Cat" in our midst. It seemed like God was smiling on us all, and it turned out that Terry was absolutely correct in his assessment of how much girls loved football players — even the little bitty ones.

We were becoming stars.

• • •

As for me, I could feel myself getting better — and maybe even stronger — with each practice. Rather than the 20 yards they were dragging me on those grim first few days, those backs — T.C. included — were only managing to drag me three or four yards by the time the season started.

We sat in the locker room after the last practice before our first game and listened as Coach Bruce announced the starting lineup. All I heard in that long list of names and positions was "Bradshaw will start at quarterback" and "Spinks, you'll start at corner."

I couldn't believe my ears. I was a starting cornerback for the fighting Trojans of Oak Terrace Junior High. And Terry was the starting quarterback. Part of that backyard dream was already starting to come true.

That first game, against the Broadmoor Bulldogs, offered up the perfect opportunity to showcase the skills Terry and I had worked so hard to acquire in all of our summer practice. And shine we did. I was riding on the backs of those Bulldog running backs, bringing 'em down all over the place, and Terry was looking amazing as the quarterback.

Then something terrible happened.

I looked over just as Terry got sacked really hard. I watched to make sure he got up. He didn't. I went closer to make sure he was OK. He wasn't. Writhing in pain, Terry clutched his arm and shoulder. The team doc came out, and then he motioned for help to get Terry to the sideline. Everyone clapped for Terry as he went out, and I just stood there, shocked. How could this happen?

We got word a little later that Terry had broken his collarbone. This news was a blow to all of us on his team, but to me it was devastating. Now what?

• • •

"So how's it going?" I approached the sofa in the Bradshaw home where Terry sat, propped with pillows, trying to read a comic book with his right hand. His left arm was in a sling that was secured to his left side. "Does it hurt?" I asked, coming around the end of the sofa to sit carefully on the other end.

"Yeah, a little," he said. "The worst part is I can't play football for six weeks and by then the season's *over*!" While the physical pain may have been under control, Terry's emotional pain was palpable.

The knot in my stomach tightened. My best buddy, who was at the lowest point of his young life, was looking to me for comfort. Not only did I have no words of comfort for this horrible thing that just happened to him; I now had to break the news that the coaches had decided I would take over his quarterback position. Me. Of all people!

I cleared my throat. *Might as well get this over with*, I thought, trying to figure out how to begin. I had practiced what I would say all the way over to the Bradshaws, but now every possible way I had thought of to break this news seemed lame.

"I have to tell you something," I began, picking the first one that came to mind. "Coach has decided that while you're getting over this," I said, gesturing to his sling, "that, um, I will take your place as quarterback." I said those last words quickly, hoping that somehow speed of delivery might help lessen the blow.

It didn't.

"You are going to do . . . what?!?!?!" Terry said. The look of total shock, betrayal, and confusion on his face made me want to die right then and there.

"I swear to you, Terry, I had nothing to do with it!" I said. This was way worse than anything I had imagined. Nevertheless, I had waded in. Might as well keep going.

"Coach Bruce called me in his office this afternoon and asked me if I had ever played quarterback before. I told him I hadn't. Then he told me I was fixin' to learn real fast."

Terry just shook his head, slowly, right to left and back again. The pain in his eyes now eclipsed what I had seen on the field just after this happened. This was pain that might never go away. As hard as it was for him to think about not playing football for the rest of the season, the news of being replaced — by anyone — was devastating. For it to be me added insult to his injury.

"I can't believe my best friend is going to take my position away from me," he said once he was able to summon actual words.

"I'm not taking your position away from you, you knucklehead!" I exclaimed, turning toward him and gathering the courage to look him right in the eye. "Terry. You have a *broken collarbone.* You can't be the quarterback right now — and *someone* has to be." I paused, deciding to go with full disclosure. "Terry, believe me, I don't want to be the quarterback. Heck, I don't even know *how* to be the quarterback."

"I can't believe you would even accept it." Terry spit these words out one at a time.

What??? I thought, confusion descending. It never crossed my mind that I could have refused. As far as I knew a ninth grader pretty much had to do what coaches, teachers, and parents — heck any adult — told him to do.

"Terry, you know even better than I do how Coach is when he makes up his mind," I said. "You know I didn't have a choice." I searched my best buddy's face, looking for some flicker of understanding to break through the scowl he was using to try and cover pure heartbreak. How could he think I had a choice?

• • •

"Coach?" I said, hesitant to interrupt. I was standing at the doorway of Coach Bruce's office before school started the very next day. I hadn't slept at all the night before, tossing and turning and replaying the conversation with Terry. *Maybe Terry is right.* I had decided sometime during the wee hours. *Maybe I do have a choice.* It was clear to me that if there was any way some other kid could take Terry's place while he was out it would save our friendship.

"Well, hello, Tommy," Coach Bruce said, looking up from the paperwork he was filling out on his desk. "Are you all set for today? Big day for you!"

"That's what I want to talk to you about, Coach," I said, taking a tentative step inside.

"Come on in," he said. "What's on your mind?"

"I've been thinking about it and I don't think I'm the right one to replace Terry," I said, all in one awkward blurt. There. I said it. I stood and waited for him to accept my resignation.

"Nonsense, Tommy," Coach Bruce said, "I've seen you throw that ball with Terry. And I've seen you take those hits from guys a lot bigger than you. You're small, but scrappy — and you're smart, which a quarterback has got to be. And you've got a heck of an arm. Why in the world would you pass up this opportunity?"

"Well, sir, you see, Terry's my best friend. And this whole thing is enough of a bummer for him without it being *me* who's going to take his place. If there's someone else who can do it until he gets well, I think that would be better for everyone." I was surprised at how freely these words came. It wasn't like me to be this outspoken — much less to talk back to adults — but with my friendship with Terry on the line I was willing to take my chances.

"I see," said Coach Bruce. "That's really kind of you, Tommy, to worry about Terry's feelings. But I'm the coach and I have to put my best team on the field for the next six weeks and that means you will be playing quarterback."

"Oh." I said. "Well, I just thought . . ." I wasn't quite ready to give up, but had the definite understanding that my initial instincts were correct. I had no say in this matter whatsoever.

"I'm counting on you, Tommy," Coach Bruce said, shutting down any further discussion of my thoughts or opinions about what should be done. "The team's counting on you. You've got to shake this off and give it your best. Terry's hurt. He'll be back. But until then, you're our quarterback."

"Yes, sir," I said. I left Coach Bruce's office that day as dejected as I had ever been in my whole life. Terry was never going to understand this.

• • •

When I stepped onto the Bradshaw's front porch that same afternoon, I had no idea what I was going to find on the other side of the door. My reason for coming back was simple: I wanted Terry to know that I had officially tried to refuse to take his place as quarterback — and that Coach Bruce had all but told me that if I wanted to play on his football team I had no choice. Knowing how adamant Terry was that I play football, my hope was he'd see that the only way out of this for me was quitting the team — and I knew he wouldn't want me to do that. Or would he? The Terry I talked to yesterday probably wouldn't even care. Most of all I knew I had to try one more time to talk some sense into him.

Mrs. Bradshaw opened the door and smiled that genuine Southern smile that always made me feel so welcome and safe. "Come on in, Tommy," she said. "Terry's right in there watching TV. Can I get you a snack?"

I smiled a grateful smile. "Yes, Ma'am," I said. "That would be nice."

"Good!" she said, beaming at me. It must have been a long day taking care of my disgruntled friend.

"Um, how's he doing today?" I ventured, just to see what I was walking into.

"Oh, honey, he's fine," she said.

Did she know about our conversation the day before?

"He's just uncomfortable and a little bit grouchy, but don't you worry," she said. "Everything will be just fine once this collarbone heals and he can get back to his football."

"I sure hope so," I said as she disappeared into the kitchen. Standing there in the foyer had been safe enough. Now it was time to go in and see if I could smooth things over with Terry.

"Hey," he said as I entered the room.

He spoke first. Is that a good sign? My thoughts raced ahead of me. *Maybe.*

"Hey," I said, matching his tone. I sat down on the far end of the sofa from where he was nested in pillows and comic books. "Terry, I went and talked to Coach Bru—"

"It's OK, Tommy," he interrupted. "I know you don't have a choice. Someone has to replace me while this thing heals," he said, jerking a thumb toward his sling, "and it might as well be you."

I gulped. *Wow. How could it have been this easy?*

"So here's what we're going to do," he said, taking charge of the situation. "We're going to run some routes and I'm going to show you some stuff and try to help you learn how to think like a quarterback." He paused. "You don't even have a week to figure this out, and the team needs for you to know what you're doing."

Mrs. Bradshaw entered the room with a tray filled with cookies and two tall glasses of milk at just the right moment to allow me to process the immense relief coursing through me. I had come here thinking my friendship with Terry might be over, and meanwhile he had done this amazing about-face and was now back to being my best friend and, on top of that, now he was offering to help me.

I really wanted to run over there and hug him, but his broken collarbone and my understanding of cool kept me rooted where I sat, munching on a cookie, watching him chug his milk.

I gestured toward the sling. "How can we run routes with you hurt?" I asked. "How can you throw with that thing on?"

Terry laughed. "Did you notice that it's my *left* arm in the sling?" he asked. "And that my throwing arm is just fine?"

Trying not to feel stupid, I said, "Oh. Well, won't moving around like that hurt?"

"I don't know," he said, standing up now. "All I know is I can't sit around here much longer. It's gonna hurt more not to be playing *any* kind of football, so I figure this will be better than nothing."

"Gee, thanks," I said, trying to come off sounding sarcastic and cool, but underneath it all feeling gratitude too immense for words. I had been concentrating so hard on my own survival and learning my own position that I had never considered what Terry did, or had to know to play quarterback. Until that moment I had not considered that come Monday afternoon, I would be the one standing out there with the ball in my hands, while a bunch of guys bigger than me tried to pound the snot out of me.

"Ok," Terry said, once we were back in our old familiar spots in his back yard. "The first thing you've got to know is that everything happens really fast out there. It's just a blur, man, and it's easy to get overwhelmed with all those guys coming at you at once. The main thing you have to do is keep your cool and just wait until you find your guy."

He took an imaginary snap and dropped back a few steps to show me the set-up, scanning the "field" for his receiver. Once his eyes locked onto an imaginary target, he sent a spiral straight into the breadbasket of the lawn chair next to the garden.

"Ok," I said, trying to lock into my memory how he moved back with the ball cocked, allowing himself just enough room. I even tried to practice the expression on his face. Then I stopped. "But what about when the rush is on and you have guys right up on you while you're trying to find your target?"

"Watch my feet," he said, "and watch my eyes." He demonstrated the footwork of moving side to side, up and back, evading imaginary rushers, never taking his eyes away from scanning for an open receiver.

I absorbed it all, shadowing his footwork, mimicking how he used his eyes to scan, letting my mind visualize the plays developing and how I would find my back or receiver without getting clobbered.

"Now," Terry said, once I grasped the basics of what to do just after the snap, "let's try to run some routes, but this time, instead of what you usually do, watch what *I'm* doing the whole time, all the way up until I release the ball."

After we ran a few routes that way, with my eyes and my mind trying to absorb every detail, Mrs. Bradshaw appeared at the back door. "Terry, honey, that's enough for today," she said. "Come on back in and rest. You don't want to overdo it and set yourself back, now, do you?"

I sighed my relief. I wasn't about to mention it, but even from across the yard I could see Terry wince as he threw the ball, and this had seemed to get worse in just the last few minutes. I was glad his mom was paying attention, too.

Reluctantly, Terry handed me the football and we trudged up his back steps. He was quiet now. I wasn't sure whether it was from the pain or if he just wanted to be alone with his thoughts.

We went inside and Mrs. Bradshaw straightened his sling and gave him some pain reliever. Then she turned to me, "Tommy, I think Terry needs to rest now," she said, "but I am so glad you came over. Can you come back tomorrow?"

Even though I could be slow to get a hint, this one came through loud and clear. "Yes, Ma'am," I said. "And thank you for the milk and cookies."

It wasn't until a few days later when I told Terry about my conversation with Coach Bruce. He laughed as he imagined me standing there trying to convince Coach Bruce to give the job to someone else. Terry knew all too well that it was way beyond my comfort zone to question any authority figure, so I think it said everything to Terry that I had tried to convince the coach to change his decision.

We spent the next few days before practice began with me as quarterback going over our plays. Terry demonstrated both physical things like footwork and demeanor as well as the mental side of how to think and run these plays from the quarterback's vantage point.

He never said what had brought about his complete about-face — and his decision to help me figure out what to do in the quarterback position, but it did not escape my notice, then or for years to come, that even at 13 years old Terry had the ability to get past his own personal setback and still be a key player to our team in how he guided me in this new position.

Even at that young age, I recognized that beyond Terry's incredible talent lay equally amazing character. I could sometimes see the ache in his eyes, tucked beneath his explanations and demonstrations, that he would not be the one on the playing field doing what he was so generously teaching me. I realized then I would never have another friend quite like Terry. He was a person I wanted to be around for a long, long time.

CHAPTER 4

Somewhere in the distance I heard the whistle blow just before I slammed into the player between the ball carrier and me. I was playing defense, which was only a marginally better experience than my attempt at quarterback. In those days, and particularly in small schools, it was not uncommon to play both offense and defense. This was the last game of our ninth-grade season, which had proven uneventful with me as quarterback. Somehow we had managed to hold our own, and somehow I made it through, week by week, without getting killed. For me, this was a victory with a capital V.

Before I could stop my automatic manners, I said to the hulking player I had just inadvertently body slammed, "Excuse me."

"You've gotta be kidding me," said the big kid, looking at me like I had just grown an extra head.

Why am I even here? I asked myself as I turned and walked back toward the sideline. I decided right then and there that when the season was over I would call it quits. My career in football would end just as it began. *I'm not cut out for this game,* my thoughts hammered. *I'm not mean enough, big enough, or tough enough.*

• • •

"How are you doing?" This question came from Coach Bruce, who had just entered the locker room and walked out of his way to the corner where my locker was located.

"Oh," I said, "I'm fine," reaching into my locker to get my books. I had just used the phone in the coach's office to call my mom to come pick me up since I had missed the school bus.

"Do you have a few minutes to spare?"

"Sure," I said, standing there holding my books and wondering what in the world he could want to talk to me about. It was the Monday after our last ninth grade game, but there were still a few weeks of offseason before the semester ended. I was planning to inform him then of my decision to move on from football.

I had told Terry over the weekend of my decision. "It just makes sense," I had said. "I tried it. It's just not for me." We were finishing at Oak Terrace Junior High and moving on to high school next year. "It's a natural break," I had assured Terry. "And now I'm going to move on to something else."

Terry had not said much when I told him of my decision. In fact, he had seemed to accept my decision pretty much without comment. To my surprised relief, he had shrugged and said, "It's your life, Spinks. Do what you need to do."

Well that was easy, I had thought.

Now Coach Bruce was standing there in front of my locker, and I still didn't connect it all in my head until he looked me right in the eye and said, "I understand you're thinking about quitting football."

My best friend had ratted me out. What a fink. "Yes, sir," I said. *Might as well get this over with,* I thought.

"Can we talk about that?"

I knew by the tone of his voice and the look on his face I wasn't going to be doing any of the talking.

Coach Bruce paused for an uncomfortable stretch of time that was probably just a few seconds but seemed like an eternity. I sensed that he was trying to choose his words as if he knew the impact those words would have on the rest of my life.

He began to talk — and after revealing his spot-on understanding of why I wanted to quit football, the subject of football took a backseat to a talk about life in general. "Son," he said, "in my life I've made a lot of mistakes — and I've seen a lot of other people make mistakes, too. And do you know what I've learned from all that?"

I shrugged, not wanting to interrupt. Something in his tone told me that these were some of the most important words I would ever hear in my life.

"Tommy," he said, "there are two kinds of people in this world." He paused as if to make sure I was listening.

I was.

"There are winners and there are those who make the choice NOT to be winners."

I noticed he was very careful not to use the word "losers." This seemed odd for a man who made his living coaching a game in which there were *always* winners and losers.

As if reading my thoughts, Coach Bruce continued, "Tommy, the only time people are not winners are the times when they choose to give up or just quit trying."

What I remember most about the rest of that 18-minute talk with Coach Bruce was not so much what he said, but how he made this young kid feel. For him to take the time to talk with me, to care what I did or didn't do — to tell me about the difference between "a winner" and "not a winner" — not only made me feel special, but it also wove tenacity into everything I did or tried to do from that day forward.

Neither of us could have known then what an impact these words from Coach Bruce would have on my life, but the older I've gotten the more I understand what Coach Bruce knew that day. Our words can have a tremendous and lasting effect on a young person's life. When I think about all of my experiences and memories that came from playing football, I realize that so many good parts of my life would never have happened if Coach Bruce had not taken the time to deliver that talk to me at that precise moment in my life.

Terry, seeing some potential in me that I couldn't see in myself, had brought about this talk by telling Coach Bruce I was going to give up on football. This was a gift from this gentle man and my best friend that would serve me well, in and out of sports, for the rest of my life. As the years went by, I realized that Terry kept me playing the game he loved so much because he knew I would grow to love it too.

• • •

We were just inside the front doors of Woodlawn High School for our spring welcome tour when Terry elbowed me and pointed. My eyes followed his direction to land on an enormous silver-armored knight statue standing guard outside the door to the main school office.

It was two weeks before school let out for the summer, on the day when all the football guys were invited to come and walk the halls of the high school we would attend the following year. This tour made it official. We were becoming Woodlawn Knights.

Woodlawn High School was brand new, with a modern layout that put hallways both inside and outside the buildings. We followed our guide into the huge open space between the two buildings, and it was my turn to elbow Terry. Surprised, he jumped sideways and stared at me, and then looked as I directed his wide eyes toward the back of the school — and just beyond that, to our first glimpse of Woodlawn's brand-new football field.

Terry's whole face radiated his excitement as he took in that field with all its red, blue, and silver flags whipping with the steady breeze. He looked at me, then at the field, and then back at me with the incredulous awe one might reserve for Christmas morning.

"Would you look at that," he whispered. "I can't wait to get out there!"

I nodded, stole a last peek, and then hurried to catch up with the tour as it re-entered the building. We turned down another hallway, past a long row of lockers punctuated by classroom doors. As the tour guide talked about the *kinds* of classrooms these were, my mind returned to that football field — and all the possibilities I knew were waiting for us beyond those red, blue, and silver flags.

I looked over at Terry. From the look on his face I knew he, too, was already on that field, lost in his imagination of our glory days to come on that beauty of a football field.

My attention was brought back to the matters at hand when we stopped right in front of the school's trophy cases. Scanning the glittery display, I noticed that the football section of the case was already filling up with awards, trophies, photographs, and other items of memorabilia.

The excitement in our group was palpable as the coaches approached. Riveted in place, we listened as each coach told a story. They talked of come-from-behind, last-second wins, perseverance despite insurmountable odds, and undersized players who reached deep within themselves, refusing to be beaten.

Not a word passed between us as we left the building and climbed onto the school bus back to Oak Terrace to finish our last two weeks of junior high. We were already Knights.

• • •

Inviting us all back to Woodlawn for the last two weeks of the Knights' regular spring training, the coaches explained that this was a chance for all incoming ninth graders from both Oak Terrace and Linwood Junior High — anyone considering playing football for Woodlawn — to practice with the team.

"Woodlawn may be the newest school in Shreveport," the head coach had said, "but make no mistake. We are a *powerhouse* in Triple A football, and every spring we start bringing along the players who will help us stay that way."

Terry and I were pretty sure he was referring to us, and we couldn't stop talking about how we were going to get out there and impress those coaches right away. Probably on the very first day.

When we stepped off the bus at the Woodlawn High School football field the very next week, we realized a few things right away. First, if we thought the *school* was huge, it was nothing compared to the size of its *football players.* We were issued practice uniforms, and after just a few minutes in that gigantic gleaming locker room, we learned that these were not boys. These were *men.* Men with hair all over their bodies. The only hair Terry and I had was on our heads. We made no mention of this, of course, but I knew without a doubt we were thinking the same thing. *How in the world are we going to be able to keep up with these guys?* And in my case, *how am I going to be able to keep them from killing me?*

The junior high boys who had just arrived at Woodlawn to participate in spring practice stayed together, moving like a pack of frightened sheep onto a field full of gargantuan wolves.

"You new guys need to report to the blocking dummies over there," one of the coaches said, gesturing to a set of dummies across the field from where we stood in the sweltering Shreveport sun.

No one spoke as we hustled together toward the blocking dummies, careful not to even look at the mammoth players of the Woodlawn football team as we jogged past.

A burst of laughter rose from these players as we scurried by. "Look! The junior high girls are here!" one of them shouted, pointing toward us. The others followed suit, laughing and pointing and saying things we didn't quite understand, but I was pretty sure were not complimentary.

After a few minutes of warming up and then standing around, we began some simple blocking drills with the dummies. One of the coaches came over and got Terry and another kid, Randy Tunks from Linwood, and gestured toward the larger group of Woodlawn players practicing across the field.

As our two buddies jogged toward certain doom, the rest of us stayed on our side of the field, blocking dummies and counting our blessings.

• • •

About three days into our Woodlawn spring training experience, something bizarre happened. A kid I didn't know picked up a rock and, out of the blue, threw it and hit another kid on the side of his helmet.

I watched, shocked. I couldn't even imagine what that sound must have been like from the inside. Being hit with anything while wearing a football helmet is really loud, let me assure you. The magnified sound of a *rock* hitting your helmet would likely make your ears ring for days. Heck, it might even bust an eardrum.

Everyone froze, staring at one another, waiting to see what would happen next.

Then it all became clear. The football players from the two junior high schools separated, an invisible line drawn between the two groups. Each young player was proudly representing his own junior high, even while wearing a Woodlawn football practice jersey.

The complete chaos that ensued next can only be described as a full-on rock war. Every helmet was a moving target. Boys were running, diving, and rolling — darting left and then right — trying to avoid the flying rocks that filled the air like giant buckshot. Big boys hid behind the little boys, using them as shields.

One kid started crying, and then the sound of evil laughter erupted from the more sadistic of these boys who were taking special delight in dealing the grief, pegging every head they could. Pretty soon it became obvious that standing frozen in place was not a good strategy, so I joined the diving and rolling, catching every rock I could reach in mid-air and then zinging it back at the attacker before ever landing on the ground. In my mind's eye, I became a Special Forces Green Beret whose only mission was keeping enemy rocks from pelting my head.

While the rock war — and the extra laps we got to run as the consequence — created the most action we junior high players had seen on the field during the entire two weeks of spring training, Terry had gotten to scrimmage with the powerhouse football team. His potential was obvious to everyone, and the coaches were encouraging him to work out during the summer.

Just before school was out, Terry told me he had promised to keep working out over the summer. The good news for me about that promise was when Terry said *he'd* work hard over the summer, it meant *we*. Because of our almost constant daily practice the summer before, we'd just use what we learned during those two weeks of Woodlawn spring training to amp up our practice sessions for the coming summer.

With a little luck and a lot of extra hard work on my part, maybe I'd get my shot when school started. Becoming part of that Woodlawn tradition — and someday part of that glittery trophy case — was something Terry and I wanted so badly we could taste it.

• • •

I stood shirtless in front of the mirror in our entry hall, examining in detail the torso that might be of better use in a biology class studying the human skeleton than on the football field with that bunch of hulks. Insecurity clawed at the back of my throat. *Why do you even think you can play this sport?* My thoughts mocked my reflection.

As clear as it was to everyone that Terry would be a star — and as proud and happy as I was for my buddy — I knew I probably wasn't even going to make the team. I pushed all that fear back down as I pulled my worn t-shirt over my head. Summer was here. Fall was a long ways away. More than anything else, I just wanted to go throw that football with Terry.

CHAPTER 5

Man-oh-man. For a teenage boy about to enter high school with a headful of dreams, there's nothing quite as exhilarating as the whole summer stretching out in front of you. The only thing Terry and I felt obligated to do that summer was to get bigger and stronger. Those looming Friday night lights of Woodlawn High School football had brought a new and tangible sense of purpose to our lives — and our only care was getting prepared.

The first thing we did every morning was go for a run, up and down the hills of our neighborhood, just looking for steps to run up and then back down. Sometimes to show off, we'd run up a set of steps backwards to give a little bit of extra work to our hamstrings. We punctuated just about everything we did with spontaneous pushups — and probably did about a million of them that summer — and any substantial tree branch within reach above our heads became our chin-up bar.

Terry laughed at me the first time I ran over to a tree and pulled myself into a chin-up. Then he watched as I lowered myself back down, hung there for a second, and then pulled myself back up. I did this over and over until my arms gave out, and then I dropped back to the ground and jogged over to where Terry stood.

"What in the world are you doing?" he asked, still puzzled.

"I've got to get stronger, especially in my arms and shoulders," I said, gasping for breath. "So every time I see a branch about the right height, I'm going to try to see how many chin-ups I can do."

Terry nodded, seeing the wisdom in this plan. He eyed the branch and then, without another word, trotted over to the tree and did his own set of chin-ups.

"I figure if I want to get some playing time this fall," I said as we continued our run, picking up our pace now to something between fast jog and run, "I'm going to have to get bigger, stronger . . . and more confident."

"You can do it," Terry encouraged. "We'll just keep working till we get there."

I hated to state the obvious, but we both knew Terry was *already* there. I also knew that bulking up and getting as good as I could this summer was my one and only chance to earn a spot on the team in the fall. If I didn't put everything I had into every single minute of my summer training, I was pretty sure I could just go ahead and take my place as the head water boy, and plan on spending my entire high school career providing ice-cold beverages to all of my hot, sweaty, hairy, football-playing buds.

No can do. My deepest resolve spoke in a voice all its own. *I am on a mission to make that team and nothing is going to stop me.*

• • •

"Is anybody out here hungry?"

The clamor of a roomful of sweaty football-obsessed teenaged boys always came to a dead standstill when my mother swooped into the room with a tray filled with cookies, sandwiches, or chicken pot pie — or whatever happened to be on her stove that day.

For this reason alone, my house became one of my friends' favorite places to hang out that summer before high school. Just one good whiff of my mom's Southern cooking, and you were hooked — a goner. You'd be back for sure.

I can still picture her moving around our kitchen in one of her favorite aprons. Her hair was always perfectly coifed, her lips a permanent shade of deep pink, and her nails were always painted a lighter shade of pink like the petals from her favorite rose bush just outside our back door.

The best part of my mom's kitchen was there was always something delicious bubbling away on that stovetop or wafting its allure from the oven. The reason my mom was always cooking was two-fold. She not only loved to cook for our family, but any time the church needed to serve a meal, she saw it as her job to make sure there was plenty to go around.

As the Senior Pastor's wife, my mother took very seriously her role in helping my dad 'grow the church.' She cooked constantly and did whatever else needed to be done, however the church needed her to serve. How she managed to cook for all of us — and always look so rested and together — is still baffling to me. I don't remember her ever complaining about being tired, how much she had to work — or ever seeing a hair out of place. And on top of that, she was always cheerful whenever a bunch of sweaty, hungry, loud teenage boys descended onto her kitchen. She'd just smile and offer whatever was cooking to whoever came.

Who doesn't love that?

• • •

As good a wife, mother, cook, hostess and force of nature as Grace Allen Spinks was, what most people didn't fully appreciate about my mother was her intelligence and talent in so many different areas. There seemed to be nothing she couldn't do — or at least figure out.

She was just 16 years old and destined to be valedictorian of her high school class when my dad, at 30 years old, whisked her away to be his wife. Of course, this didn't sit very well with my mom's mom, Gran, and that, as the story went, was the main reason Gran didn't like my dad too much, at least in the beginning.

Even as young as she was, my mother thrived as a preacher's wife. She led children's Sunday school classes, women's Bible studies, and with the incredible God-given ability to play the piano by ear, accompanied the choir and anyone else who wanted to sing for the church.

So it goes without saying how proud I always was of my mom. She was a classy southern woman. *Gone With The Wind*'s Scarlett O'Hara had nothing on her in the accent department.

But as good a cook, as warm a hostess, and as sweet and kind as my mother was, she also had a feisty side — and a wicked sense of humor. She also took no prisoners when it came to protecting my dad.

Now make no mistake, my dad was a good man — as good as they came — and he rarely needed protecting. As far as I can remember, Otis Spinks never raised his voice or said an unkind word about anybody. However, being the preacher in a church for some reason sets you up for criticism nobody deserves, and that was one part of his job that my mother could never handle.

I remember standing outside of the church just after the service let out each Sunday. My dad, with my mom at his side, would greet the parishioners and connect with them however he could or needed to, depending on what was going on in their lives. It was a pretty small congregation, and Dad prided himself on knowing each face, each name, and a little something about the current situation of nearly everyone who came through those heavy wooden doors each Sunday.

It was there on the steps of that church that I learned to recognize the quiet rise of white-hot indignation beneath my mother's Southern smile as a "well-meaning" church member offered my dad "constructive criticism." She would smile on the outside, but on the inside roiled molten lava that would wait to erupt until we were safely back inside the closed doors of our home.

• • •

"For the life of me, Otis, I cannot belieeeeeve the nuhh-hhrve of that woman!" Mom said, stretching out the one-syllable word, nerve, into three.

Mom had just found out that the notorious busybody, Mrs. Honeysucker, had been speaking ill of my father to some of the other women in the church. Apparently, Mrs. Honeysucker didn't feel that my father's preaching of The Word was up to par.

They were behind the closed doors of my parents' bedroom, but those doors only served to take the edge off the volume. Each word came through crystal clear. I knew I probably shouldn't be listening, but I was riveted to that conversation.

"How much fasta does she think a man can grow a church?" she fumed. "What does that Gladys expect you ta do?"

"Now, Grace," my dad said, as if the calm in his voice could coax her to follow suit, "she is a good person with a right to her own opinions. We can't judge her harshly for her opinions, even if those opinions are directed at me." My dad paused. "Mrs. Honeysucker is a Godly woman who does a lot of good in our church; it's just that her strong opinions about things can be a little bit hard to take. We have to remember that actions speak louder than words."

There was a moment of quiet, and then I heard my mother say, frustration spilling over into every word, "Otis, when people's words ahhh so loud, I can't think about their actions — or tell which scriptchuh they ahhh reading."

When people's words are so loud, I can't think about their actions. That one, quick-off-the-tongue remark has stayed with me my entire life. Being a preacher's kid, I grew up around people who loved the Bible, studied the Bible, and often times quoted the Bible. However, it was the people who lived the Bible who had the biggest impact on me. I wanted to be that kind of Christian, that kind of person.

• • •

"I've been working my butt off and eating everything in sight, and still I can't seem to get any bigger." This complaint came not from me, but from my friend, Ronnie Brown, who, like me, was a little low in the bulk department and similarly driven to use this summer to gain not only the skills the coaches would be looking for, but also the size we needed to go along with it.

Ronnie and I, being in the same boat — both in terms of stature and our pure determination to do something about it — had spent a lot of time that summer exchanging ideas, considering various popular and obscure ideas for bulking up, getting stronger, and developing new strategies to make us seem bigger to our opponents. We were always on the lookout for anything that would make us valuable once fall rolled around and we were on that Woodlawn football field for real.

Ronnie's expressed frustration over our lack of progress came out just a little bit louder than he expected as we entered the house. Ronnie looked sheepish as he then saw my mother swooping toward us from the kitchen. "Now Ronnie, you know we don't say, 'butt' in this house," she said, smiling at us.

"Yes, Ma'am," Ronnie muttered, blushing.

"Now who wants smothahd steak?"

Without waiting for an answer, my mom disappeared into the kitchen, and then returned seconds later with a long rectangular dish of what could only be described as heaven on earth.

The murmur of collective appreciation as everyone found a place at the dining table was all the encouragement my mother needed. In no time, placemats, plates, napkins, silverware and iced tea glasses were on the table and she began ladling out the thick juicy pieces of meat, covered in just the right amount of gravy and loaded with wedges of tender, sweet onion.

As mom fluttered around the table, serving each of my buddies in turn, I couldn't help but feel grateful. The names and faces varied from day to day, but today it was Terry, Bobby Waddell, Ronnie Brown, Donnie Baughman, and Jimmy Buckner who had gathered around our table after a long morning of grueling, self-inflicted practice sessions. They came over to hang out — and mostly to enjoy my mom's cooking.

"Now boys, y'all wait just a second and I'll bring out some of those black-eyed peas and collard greens from last night's suppah, and let's see . . ." Her voice trailed off as if trying to remember all that was actually available that day in her kitchen . . . "I think we may still have a little cornbread."

My buddies looked at one another as if they couldn't believe their ears — or their good fortune.

"Now Ronnie," My mother continued as she re-entered the dining room with a ladle already moving to add first the black-eyed peas and then the collard greens to each plate, "Ya problem isn't ya size."

We all looked at Ronnie to see what he'd say.

He just looked at my mother, waiting for her to go on.

"It's not ya ability or skill level, eithuh. Ya have mounds of both of those things, honeh." She didn't look at Ronnie as she made this pronouncement; she just kept ladling out the vittles.

Ronnie, clearly unsure exactly what to say, stared at his plate.

I glanced around the table, amused at the shock on my buddies' faces. I could tell that at first they wanted to laugh it off and ignore this Southern woman who was offering up football advice along with our lunch. But something in her tone was making them sit up and listen.

Just wait, I silently advised them. I knew what was coming and was happy just to sit back and enjoy the show. If my mother knew anything, she knew her football.

"Ronnie, ya problem is all in ya head," my mother declared, returning her ladle to the pot. "Even though at this point in ya life, ya might be smaller than those other boys, believe you me, that'll all change over the next few years, so you need to quit your frettin' about all that."

Ronnie looked at my mother as if seeing an apparition. The rest of the guys sat riveted.

"Go ahead an eat, boys," she said, waving her hand at the rest of us and laughing that easy laugh that made them all dig in at once. Then she turned back to Ronnie. "I know how concerned ya are about ya size, but I'm gonna tell you the same thing I tell my Tommeh all the time." She looked across the table and smiled at me.

"For now, you boys gotta learn how to let ya smaller stature work for ya, rath-eh than against ya. What you need to spend ya time workin on right now is getting quickah and smartah." She paused to let this sink in, and then continued, "You gotta play like ya know their plan — even before *they* know their plan."

Now she had everyone's attention — and she knew it. She smiled, walked around the table as she talked, using the slotted spoon in her hand for emphasis. "Ya may not be as big as they are just now, but all that means is ya gotta be bettuh prepared than they are." Then she stopped, turned back toward Ronnie and tapped her temple with a dainty pink painted fingernail. "Ya gotta learn how to think ahead — way furthuh ahead than any of you are used to thinking now."

What? We all sat there like cartoon characters with question marks over our heads — and not one of my buddies moved a muscle. And none of us dared to look at Ronnie, who was staring back at her as if she was speaking directly into his soul.

"Ya see, yo responsibility to yo team is to contain those offensive players until they start to re-think their plan." She paused, making sure they were all still with her. They were.

"So any time the offense goes to throwin' a deep pass," she continued, "or if the offense puts a blitz on that line, that's where ya speed and ya smarts — not ya height or strength — will make 'em fear ya presence on the field."

"When ya ah quickuh on ya feet than they ah — and ya show 'em ya know what they're gonna do before they do it, that's what'll set ya apart in those coaches' eyes."

Looking around the table I saw the same flicker of recognition in everyone's face. They just realized my mother knew what she was talking about — and that she was spot-on.

Mom smiled at the group now eating out of her hand. "Boys, when ya can stop ya opponent's progress toward the end zone every single time, those coaches will see that talent of yoas in a whole new light." She looked around the table and then let her eyes come back to rest for just a moment on Ronnie. "Ya brain and ya speed — THAT'S what's special about ya, Ronnie. Ya need ta remember that and figguh out how to use it to ya advantage. That's the sort of drills y'all need to be runnin this summah."

She reached for Ronnie's glass, "Mo sweet tea, honeh?"

The fellas all finished their lunch in silence, processing, I suppose, the football wisdom my mother had just bestowed upon ole' Ronnie. After adding a thick slice of apple pie to each plate, my mom waltzed back toward the kitchen, leaving an atmosphere of impressed silence in her wake.

For all her beauty and many other talents, my mom always spoke our language — food and football.

• • •

As great a life as my mother always seemed to be living, those of us closest to her knew all too well it wasn't without heartache. Dad always said that watching my mother's heart break when her only sibling, her sister Peggy, died from cancer was one of hardest things he had ever witnessed. And in his line of work, that meant something. Aunt Peggy was only in her forties when it happened, and he said my mom never really got over it. Sometimes even when she was smiling, I could see a shadow in her eyes and feel a glimpse of the grief that never left her completely.

Mom and Dad always said that my sister, Betty Carol, and I were surprise babies. I didn't understand exactly what that meant until I was old enough to know that my mother had many miscarriages before we were born, some of them full-term stillborn babies. That grief weighed on both of my parents at different times and in different ways — shadows of my lost brothers and sisters we never talked about, but who had an unspoken place in our lives and in my parents' hearts.

As painful as all those losses were for my parents, Mom would always say that the key to surviving any great heartbreak is returning to the center of our faith. "Life eventually falls into place if you just remain faithful and patient," she liked to say. The way she said it, and as surely as she said it whenever the grief would make an unscheduled stop at our house, I knew she was right.

• • •

One of the best things that fell into place as my mother predicted was my oldest sister, Peggy Ann. Had it not been for all those miscarriages, she and dad would never have adopted Peggy Ann, who was named for my mom's sister. Because Peggy Ann was almost 11 years older than me, it was like having a second mother during my youngest years. My dad always said that Peggy Ann earned the nickname "Mother Nature" because she ruled everything in our house once she arrived like a storm. She was fun and dramatic, with a sarcastic wit. From my earliest recollections, being around her was an unexpected delight.

Even though Peggy was strong-willed and could be a little dramatic, she always had a soft spot in her heart for me — and we had a wonderful relationship. By the time I was old enough to realize how her eccentricities made her special, Peggy was married and having children of her own, and she even named her middle son after *me*.

"Now remember Tommy," she'd say as a way of keeping me in line when she thought I was acting up a bit too much, "Ya gonna need to be a role model for *our* little Tommy. He's watching every move ya make."

Because she so believed in me and in my capacity to be someone's role model (whatever that meant) I took that responsibility very seriously. I always loved Peggy Ann, and I loved that she was my sister.

• • •

"Climb on up there on my handlebars, Tommy and I'll give you a ride to town." Another thing that fell into place because of my mother's faith and patience was my other older sister, Betty Carol. About 7 years after adopting Peggy Ann my mom gave birth to Betty Carol, whom even mom didn't realize was just her first "surprise baby."

I loved listening to Betty Carol laugh and talk to me as she pedaled. She told me all about the town, where we were going, and I lived for the moment when she said, "Ya ready ta stop and get a Coke?"

We'd then sit on the curb and drink our Cokes and talk about what we'd seen that day, then she'd say, "Ya ready?"

I'd nod and climb back up there on those handlebars and away we'd go. Betty Carol must have pedaled a million miles with me sitting on those handlebars.

"You want me to pedal a while and you can ride?" I'd ask from time to time as I got older and bigger and heavier, especially when I caught up to her in weight. Even though I was always small for my size I must have been quite a load for those handlebars.

"No," she would always say without a second's hesitation. "You're my baby brother and I wanna carry you."

And she always did. Always.

Years later, we laughed about how much work that was for her. She never complained and never asked me to switch places. "You were my baby brother," she'd remind me in the years to come. "I took my job of carrying you around very seriously!"

I can still picture us riding double on that old bike, with her looking around me, trying to see where we were going with me blocking her view. I can still hear her laughing, talking and telling me things she thought I should know about the town, where we were going, even life itself. Even though by today's safety standards that may not have been the safest way for two kids to travel, I can't ever remember feeling safer, more special and more taken care of in my life.

• • •

I grew up feeling pretty sure I was my parents' favorite. Maybe it was because I was the baby. Or maybe because my dad was 50 when I was born. In considering all the ways my parents took care of me, spent time with me, and made sure I had everything I needed, I knew it must be because I was the most special.

It wasn't until years later when I was grown, married and a father myself that I realized the mark of great parenting is being able to make each of your children feel like they are the favorite. Even then, however, and understanding that Peggy Ann and Betty Carol felt as I did, I'm still pretty sure I really was the favorite.

One thing I knew for sure, then and even now, was that Otis and Grace Spinks genuinely loved everything I loved and liked everyone I liked — and out of all those things and all of those people, they especially loved Terry. To my parents, Terry was like another son. And, truth be told, he might actually have been the favorite.

CHAPTER 6

"What is that wonderful smell?" Terry boomed, taking a long, dramatic whiff with his head turned toward the kitchen. Terry always had a way of entering our house like the prodigal son. The very hungry prodigal son. He'd walk in, hug my mom, and then start with the flattery of her cooking.

My mom came in from the kitchen for the hug. Predictable.

"I don't suppose you have any leftovers of whatever that is for your favorite kid, do you?" Terry said, giving my mom his most charming smile.

I rolled my eyes. "And he calls me Eddie Haskell," I muttered to myself.

My mom threw back her head in laughter — probably at both of us. She knew this routine well. "Well, honey, I'm cooking about a hundred and fifty miles of chicken pot pie for the church supper tonight, but you know what?" she said, stepping back and beaming up at him, "I betcha I can squeeze out a couple of bowlfuls for both my favorite boys."

What a diplomat. She knew full well that by "favorite kid", Terry had meant himself — and I, of course, was her only son. Clever woman.

My parents liked all of my friends, but they loved Terry.

"I am just smitten with that boy," my mom liked to say to anyone who would listen. My dad was completely captivated by Terry from the day they first met — and most especially by his sense of humor. Nobody could make my parents laugh like Terry. Sure, he was always polite, well mannered, and considerate, but of utmost importance in my family is Terry could make us all laugh like nobody else. Humor, my family always believed, is key to living a good life.

• • •

Terry stood at my mother's ironing board, taking one garment after another out, ironing it with impressive mastery, and then hanging it over the door. This was a common sight in my house. Anytime Terry was there and the ironing board was up, that big goof would go over there and just start ironing our clothes. Don't ask me why. I never could figure it out, except that my mother loved it. And more often than not it would work its way into an unflattering comparison with yours truly.

Mom whisked into the room, in a big hurry to do something and stopped dead in her tracks when she saw Terry there at the ironing board. This was not new. It had become their bit.

She smiled at Terry, "Well I declare, it sure is nice to have some help with all that ole' ironing," she began, and then, without even turning in my direction, added, "Tommeh sure could learn a thing or two from you, Terreh."

Terry put on that great big smile of his and said, "Mrs. Spinks, it's the least I can do to thank you for all of the meals that you generously provide for me."

"Lame," I said, glowering. This, too, was part of the bit.

Then my mom waltzed out of the room, charmed to her toes.

I glared in Terry's general direction.

"And THAT, my son, is how you do it," he said with that mischievous grin.

Somehow, a couch cushion slipped right out of my hand and headed straight for Terry's head.

• • •

"How's it going, there, Big Arms," Terry greeted my dad as no one else greeted a preacher ever. I'm not completely sure how all this got started between them, but I think it was mainly because my dad's arms were very much the opposite of big.

"Son, is that the way you greet a preacher?" my dad would ask, giving Terry a playful shove. My dad loved that boy, and loved that Terry could make him laugh.

"You know, Mr. Spinks, if you ever want to become a real preacher you're gonna have to become a Baptist."

My dad just stood there, looking stern.

And then, without any sort of warning at all, my dad just burst out laughing.

Terry laughed, then, too, seeing how tickled my dad truly was. Not wanting to be left out, I beg9an laughing then, too.

I looked over at my dad, who was by then laughing so hard he sounded like he was having an asthma attack. Every time he was just about to get it under control, he'd wipe his eyes and take a breath, look at Terry and start to say something, and then it would hit him again and he'd throw his head back and forth and slap his knee with his hand, struggling to catch his breath between fits of laughter.

Just like the ironing thing with my mother, this became their bit. Terry loved making my dad laugh to the point that he had to struggle to catch his breath. This strange bond lifted the spirits and fed the souls of both of them to such a degree that Terry looked for opportunities to keep the one-liners going until my dad was physically exhausted from laughing so hard.

• • •

"You know," Terry said, pushing himself back from the table after another of my mother's fabulous meals. "I really think Tommy here could be of more help to you around the house," he said, looking straight past me to my mother.

"Well, Terreh, I do believe you're right about that," my mother played along. "What kinds of things do you think he could be more helpful with?"

Which one of them is the bigger traitor? I pondered internally as I played with my mashed potatoes and began planning my revenge.

"Oh, gee, Mrs. Spinks," Terry said, scratching his chin. I don't know. "What kinds of things do you need more help with? Laundry, perhaps?" He looked at me and tried to catch my eye.

Nothing doing.

"Well, since I'm already doing a lot of the ironing for you," he continued, still determined to get a rise out of me.

Not gonna happen.

"Maybe Tommy could put the wash out on the line for you."

"Why, Terreh, I think that's a wonderful idea," my mother cooed. "Tommeh, don't you think that's a wonderful idea?"

Oh boy, are you going to get it next time we eat at your house, I silently vowed. Terry loved any conversation with my parents that could be focused on any of my inadequacies — or give me more to do around the house.

Good friend that I was, I always tried to return the favor when we were at his house, making sure his parents knew all Terry was capable of — and all the specific ways he could be of much more help to them around their house.

Our families, and the way we lived our lives, were so much the same that this sort of running banter amused both households for years — and gave us all plenty of stories to tell.

• • •

"Going to church tonight?" I asked Terry as we wound up our afternoon practice in the vacant lot down the hill. We liked throwing the ball there and then running backwards up the steep hill toward home. Hamstring work and transportation home — you can't get more efficient than that, right?

"It's Wednesday, isn't it?" Terry said, grinning as we jogged backwards up the long hill. "Where else would I be?"

"Man, Bradshaw, sometimes I think you go to church even more than I do, and I didn't think that was possible!" I said.

We jogged on until we reached the top of the hill, and then, looking at his watch, Terry made an unintelligible sound of startled distress and then spun around and took off at warp speed across the dozen or so lawns that separated us from his house.

"See you tomorrow!" I hollered after him as he bolted for home. Looking at my own watch, I gave a low whistle. He was cutting it pretty close on time to shower before Wednesday night services down at the Baptist church.

Growing up as a preacher's kid, it pretty much goes without saying that I had to be at church every time the church doors opened; Sunday school, morning service, night service, vacation Bible school, and revivals. Basically, I was exposed to more religion than one kid could handle.

So I guess I was pretty much known as a goody-two-shoes, and maybe I was one. With the parents I had, I was well-sheltered from the evils of the world. As far as I knew, looking at dirty magazines, watching dirty movies, smoking, and drinking were only done by people boarding a fast train to hell.

• • •

"Hey, Spinks, come look at this!" one of my buddies shouted across the parking lot where we were gathered to do some conditioning drills.

"Don't show him that, dummy," another one said. "Are you crazy?"

Show me what? I wondered, ambling in their direction.

Whatever it was got put away with the greatest of haste.

Whatever. Being among teenage boys with natural teenage boy curiosity, this kind of thing happened fairly often. For some reason, no one wanted to include me — or Terry, for that matter — in the viewing of whatever contraband they had managed to get their hands on.

I guess it was luck or providence or the hand of God that brought Terry and me together as best friends. Our households were very much parallel in terms of how we were raised, how we were treated and taught to treat others, and most of all the sense of humor that kept us all laughing and looking on the funny side of things.

But that doesn't mean we weren't curious.

• • •

"Hey," Terry said with an expression on his face I couldn't quite identify. We were standing in line in the school cafeteria, and Terry looked around to make sure no one was listening before he continued, "Gary Neely has a picture of a naked woman in his billfold. He's going to show it to me right after school — just outside the back corner door of the gym."

I made a mental note to be there.

After what seemed like about seven years, the final bell of the school day rang. I hurried outside to the exact spot Terry told me he and Gary were meeting to look at the picture. Then, rounding the back corner of the gym, I learned that about 300 hundred other boys had made that same mental note.

"What's going on out here?" Coach Bruce thundered, bursting through the gym door to break up what he assumed was a fight.

"Nothing, Coach . . . Sir . . ." said a polite voice from somewhere in the crowd. "We're just hanging out."

After Coach Bruce peered at enough faces in the gathered throng to satisfy himself that there was no fight to be broken up, he turned and went back into the gym.

Our eyes all followed him as he disappeared back into the gym, then a silence floated among us as if each of us was deciding what to do next. Then, without any sort of preamble, a sort of hushed frenzy of excitement erupted near the edge of the crowd. The wave of this frenzy grew larger, louder, and more intense until any semblance of order evaporated.

From where I stood at the back of the crowd, I couldn't see what was causing this excited ripple until my eyes caught a glimpse of what I could only assume was the picture, making its way through the crowd and leaving in its wake an unruly mob of young men who were frantic for another look.

The picture seemed to be heading my way and I braced myself for what I was about to see. There was no way I wasn't going to look at that picture, but all my upbringing kicked in about then to create an uncomfortable stir in my gut. Then, just seconds before my turn to see the picture, Thurman Jones grabbed the picture and took off.

Just like that. One minute the picture was just beyond the reach of my outstretched hand — and the next minute it was being carried off at a dead run by a lunatic! The mob followed him, and as boys of all ages and sizes caught up and surrounded Thurman, trying to get even a quick glimpse of the naked lady picture, the inevitable happened.

By the time I caught up with the mob that picture was torn into a thousand pieces.

"Here, Spinks," one of my buddies said, passing me a piece of the picture. I gulped, gathered all my courage, and looked at the torn picture remnant now in my hand. *Is that her . . . ear?* I wondered. Still, I felt my face getting red.

"That's nuthin,'" came Terry's voice behind me. "I got to see the whole naked lady," he bragged. "It was really something." He whistled. "You shoulda seen it, Tommy," he added, eyes huge. "You could see . . . everything."

You would have thought he saw that naked lady in person. I just looked at him. "Freak," I muttered.

I was so mad at Thurman Jones, as was the rest of that pack of disappointed ninth grade boys. The injustice of it was almost too much to bear.

• • •

"Boy, do I remember my first time," Terry said, holding court as he often did in his corner of our junior high locker room. He smiled and closed his eyes like he was taking it all in once again.

As ninth graders, we were becoming somewhat nonchalant and confident in the locker room — and even though some had become nonchalant and proud, others of us still took quick showers, toweled off even quicker, and got our underwear on in world record times. It was only once the underwear was on that you could finally relax a little bit. THIS was when the "big talk" started in the locker rooms, where some of the boys would brag — and most likely lie — about their sexual experiences.

Terry was joining the ranks of this particular locker room ritual now, and everyone leaned in close, not wanting to miss any of the details of Terry's first sexual experience.

Terry flashed this big cheesy grin. He paused for what seemed like an eternity and then said, "I was alone at the time."

The whole locker room broke out into a consolidated roar of laughter, with all these big ole' boys doubled over, laughing until all of the oxygen had left their lungs, and then punching each other in the shoulders. I guess Terry's story struck home in this most hilarious way because his story was pretty reminiscent of their own "first experience" as well.

Once things began to settle down, Terry couldn't resist telling that roomful of boys the rest of the story. "You see, my brother Gary, and I were playing hide and seek at our house," Terry began.

You are not going to tell that story, I begged silently. It didn't matter. Terry was rolling now.

"So it was Gary's turn to be 'it,' and I went off to find the perfect place to hide." He looked around the room, clearly enjoying the rapt attention of every boy in that locker room. "I decided to hide under the bed, so I got flat on my stomach and started to shimmy under the bed railing."

Dead silence in that locker room. I wished I could teleport myself to somewhere else. Anywhere else. In the whole world.

"And then I got stuck," Terry said. He paused for effect. "It was when I started wiggling to break free that I suddenly realized the more I wiggled, the better it felt." He winked at the crowd of boys. "Then I began to wiggle just to wiggle. By the time Gary found me I was one glassy-eyed, happy boy. Gary told me it was my turn to be 'it,' but I really just wanted to stay right there and take a nap."

One of the things people loved about Terry was that even at that young age, he could share a story that no other boy would have the confidence to share — in a way that made people listen and relate. He also had no problem making fun of himself, an endearing quality very few boys in ninth grade had.

CHAPTER 7

The whistle sounded and Coach Bruce motioned me toward the sideline. I looked over at Terry, ready to come in, and I gave him a thumbs-up. He grinned, sent back a mock salute, and trotted toward the line of scrimmage.

This was the rhythm of our sophomore year — Terry and I alternated as quarterbacks on both the sophomore and B teams — and man, oh man, was the year flying by. My job was to go into the game and keep the ball on the ground. Hand off here, hand off there — maybe keep it myself, especially when we were close enough that I could then slip the ball across the goal line into the end zone. Terry would go in and fire that football all over the place. First down, throw it. Second down, throw it. Third down, throw it. Fourth down, look over at the coaches on the sideline, and if they weren't paying attention, throw it again. When the coaches were quick enough to motion for him to kick on fourth down, he would drop back in punt formation and look for an opening to run for a first down. If there were no openings, he'd go ahead and kick the ball.

"You know what I think we need to do?" Terry asked one afternoon on the way home from school just after school reopened after Christmas break our sophomore year.

"I don't know," I answered, "Go throw the football?" it seemed like a reasonable guess because that's pretty much all we did when we weren't in school. With our sophomore football season now in the rear-view mirror it was hard not to be antsy.

"Well yes, of course," he said, grinning, "but also I was thinking . . . We should go out for track."

"Track?" I repeated, leaving off the "have you lost your ever-loving mind?" part of my response. "Isn't football plenty? Why in the world would we go out for track?"

Terry was always so aggressive, always attacking. He was this way with everything in life. He loved any chance to challenge himself. He simply loved the idea of getting better — at anything he did. "I think it would help us stay in shape, pick up some speed, and heck, it might be fun," he reasoned.

He had a point. Having that daily conditioning and practice routine would keep our bodies strong. And of course we'd still throw the football and do our own drills every day as we always had. So I agreed.

As fate would have it, we both made the traveling varsity squad, where Terry became a champion javelin thrower and I qualified for pole vault, triple jump, and broad jump.

It was funny to me how these events mirrored our football talents perfectly. Terry could already chunk that javelin with amazing distances and accuracy — and, following my mother's football wisdom to use my speed, quickness, and smarts on the football field — adding to my arsenal the ability to leap into the air, jump over and across a target area bar hurtle myself over a barrier just seemed like good sense. Terry was right. Again.

• • •

How we learned that Terry was a natural javelin thrower happened not during those track and field tryouts. It was still early spring and it seemed like all Terry ever wanted to do was fish. Terry loved to fish almost as much as he loved football.

So when I couldn't find Terry at his house, I rode my bike down to a small pond about a mile from Terry's house, just off Kingston Road. There he was, chest deep in that murky, slimy, snake-infested pond, looking once again for "Thor." Thor, you see, was Terry's name for the biggest bass in any pond. That boy could fish for hours. He had incredible patience. He would fish from a boat, the bank, or would wade in to get to whatever spot he decided "Thor" might be that day.

"I think he's under that brush right over there," Terry said, flipping an expert cast right at the edge of the brushy growth he indicated.

"I think you're crazy," I said, wrinkling my nose at the color of that water. "There've got to be all kinds of snakes in there."

"Weenie."

"Smarter than you."

"Be quiet. I need to concentrate. He's in there. I can feel him."

I picked up a small flat rock and sailed it expertly across the other side of the pond from where Terry was stalking Thor. I knew from experience this could be a while. Still, I asked, "How much longer?"

"As long as it takes," Terry replied, not looking up from his casting. He picked a piece of moss off his fishing line. Still not looking at me he said, "I don't know why you don't like to fish," he said. "It's good for your soul."

"My soul is just fine," I said. But my feet are a little cold. "Aren't you cold out there in that water?"

"Nope," he said. "I have waders."

"Are they heated?"

He turned his back to me then and approached Thor's hiding place from a different direction, expertly placing his bait just under the edge of the brush. I just wished he'd catch the dang thing so we could go do something else. Anything else, at this point, would be better than standing there shivering in the late winter sunshine.

I tried fishing. I wanted to love it as much as Terry loved it. He was so sure I'd love it. He'd been right about football, after all. But after just a few outings to fish with Terry I learned two important things about myself. First, I had no patience for it. If the fish weren't biting by about the third cast, I was outta there. Gone. History. Done. Second, wading into a dark, slimy pond, stepping on God-knows-what, and feeling that mud and slime squish between my toes felt completely insane.

After what seemed like seven hours of my skipping rocks and nagging, Terry finally sloshed his way to the shore, defeated once again by the wily Thor. "Ok, let's go," he said as he reached the bank.

"Oh," I said, chunking my last rock, "so soon?"

Terry rolled his eyes. "I still don't get why you won't fish," he said.

I picked up my bike and hopped on. "I think it's because I hate fishing," I said, standing up on my pedals to get moving as he walking beside me.

We moved along in silence for a few blocks and then Terry turned to me and said, "I bet you a dollar I can throw this cane pole past that mailbox up there." He pointed at his target, a mailbox about 200 feet away."

"You're on," I said. That seemed like a long way to chunk a cane fishing pole.

Terry stopped, took a few steps back, and then let that cane pole fly. And fly it did. Who knew those things could fly? I watched in awe as that pole not only reached the designated target mailbox, but passed it right on by and continued about another 100 feet.

When the pole finally did descend, to our horrified amazement speared straight through the back window of a school bus. And this wasn't just any school bus, we discovered in our speechless escalating panic. It landed in the school bus of the toughest, scariest broad in town . . . Mrs. Bell.

Yep, our excitement over the incredible distance that cane pole flew was immediately squelched as we realized that the person we were going to have to explain this to was tough-talking, trouble-stalking, waddle-walking, Mrs. Bell. Every kid at Woodlawn who had any sense was scared to death of Mrs. Bell. Of all the people and buses in this entire world, why did the bus driven by Mrs. Bell have to be the one skewered by that runaway cane pole hurled by Terry's ridiculous throwing arm?

"We're dead ducks," I said.

Terry whistled. "Don't I know it."

We knew without any further discussion that this just might be the end of us.

There were about a million thoughts swarming around in my brain as we walked closer to the wounded bus. Toggling between awe of the distance my buddy threw that pole, and wondering how in the world fate could allow it to land in MRS. BELL'S bus, of all places! I couldn't even begin to imagine how we were going to get Terry's fishing pole back. With the bus parked right outside of Mrs. Bell's house — and that big picture window facing the parked bus — we knew in an instant there was no way to retrieve Terry's favorite fishing pole without being caught — and most likely killed — by Mrs. Bell. The worst part, for Terry, was that he could never brag about that amazing throw, because the news would surely spread in our corner of town — and it wouldn't take much for it to get back to Mrs. Bell.

Little did we know then, but that first throw was just a taste of what Terry was capable of doing with a pole. I don't think we ever told anybody about that incident, but I think it was that afternoon when Terry decided track and field was something we needed to explore.

He was right. By the time we graduated from High school, Terry had broken the National High School record for throwing the javelin with a throw of almost 240 feet. Not one to be outdone, I, too, took ownership of a high school track and field record myself — as a pole-vaulter.

As much as Terry enjoyed our track and field adventures, our first love was always football. "Do you guys ever talk about anything else?" one of our teammates chided, turning around from the seat in from to us. "We need to be getting psyched for today's events." We were on the bus to a big track and field meet, and while the rest of the team was "getting psyched," our only concern was the upcoming NFL draft.

Terry waved his hand in the general direction of our teammate. "We stay psyched," he said, not even looking in the kid's direction. Then he paused, looked at the kid's shocked expression and then busted out laughing.

Terry reached over and tousled the skinny kid's hair. "Just messing with you son," he said. "But really, don't worry. We're ready, right Tommy?"

I nodded solemnly.

The kid turned back around, clearly annoyed. Terry and I looked at each other and shrugged, then returned to our discussion of all the stats and what ifs that made our eyes and imaginations light up, even as they drove the lives and careers of our football heroes.

Those kinds of discussions between Terry and I were ongoing — and they marked some of our most special memories and spectacular dreams. We dreamed together on those track and field trips, and our dreams already felt so completely real to us — even though they were still years in front of us. We each believed, with every fiber of our being, that these dreams were ours to attain.

• • •

As spring spiraled into the glory of summer once again, the failing algebra grade on both of our report cards heralded a stint in summer school — for both of us. We took some comfort in having to endure this agony together, and I agreed to pick Terry up each morning in my green 1951 Nash Rambler so that we could serve our sentence.

On that first morning of summer school, I chugged to the front of Terry's house in that green beauty that had about three million miles on it.

"We may have to stop for gas," I said as Terry jumped in.

"And oil. And water," Terry said, grinning, "what? About every 10 miles?"

"Something like that," I said, pulling out into the street to hiccup and rumble toward the school a few miles away. "But lame wheels are better than no wheels, wouldn't you agree?" I asked Terry as we turned into the parking lot.

"I would indeed," Terry said with a chuckle.

Our summer school teacher was Mr. Jim McLain. Mr. McLain was a huge man who took his job very seriously.

"You can call me Mr. Mac," he told the class on that first morning.

"Yes, sir, Mr. Mac," the class responded in unison.

"I'm here to help you learn algebra," Mr. Mac said, pacing back and forth in front of the class. "I will give you all the time and attention you need to get a passing grade and understand this material so you can move on in your math studies," he continued, looking each one of us in the eye. "But what I do not have time for is bad attitude, rude behavior, or short attention spans."

We believed him. Well, at least some of us did.

As we neared the end of that first summer school day, Mr. Mac's shirttail was untucked and chalk covered his pants and shirt.

He was in the middle of writing an algebra problem on the blackboard when, all of the sudden, there were voices coming from the back of the classroom.

All eyes turned to discover the culprit, a punk kid in the back of the class who continued to laugh and talk to the unsuspecting person across the aisle. He seemed oblivious to the wrath he was provoking.

Terry and I kept our eyes on Mr. Mac, who was still trying to explain the algebra problem on the chalkboard as he wrote.

Then Mr. Mac stopped talking. And he stopped writing. With his hand still high over his head, chalk still pressed tightly against the chalkboard mid-stroke, he tilted his ear ever so slightly to the left.

This, I recognized right away, was a warning to back-row Joe that it would be in his best interests to zip his mouth.

Unfortunately, this kid didn't quite catch that subtle signal, and he continued yukking it up with that poor kid beside him, who had his eyes fixed on the chalkboard.

So Mr. Mac, once again, stopped writing on the board.

Terry looked across at me now and mouthed, "Uh oh."

I nodded. There was no way this was going to go well for that kid, who was either brainless or bolder than anything I could imagine. I wasn't sure which was worse.

You could cut the tension in that classroom with a knife. No one moved or spoke, and yet that kid just kept on talking as if his buddy across the aisle was holding up his end of the conversation.

Then, like a streak of lightning, Mr. Mac wheeled himself around and fired that piece of chalk in his hand toward that kid as if he was Satchel Paige himself. The white bullet of chalk whizzed about three inches above the kid's head and exploded off the back wall.

In the stunned silence of that full classroom, giant eyes stared back at Mr. Mac from every vantage point — including the two very wide eyes of the punk kid.

Terry and I looked at each other, then back at Mr. Mac.

"What an arm," Terry mouthed, putting into words exactly what I was thinking.

While the enormous grins we could no longer contain were probably highly inappropriate for the situation, we couldn't hide our admiration. Mr. Mac was a stud. In a single instant of this teacher's utter frustration two things became clear to Terry and me:

1. Don't mess with Mr. Mac, and

2. Dizzy Dean ain't got nothin' on Mr. Mac. The man could throw. And hard.

We talked about that legendary throw for years.

• • •

The bell rang, as it did every day, to herald our 30-minute summer school break.

As was our practice, Terry and I walked calmly to the door of the classroom, and then sprinted down the empty hallway, down the stairs, and out the back door. Passing up most of the other kids who liked to use that break to hang around and talk, go downstairs to walk around or get some fresh air, Terry and I grabbed a football from the coach's office and hurried out onto the football field.

The excitement of having thirty free minutes to throw the football right in the middle of our summer algebra experience completely erased any concern over throwing the ball in our school clothes or the 110-degree heat.

"Dang!" I said, looking at my watch after what seemed like five minutes but was actually 25. "We gotta get back in there."

"Oh, man," Terry whined, "I was just getting warmed up good. A few more," he said drilling the ball into my chest.

The few more turned in to 10 extra minutes, so we sprinted all the way back to the classroom, dreading whatever was about to befall us at the hands of an annoyed Mr. Mac. The chalk incident of the first day was still burned into our brains.

Tucking the football we hadn't had time to return as discretely as I could beneath my arm, I followed Terry into the now quiet classroom. All eyes turned toward us as we entered, dripping sweat from every pore, and followed us to our seats.

We sat quietly, trying to calm our breathing from the sprint, and made eye contact with no one.

Mr. Mac watched us enter and sit down, but didn't say a word.

I tucked the football under my chair and opened my notebook. Whew, I thought, taking care to look studious and trying not to think about what we probably smelled like. As class got underway once again, I couldn't help but glance at Terry from time to time to see if the paper was sticking to his arms and hands as bad as it was mine. It was.

Years later, we asked Mr. McLain why he never got mad at us for those times when we sprinted back to his classroom stinky and late after our breaks.

"It's very simple," he had said to our surprise. "Boys, I could spot a dream taking shape when I saw one, and I saw that happening with the two of you. I wasn't gonna interfere with that process, and in some small way I believed I was helping you with your journey."

This one statement by a teacher I had for one half of one summer stayed with me for the rest of my life. These words and Mr. Mac's reasoning have played and replayed in my mind so many times to guide me and help me remember how important it is to be observant of others' dreams. I think it was because of Mr. Mac that later on in life if I was ever in a position to help someone's dreams take shape, then that's what I was going to do. Mr. Mac's legacy will forever live through me.

CHAPTER 8

Just as I opened my eyes to look at the alarm clock, it went off, jangling me into my junior year with the August 15 beginning of our dreaded two-a-day football practices. As much as I loved playing football, and even as much as I appreciated what these intensive periods of practice did for me physically, there was just no way not to hate two-a-days.

Even though this torture only lasted for two weeks, while you were in those two weeks it felt more like six months. I pulled on my clothes, brushed my teeth and headed out the front door.

Because my Green Goddess of a car had grown even less dependable over the summer, and since Mack Ramsey, my neighbor and teammate, had a much more dependable car — meaning it would start — it made sense to ride with Mack.

"Hey," Mack said, coming out his front door just as I got to the steps.

"Hey," I said, following him to the car.

We rode to the high school gym in silence. It was too early for words, and neither of us really wanted to admit the dread we were feeling, deep in the pits of our stomachs. We knew that once we got into it we'd be OK, but the idea of beginning this infamous and grueling conditioning experience was daunting.

We arrived at the school, and along with a pack of other sleepy reluctant guys, entered the gym. We greeted one another, trying to keep a lid on any enthusiasm — we'd need every bit of energy we could muster to get through the morning ahead.

"I just hate this," someone said from the back of the locker room as we dressed in silence.

"And it's not like we're not in shape," said another. "Why do we have to kill ourselves these first two weeks when we already know what's what?"

"I think it's just a sick tradition," came another voice. "Someone started it for a bunch of out-of-shape wimps and now nobody knows why we still do it when we've got a good solid team like ours."

You see, the universal rule among all football players going through two-a-days is to start complaining, immediately. Literally, as you are putting on your uniform, the morning ritual of complaints begins, and everybody chimes in. Looking back, I think it must have been a sort of bonding ritual more than anything else.

"Why we gotta do this so early?" a big lineman whined as we entered the field. "It's too early in the morning to practice football. My brain's not even up yet."

This drew a chuckle from several of us. Terry and I pretty much listened, nodded our agreement and laughed at the best ones. We probably didn't hate it as much as everyone else did because we practiced all the time — and anything having to do with football was pretty much OK with us, but we did our part. And they were right. It was too dang early.

"Look at that," someone said in the pack walking behind me, "there's still dew on the field. It's too wet. It's gonna be slippery."

Throughout that morning, the complaining continued. The coaches. The equipment. The short water breaks — and about once every 30 seconds — someone took their turn complaining about the hot, humid, Louisiana heat.

• • •

I slammed into the tackling dummy, feeling the heat pounding in my head and coming through the soles of my cleats. It was getting close to the midday break and the sticky Louisiana heat had already lived up to its curse words.

On one hand, it seemed wrong to pray that someone would have a heat stroke as we struggled through drill after drill. But we were in survival mode, and any sound of that whistle was as welcome as the lukewarm water we chugged from our water jugs any time we got a chance. Besides, a random heat stroke or any other medical emergency would mean everyone could take a nice, long break.

Our manager, the big wimp, stood over to one side of the field in the shade, sipping from his water jug, watching his clock to signal that it was time to move to another segment of practice. He was a nice enough guy, but in that role we hated him. Until, that is, he blew the whistle signaling the end of a session.

• • •

"EVERYBODY UP!" These, the sweetest words in the whole English language, were hollered by Coach Bruce himself when the end of morning practice had at last arrived.

With energy none of us realized we had left, we all started yelling and clapping as each of us, in the silence of our own hearts, thanked God that another chunk of this two-week beating was behind us.

"What's for lunch?" Terry said, catching up to me as I waited for Mack. Everyone piled into whatever car they could get a ride in to go home to eat, rest, and then drag themselves back to the field and start all over again.

• • •

"Wanna throw?"

One of the funny things about those grueling two-a-days was that every day of those two weeks, before practice got started and in the evenings after we were done, Terry and I somehow always had enough energy left over to throw the football. We threw every day after school, during football season, during basketball season, during track season and baseball season. We threw in the rain, the sleet, and even in the rare Louisiana snow.

Throwing the football was like breathing for us. It was all we wanted to do. And as we threw we became so in sync with each other that it felt as if we could read each other's minds. We literally lived and breathed football. Football made us brothers.

• • •

The speaker crackled overhead, jolting us out of our world geography daze. The well-meaning teacher had just about bored us out of our socks, and I was lost somewhere in my NFL daydreams when the telltale sound heralded incoming daily announcements.

"Attention students, we have some very special announcements today . . ." Blah blah blah . . . I slipped back downfield in my mind, waiting for the game winning pass . . . "And Tommy Spinks and Terry Bradshaw."

Wait. What?

"Congratulations, Tommy!" The teacher looked right at me and smiled. "It's such an honor to be elected by our *whole* student body to be in the Accolade Pageant," she said. She began clapping and the whole class joined in.

Well, then. I thought, grateful for the recap. For whatever reason, the Accolade Pageant was a very big deal at Woodlawn High School. Eight seniors, six juniors, and four sophomores — a mixture of boys and girls — were chosen to sit on a court where there would be a Senior King crowned and a Senior Queen crowned in what they called the "Knighting Ceremony." The evening then ended with a "Knight's Ball" held at the American Legion Hall.

This was A Very Big Deal. And Terry and I were in. I wasn't sure what all that entailed, but I knew enough to be excited about it. I couldn't wait to see what Terry knew about it. He always seemed to have the inside information on things. I had no idea where the inside even was.

• • •

"Ok, girls, file in from the back right corner," said the pretty young teacher with the bullhorn. She gestured and pointed a dainty finger, "over there." She took a quick look around at the students gathered in the auditorium and found the group of boys laughing and cutting up and not paying her any attention at all.

"Boys," she said, a little bit louder than she had addressed the girls. She waited. No response. "BOYS!" she said, putting some oomph into the word this time. A few of the boys looked around, and then elbowed the others into attention. She nodded, "Boys will file in from the back left side." Again she pointed to the left in case we had trouble discerning left from right. Wise woman.

In the days leading up to the Accolade Pageant, we had to rehearse every day in the auditorium. Once we got the who-files-in-where part straight, we progressed to the part where each boy and girl from the same class would meet in the middle, and the boy would escort the girl up the stairs onto the stage. Then we would all take our places in the chairs on either side of the King and Queen.

It seemed pretty straightforward, but one should never assume any such thing with a group that contained teenaged boys, and especially one that welcomed both Terry and me.

• • •

I watched the junior girls file in from the right as we junior boys filed in from the left, and I couldn't help but notice that Barbara Ann Lindsay was one of the junior girls elected to the court. I didn't know Barbara, but I knew that Terry had been out on a date with her once before.

"She's a square," he had reported when I asked about the date. "A real prude, but a sweet girl."

Barbara was also exceptionally pretty, and I admired Terry's courage in asking her out. I also liked knowing this about her, and I decided the first time she walked in that I wanted to be paired with her.

As we began walking towards the stage, I heard this strange little popping sound. It seemed to be coming from the same direction where Barbara was. With every step she took, something kept pop, pop . . . popping. As we met in the middle, I leaned over and whispered out of the side of my mouth, "Is that . . . I'm sorry, is that your toes making that popping sound?"

Barbara threw her head back in laughter. I wasn't sure whether she was laughing at the goofy look on my face or at me for thinking that sound might be coming from her toes. Her laugh was an amazing sound — this loud, melodic lilting music-to-my-ears sound that pretty soon had every head in the room turning in our direction.

Then her face got beet red. Still laughing, she nodded her head vigorously, and then, suddenly realizing how loudly she was laughing, Barbara clapped her hand to her mouth, as if to muffle the sound.

I never wanted anything to muffle that laugh ever again. In fact, I knew in that single instant that I wouldn't mind hearing that sound for the rest of my life. I was hooked.

• • •

We were all dressed up and stuffed into the cramped backstage area. There was muffled small talk and nervous anticipation as we all waited there for the pageant to begin.

After weeks of rehearsal, Accolade Pageant day had at last arrived. I'll have to admit, this deal had changed for me from one of those things to suffer through to something I looked forward to from the moment I opened my eyes every morning.

The reason for this change of heart? Oh, that's simple. From that first exchange with Barbara Ann Lindsay, all I thought about was how to get another chance to talk to her again.

I said nothing of this to Terry, of course. He'd just make fun. And besides, after his assessment of Barbara's girlfriend potential, he probably wouldn't approve, anyway. Wait, I had to stop my runaway thoughts. Who said anything about a girlfriend? Still, Barbara Ann and that infectious laugh of hers had gotten my attention like nothing else.

I craned my neck toward the door. Is Terry here yet? I wondered. Then I silently asked the question that was really on my mind: Where's Barbara? I tried to look around the room without being too obvious, scanning the girls' side for any glimpse . . . Using my peripheral vision as I pretended to be studying the drapes, the wall socket — really anything I could fix my face on and let my eyes do the walking.

Then an explosion of laughter rose up from a group of girls across the backstage area. Following that sound to its source, I found Barbara, hand covering her mouth, trying to contain the laughter I was desperate to set free.

To say she was stunning in her floor-length gown would have to be about the understatement of the year — or maybe the century. I knew my time for contact was limited, so I p every opportunity to make my way closer to her, thinking nothing else but how to strike up a conversation.

"Uh-oh, Helen, is this your pin on the floor?" I inquired, stooping over to pick up a pin and then extending it toward Helen.

Helen shook her head "no" and continued her conversation.

"Oh, it's not?" I replied, taking a casual side step closer to where Barbara was excitedly talking to her friends. I turned the other direction toward the group gathered there. "Hey, anybody lose a pin over here?" I asked, taking a step backward without so much as looking to see whom I might be stepping on. The only concern in my mind was closing the real estate gap between Barbara and me. "Okay, then," I said, waving and smiling, "I'll hold onto this pin in case anyone needs it."

Then I turned to a girl I sort of knew from history class and said, "Patty, does my tie look straight?"

Patty took a step back and examined my tie. "Yes," she said.

"It does?" I said, feigning complete shock, then relief. "Oh good," I said, patting my tie. "I guess it just feels crooked."

Catching sight of another acquaintance close enough to engage, I took another sidestep, putting myself well within conversation range of Barbara.

"Hey Marcia," I said, "I just saw your parents out there. They are front and center." I gave her a thumbs-up. "You ready?"

With every attempt I made to get noticed by Barbara, I seemed to get noticed by everyone BUT Barbara. And, with each step in her direction, I would ever so coolly glance her way to see if perhaps she was looking my way, too. She never was. She was too busy laughing at whatever someone *else* shared with her.

I was getting desperate to be on the receiving end of that glorious sound.

Normally, I prided myself on being somewhat "cool" around the girls, but around Barbara, I was just the opposite — a goofy and ridiculous klutz.

"You ain't got a chance, brutha," Terry whispered, giving me a nudge in the ribs with his elbow. "She don't even know you're alive! But it sho is fun watching you try!"

Terry had joined the backstage group and, knowing me as well as he did, quickly sized up the situation — and caught on to my charade the minute he spotted me working the room in an attempt to get closer to Barbara. He smiled that Cheshire grin of his, and then cackled like he was watching some hilarious scene in a movie.

I got so tickled at how he was laughing at me that I couldn't help but laugh right along with him.

That's when it happened.

Somewhere between my laughing at my ridiculous self and my laughing at Terry laughing at me, my eyes met Barbara's from across the crowd.

While Barbara had no idea why I was laughing or what was so funny, her amusement danced in those beautiful eyes until she couldn't stifle her own giggle.

I smiled at her and shrugged.

She smiled back at me and my heart melted to the floor.

The pageant then began.

• • •

In the days and weeks after the Accolade Pageant, I would see Barbara at school, usually talking with her friends in the hallways between classes. Sometimes these sightings occurred naturally. Often, I went out of my way to make it happen.

I took a casual stroll, as I did about the same time every afternoon by Ms. Loper's shorthand class. I was quick to spot Barbara — and then look away — as I slowly sauntered past the classroom. As I did this, I kept my head facing forward, using my peripheral vision to determine whether she saw me, too. I was playing it cool and my plan seemed to be working well. I would later learn that she saw me, too, but thought I must have a small bladder because I needed to leave during class for the bathroom every single day. So embarrassing.

It was spring of my junior year, and baseball and track season were in full swing. I played shortstop for the baseball team and was the only pole-vaulter on the track team. It surprised me that as eaten up as I was with baseball as a younger boy, playing shortstop for my high school was by then just another fun thing to do. Baseball season came and went, just like track and field. My heart belonged to football. And now, I also had a constant case of Barbara on the brain.

• • •

"So, Tommy," said the cheerleader leaning against the locker next to mine, "who are you going to take to the Spring Picnic?"

This was about the eleventh time that week someone had asked me that question. Some were bold and came right out with it; some slipped a note into my locker vents between classes — or into my hand in the passing period between classes. Still others whispered their suggestion in my ear just as class was about to start.

"I don't know," I told her, trying not to look for too long at her big, imploring eyes. "I haven't decided yet."

The problem with all this was that I had decided. Without question. But not one of those inquiries or suggestions ever mentioned Barbara's name. If Barbara Ann Lindsay was the least bit interested in going to the picnic with me, she definitely did not let it be known by way of the substrate network most girls used to let their love — or even "like" interest be known.

So while I knew for sure I wanted to go to the picnic with her, I didn't have a clue how to make that happen . . . in a cool way. Or, to be honest, in any way at all.

Because I still had not said a word about my secret infatuation to anyone — and most especially not to Terry after that pageant exchange — I was completely on my own. So when I heard one of her best friends talking in the hallway about a bunch of them going to study in the library, I decided my studies needed some library attention as well.

The plan that I hatched on the way to the library was to casually walk up to her, turn on my charm and make her laugh, and then ask her to the picnic. She wouldn't be able to resist saying yes, right?

I walked into the library, sat down at a table across the room from where Barbara was studying, and opened my books. I decided to play it cool by "studying" for a while, and then, with a need to "take a break" I would stretch, get up and stroll over to her table and strike up the conversation that would end with her saying yes to going to the picnic with me.

The only trouble with that plan was the moment for my "study break" never seemed to feel right. I sat there and feigned studying as I listened to my thoughts bouncing around inside my head like charged ping-pong balls. *Ok, go over there now. No. Not now. Why not, you big wuss? Just go over there and talk to her. No, I need to wait. She really looks like she's concentrating right now. I know what I'll do. I'll wait until she gives some sign of needing a break. What would that look like? Maybe she'll fidget or put her pencil down or something. Ok. That's the plan. Wait. Where's she going?*

To my complete dismay, Barbara never showed any sign of needing a study break at all. Then, after an hour or so, and without any warning whatsoever, she closed her books, got up and headed toward the door, turning toward me just as she went through those large wooden doors to give me a small smile and a dainty wave.

Agony. *You idiot*, my ping-pong thoughts chided as I sat there for long enough that I wouldn't appear to be following her. You blew it!

The next opportunity I had to ask Barbara to the Spring Picnic appeared quite unexpectedly. Class elections were coming up and in those days it was a tradition for people to host "poster painting" parties for their friends who were running for office. There was always lots of food, unlimited soft drinks and great music. It was as much a chance to socialize as it was to actually paint campaign posters for the school hallways and gym — but that work got done, too, and it was always a lot of fun for everybody.

I learned through the grapevine that Barbara was going to be at Ronald Carlson's poster painting party. I had figured out where to be between classes and how and where to listen to get some idea of Barbara's intended plans. I was in love. I was also trying to find the best way to ask her to the Spring Picnic — in a cool way, of course.

Even though one of my best pals, Bobby Waddell, was also running for office and hosting a poster party at his house at exactly the same time as Ronald's, I figured that my help would be more appreciated at Ronald's house. After all, it looked like Bobby and his crew had everything under control. Ronald and Barbara had been friends since early childhood, and I just had a gut feeling that Ronald needed a little more help. With that selfless intent, I headed over to Ronald's house.

I felt a little bit nervous as I walked into the front door of Ronald's house. The place was a hub of activity — music blaring and the smell of school-grade poster paint wafting in from the dining room where a few kids were gathered around, carefully filling in large stenciled letters with splashes of vivid color. I glanced around the room. No Barbara.

"Food and Cokes are in there, Tommy," someone shouted over the music. "Help yourself and then come on in here and make yourself useful!"

"Sure thing!" I responded, continuing to scan the room for any sight of Barbara or her friends.

Seeing no trace of Barbara or any of the rest of her group, and unwilling to expose my interest by asking, I stood there nibbling on a potato chip. Now what? That picnic was drawing close, and I knew I'd better ask Barbara before someone else did. With my recent library failure fresh on my mind, today just seemed like the day. But first I have to find her. Is she coming? Did something happen? Was my intel wrong?

My silent questions were answered in a stoke of sheer luck as I heard two girls talking down toward the end of the table.

"Who else is coming?" one asked, taking a bottle of Coke from the big tub of iced-down drinks and opening it with the bottle opener that was dangling by a string tied to the handle of the tub.

"Well, Barbara, Rita, and Nancy were here earlier," the other girl replied, "but then they left."

PAY DIRT! My thoughts yelled, as if I didn't already know that. I tried to lean closer without letting on I was listening so hard for any other details about Barbara's whereabouts. I studied a tray of cookies like it was my job, and then took great care in selecting just exactly the right one. Why did they leave? Where did they go? My thoughts conducted a silent interrogation.

"Are they coming back?" the other girl asked, taking her own Coke from the tub and opening it.

Yeah . . . Are they coming back? My thoughts chimed in.

"I don't know," came the answer. They said they were going to go over to Bobby's to see if they need any help over there. So they might be. It just depends."

After eating my cookie and watching all the fine work going on in Ronald's dining room for a respectable amount of time, I decided that Ronald and his crew seemed to be in pretty good hands. It seemed like an excellent idea, then, to head on over to Bobby's house. After all, Bobby is one of my best friends, right?

When I arrived back at Bobby's house, I was greeted at the door by Terry and a bunch of my teammates, as well as some other kids from school I really enjoyed hanging out with. Everyone was there, of course, except the one I was really looking for. Once again, I found out just by being quiet and listening to the conversations around me that Barbara and her pals had been there, helped out, and then left. She was, at that very moment, on her way back over to Ronald's house.

"I'm going home," I said to no one in particular, dejected beyond words or the ability for pretense.

• • •

The next few days seemed to be one continuous missed opportunity to ask Barbara to the picnic. It was also the week that our Woodlawn baseball team would be playing against one of our archrivals, Byrd High School. I was playing shortstop.

This game was intense from the very first pitch. And, because it was such a rivalry, lots of the student body from both schools turned out for the game. It came as no surprise to anyone when the game went into extra innings.

I was crouched down at shortstop, hand in glove, waiting for the batter to swing. For a reason I will never understand because my focus was fully on that batter, I glanced up into the stands. There she was. From my position on the field, I had a perfect line of sight toward the most beautiful girl in the whole school. And she was smiling at *me*. Me! Somehow I knew at that moment that she was there to see me . . . only me.

For the rest of the game I had to make myself stop looking up at the stands. It was like a reflex that hit me between every single play. I realized I wasn't looking too cool about it, either, because on about the 100th time I looked there I saw her throw her head back and laugh. Stop looking at her! Get your head in the game, Bozo. Be cool! My thoughts scolded.

We went on to win that baseball game by one run in what seemed to be like the 27th inning. Trotting off the field after that final out, it was all settled in my head. I would get out of the locker room as quickly as I could, go talk to Barbara — because now I knew she would be waiting for me, and I'd just ask her to the picnic. Simple as that.

Once the coach finally finished talking — and I hadn't really heard a word he said — I shot straight toward my locker to change. And, while normally I'd want to hang out with the guys and relive all the big moments of such a long and nerve-wracking game, all I could think about was getting out of there and finding Barbara.

"Where you going in such a hurry?" Terry asked me as I stuffed my uniform into my bag.

"I need to get home," I said, zipping the bag closed. "Lots of stuff to do."

"Right," Terry said, grinning that know-it-all grin I knew only too well. "Let me know how it goes."

How does he know? I wondered as I hurried toward the locker room door without dignifying his knowing comment with a response.

The door of the field house banged behind me as I looked first toward the stands. Empty. No one left but a few parents chatting and laughing.

My dad waved, thinking of course that I was looking for them. "Great game, Tommy!" He hollered across the distance. And even from that distance I could see my mother smiling. She loved football, but she still secretly loved watching me play baseball better than anything else in the world. I wondered for an instant if she still kept that scrapbook during baseball season.

Returning my thoughts to the business at hand, I shifted my focus to the parking lot where some cars were starting up and filing out as others sat while their owners visited across the hoods and tailgates.

Barbara was nowhere to be seen. *I blew it*, my thoughts berated, *I looked at her too much. I looked like a wimp to her. She'll never go to the picnic with me now.*

Feeling more defeated than I ever had in my life, even after that big win, I turned toward my car. As I did this, I took one more wistful glance across the parking lot to where Barbara and her friends usually parked.

There she was. She was heading towards her car, parked deeper than usual in the parking lot. I felt my feet moving that direction. Not exactly running, but not exactly the cool saunter I would have hoped for, either.

I knew right then as I shuffled madly toward her that there was no way I was going to let her leave without asking her to that dad-gum picnic. Time to man up, my thoughts urged, changing timbre to the self-coaching that always got me through tough situations on the football field. I have to do this, once and for all.

Getting closer, I slowed my steps to something a little bit closer to the cool saunter I had planned. "Baaaaarrrbbaaraaa!!" I managed to say. The raspy sound coming out of my mouth sounded more like a 12-year-old girl with the croup than any man voice I'd ever heard. All plans for cool evaporated in that squeaky delivery.

So what did I do about that? I began to sprint through the parking lot as fast as I could, the unmistakable sound of metal cleats grinding against the pavement as I ran.

With the sound — and possible sparks — of my parking lot dash so loud and so distinct, not only did Barbara turn around and look my way, but so did every other person in that parking lot. It was also a lot further than it looked. By the time I got to her — even in the supreme physical shape I was in — I was having what felt and most likely looked like some sort of hyperventilating panic attack stroke.

With profuse sweat pouring from my face, I bent over and put both hands on my knees, trying to catch my breath.

Barbara said nothing during all this. She just stood there looking at me.

Gathering what composure I could, I attempted to speak in my real voice. My mind searched frantically for the words, but the right words just didn't come.

It was Barbara who broke the awkwardness of this moment. "You played a great game, Tommy," she said. "I'm just so happy that we won!"

As she spoke, my mind kept trying to think of a response to her words, but meanwhile my heart was screaming, 'Go to the picnic with me! Please, Barbara, please! Just say you'll go to the picnic with me!'

"Thanks for coming," were the only words that would come out of my mouth. I smiled my coolest smile while my thoughts raved, *You big idiot! Just say it! Just ask her! She likes you! Do it, dummy!!!* Knowing in my bones I was just about to once again miss my perfect opportunity to ask her to the picnic, I somehow sputtered, "Will you go to the picnic with me?"

She smiled that drop-dead gorgeous smile that haunted my dreams.

I held my breath, bracing for her answer.

"Yes, Tommy, I would love to go to the picnic with you", she said, still smiling.

My knees went weak. "Good," I said. Somehow, I kept it together while she got in her car. I waited for her to get in and I shut the door for her. I smiled and gave her a super-cool half-wave as she drove away.

Once Barbara was out of earshot — and eyesight — I came back to life as Tarzan, King of the Jungle. I even let out a long, yodeling Tarzan yell, and the people from all across that humongous parking lot looked at me like I had just lost my mind.

I had lost my mind. And also my heart. I began beating my chest like a drum and yelling random niceties to strangers still left in the parking lot:

"What a beautiful night!"

"Isn't the moon magnificent?"

"Thank you for coming to the game!"

"Hope you tried the hot dogs in the concession stand, they're absolutely great!"

With no idea of what was going on or whether I was having some sort of mental breakdown, most of the people just hurried to their cars.

"Tommeh, honeh, you need to get in the car," my mother said, arriving only for the exuberant parking lot attendant portion of my program. I'm sure she thought I was just working off some post-game exhilaration.

Something new had been breathed into me. I knew right then that my crush on Barbara Ann Lindsay had just blossomed into full-blown love. And she was going to go to the spring picnic with me. It was going to be perfect.

• • •

That afternoon of the Woodlawn High School Spring Picnic of 1965 is still etched in my mind as if it were yesterday. Sitting together on top of a picnic table close to the water's edge, Barbara and I faced the lake. I know we were talking the whole time we were there, but I honestly couldn't tell you what we talked about — all my mind could absorb in that moment was how, with the afternoon sunlight behind her and the slight breeze that gently moved her hair, she looked every bit the angel from heaven I would know her from then on to be. Noticing how the sunlight settled around her like a well-deserved halo, I couldn't help but touch her face and brush back the strand of her hair that the breeze placed across her brow. I knew right then I would be in love with Barbara Ann Lindsay forever.

CHAPTER 9

"Tommy, I swear, you have THE greatest hands of anyone I have ever seen," Terry said in the best motivational voice he could muster. Then he added, "You can catch better than any other receiver Woodlawn has EVER had."

Now remember, it was still our junior year — and I was still playing both defensive back and quarterback. In some strange twist of fate, after Terry and I did such a good job alternating the QB job for Woodlawn's sophomore and B teams, I — and likely the coaches — just assumed we would continue this practice for the upcoming football seasons. Why change a winning combination? But in truth we were two best friends who both wanted that quarterback job, so I suppose the coaches thought this was the best solution all around, especially since it was working so well to keep our opponents off balance. Except that now my best buddy, Terry, wanted this to be his job — and only his job.

So, I looked at him and grinned. "What are you talking about?" I knew full well what he was up to, but wanted to see just how far he'd take it. There were few things in my life more fun than getting inside Terry's head and romping around.

Terry grabbed the football, darted back a few steps, and then pointed across the field, yelling, "Spinks! Run a quick route!"

I ran my favorite route and caught the ball.

"WOW! Oh Man!" Terry said, jumping up and down and slapping his knee. "What a catch! You are incredible!"

Okay, with that piece of entertainment behind us, it seemed like time to play my next card. "Terry, you know, you, too, have incredible hands," I said, dropping back a few steps and cocking my arm as if getting ready to throw. "How 'bout now you run a quick route?" I pointed down the field. "It's my favorite combination — Spinks to Bradshaw!"

Realizing I'm on to his game, Terry shrugs and trots back toward me, shaking his head. "No," he said, going around behind me to pluck the ball out of my throwing hand, "I think Bradshaw to Spinks just makes more sense."

"Why not Spinks to Bradshaw?" I persisted. I loved watching his ears turn red.

"Because I thought of the idea first!"

"Oh, Big Deal," I said, putting my hands on my hips and looking him right straight in the eye. "Just because you said it first doesn't mean that that's the way it has to be."

"It's always been Bradshaw to Spinks," he said, meeting my glare head on. "Bradshaw to Spinks. Bradshaw to Spinks. That's what it was, what it is, and what it needs to be."

He then did some kind of mind ninja move on my brain, and I'm not quite sure how it happened, but I heard myself say, "Well Bradshaw to Spinks just makes more sense to me."

Just as my words fully registered in my own mind, Terry looked at me, wide-eyed, and then flashed that mischievous grin of his, "You are absolutely right, Tommy," he said.

He got me.

• • •

I remember vividly the day it really happened. The day I would no longer be playing football as a quarterback.

We were at spring training, which was at the end of our junior year. We were in the middle of a scrimmage and one of our receivers got hurt. I saw Terry talking to Coach Hedges.

"Spinks, let's have you line up as receiver for a few plays," Coach Hedges said after he motioned me in to the sideline. It was the next practice after our Bradshaw to Spinks, Spinks to Bradshaw exchange, and I had watched with great interest Terry's long sideline conversation with Coach Hedges just before practice began.

Coach Hedges was a man of few words — and a great influence in my life. A real man's man, he was stoutly built with a short crew cut and rugged, angular good looks. He had not only earned the respect of every single football player on our team, but he also held the greatest respect of players and coaches from opposing teams as well. Coach Hedges expected nothing less of us than our very best, and if he said, "jump," it never occurred to any of us to ask, "how high?" I think we all instinctively knew that the answer was, "as high as you can. And keep jumping until I tell you to stop." There are few things in this world that matter more to a young athlete than what a coach like Coach Hedges thinks of your abilities — and what he thinks of you as a person. I would have jumped over the moon if Coach Hedges asked me to.

So I lined up as receiver without so much as another thought. It was at that very moment that my career as a wide receiver began.

I'll always believe that Terry somehow knew deep inside that not only would he ultimately beat me out of that quarter-back position, but that greater things would be in store for me in catching and running that ball. I can't help but look back to that moment of our long friendship and smile, realizing what my best friend did for me. Not only did he spare me the embarrassment of losing that position to him, he helped me find my greatest strength and encouraged me to run that ball instead. And run, I did.

Thanks, Bud.

CHAPTER 10

"This ye-ah," our principal began his address to our senior class during our very first assembly, "as the senior Knights of Woodlawn High, you will enter a magical time we like to refer to as 'Camelot.'"

Terry elbowed me and grinned, imagining, I'm sure, something quite different about Camelot than our principal was intending. Nevertheless, his fairytale-ish metaphor had captured our attention. And, as it turned out, was the perfect way to describe our senior year at Woodlawn.

In this magical time, students and faculty came together in surprising, amazing and heart-tugging ways to make each moment the very best it could possibly be. Nowhere was this more evident than on our Woodlawn Knight football team. In every moment of that year we felt both the tangible support of our Shreveport community and the amazing strength of football as our bond.

• • •

The sound of voices talking excitedly somewhere in the near distance was unmistakable. But every time I scanned the hilly terrain surrounding our practice field, I didn't see anyone — or anything. Am I going nuts? I thought as I looked in the one direction the sound seemed to be coming from for about the millionth time. Terry drilled another pass into my chest and I barely caught it before it did some damage.

"Where'd you go?" He called across the distance between us. He could always tell when my focus wavered. A strange connection forged from years of throwing the football almost every single day. The sun was starting to fade behind the football field and these last few golden minutes of practice were always bittersweet.

Today, however, was different. After weeks of trying to identify where those voices were coming from, we discovered the answer. I motioned to Terry to follow me, and I hopped the low fence at the far end of the field closest to the end zone. Trotting over the top of the hill, I discovered a large group of younger boys were gathered there with their footballs.

"Hey," I said, trying to keep it casual.

"Hey, Tommy," a few of them chimed in unison.

How did they know my name?

Looking past me, they spied Terry topping the hill just behind me.

"Hey, Terry!" one of the braver ones chirped.

Ok, this is just weird.

"Hey! What are y'all doing over here?" Terry asked, joining us.

A lanky kid at the front of the pack clutched his football. "We're just watching y'all throw," he said.

"Well, why don't y'all come down here and throw with us?" I asked, as if that were the most natural thing in the world to suggest.

Their eyes opened wide and they turned to look at each other as if to ask, "Is he kidding? Is this really happening?"

Then I hollered, "Come on boys! Let's play some football!"

You should have seen those kids running full-speed down that hill, trying desperately to outrun each other to get there first. Terry and I stood there laughing at the sight of them sliding, falling, and sprinting to get to the bottom.

We threw with those boys that afternoon until it was too dark to see the football. "Boys, Terry and I like to come out here and throw after practice. How about if y'all come down and play a little catch with us before the sun goes down?"

"Sure thing!" A few of them chirped in unison. Others, too overwhelmed to speak, just bobbed their heads in agreement.

So from that day forward, the boys would huddle together with their own footballs just outside the fence. They'd wave when we looked their way, and when I put my fingers to my lips and whistled as loudly as I could, they'd begin whooping and hollering and jumping up and down as if a fire was lit under their feet.

At the end of each of these sessions — just minutes before the sun disappeared for the day, Terry would yell out for one final play, "Somebody go long. I gotta unleash a big one! Go all the way to the end zone!"

They'd all take off then, like bullets from a gun. I'd run with them as Terry let go of a cannon.

That first day, however, that final pass from Terry came down right into the chest of a 10-year-old kid, and the power behind that throw knocked the kid clean off his feet. He was down for the count.

Terry and I looked at each other, expressions of both worry and amusement toggling on each of our faces. While it was kind of funny to watch this poor kid fly off his feet from the sheer impact of catching that ball, well, gee, we sure hoped we didn't break him.

All of the boys ran over to see if the kid was okay. He most definitely was. We reached him just in time to see him lying there, the ball still embedded in his chest, with a giant smile on his face, grateful eyes looking towards the sky. "I can't believe I caught that," he whispered as soon as he could gather enough wind.

Then his buddies began to laugh and re-enact the catch by falling flat on their backs. Laughing at them laughing at him, I extended my hand to help him to his feet. "Wow," I said, "NO one your age has EVER been able to catch one of Bradshaw's bombs. You were incredible out there."

His buddies quit laughing then and gathered around. As he continued to catch his breath, I continued, "Kid, I'm just thankful you aren't old enough to come to Woodlawn just yet. I'm afraid you'd take my job away from me."

As these kids began walking back toward their neighborhood, the kid turned and looked back at us one last time, giving us a grin and a thumbs up. Terry and I stood and watched them disappear over the hill.

"I wonder how he's gonna explain that bruise to his parents," I said.

"I dunno," Terry said. Then he grinned. "How did you explain it to yours?"

• • •

I guess word spread about our impromptu catch sessions with those neighborhood boys. Soon after that, following the first football game of our senior year, there was a line of young boys waiting outside the field house with footballs and autograph books clutched tightly in their hands.

They wanted our autographs? What in the world?

We were barely more than boys ourselves, and yet these kids were making us feel like NFL stars. Looking back now, I wish I had let them know how much we appreciated their constant support. It was an amazing feeling.

After the next game, a big win against Byrd High School, that group of boys had almost doubled in size. As Terry and I, along with a few other teammates who wanted in on this fun, were signing the outstretched autograph books, I tried not to laugh as I noted the seriousness and intensity in this group who also offered up their arms, slips of paper, or whatever else they managed to get hold of during the game.

Looking up from the pack that surrounded us, I noticed a kid in the back of the group with my number — #11 — taped on his shirt in yellowish masking tape. To this day I can think of no greater compliment I ever received in football than this young kid taping my number on his shirt.

I smiled at him. "What's your name, kid?" I asked.

A hush fell as all the boys stopped and turned to see who I was talking to.

The kid was too shocked to reply.

Without waiting for his answer, I asked, "Do you play football?" He seemed overcome with shyness, and rather than drawing the laughter of his buddies I wanted to make sure he felt as special as he had made me feel.

He slowly nodded, and then said, "I'm gonna play for the Woodlawn Knights one day like you." He looked down at his homemade jersey. "I hope I get to wear your number."

"Come on up here to the front of the line," I said. I then signed his autograph book with my name, jersey number, and a quick scrawled message to the future #11. Then I reached over and handed Terry this kid's autograph book as well. Terry peered at the kid for a moment, then made a big dramatic show of autographing his book. He handed the book back to the kid and grinned at him. "Keep up the good work," he said.

We continued to sign autographs until every last kid was gone, and out of the corner of my eye I watched a smaller crowd gathered around the future #11 to see what we wrote in his book.

At the next game, and after every game for the rest of that season, an entire slew of boys showed up after the game for autographs with Terry's jersey numbers and mine taped to the fronts and backs of their shirts.

• • •

When it came to football, it really didn't matter how many people lived in Shreveport. It became a small town in all the right ways. On Friday nights, the town shut down. The owners, realizing that not only were all their patrons at the game, anyway, by closing their shops they could be at the game as well.

This was especially true in the area of town surrounding Woodlawn High School. The shopkeepers all knew our names. It seemed as if we were always wearing our jerseys, because townspeople called out to us by name or number any time they saw one of us. People driving down the streets would wave, honk, and whistle when they saw any of us in town. With that kind of support and adulation from the people of Shreveport, we worked even harder to never let them down.

As predicted, our team made it to the final round in the state playoffs against Sulphur, Louisiana. Electric excitement crackled in the air and through our veins. This was going to be a great game — and we were favored to win.

The preparation for the big game was enormous. Our 200-girl pep-squad was relentless in practicing their new routine using giant flash cards. The band, too, practiced twice a day. The cheerleaders were everywhere, making and hanging signs, and selling ribbons, buttons, and badges to every student, faculty member, and person in town. The stores and restaurants all across town wrote messages of hope and encouragement to us on their storefront windows.

It was amazing to be part of something of this magnitude. No words can begin to describe the excitement leading up to this climatic event.

On the day of the state championship game our team boarded the bus for the State Fair stadium in Shreveport, arriving early to get our jitters settled and our muscles warm in time for the evening game. We arrived, unloaded, and suited up. After initial instructions from the coaches, our team took the field for our usual pre-game warm-ups. We were quiet as we began stretching and warming up, trying to quell the nervous energy enveloping us.

"Uh . . . Guys . . ."

As I held a deep hamstring stretch, the voice of my buddy, Ronnie Brown interrupted my thoughts.

Before I had time to look up, Donnie Baughman said, "Holy Crap!"

We all stopped mid-stretch, and our eyes followed the stares of Ronnie and Donnie. I'm pretty sure I stopped breathing and chills ran from my head to my toes.

As we stared in awe, what seemed like at least 100 chartered buses turned into the parking lot of the stadium, one by one. And behind all those buses came what seemed like hundreds of cars. With every bus and car that turned into that parking lot, I felt the strength and determination of our team grow stronger. With my eyes welling against my will, I continued to count the buses as they rolled in.

Busload after busload unloaded our fans, band members, pep-squad, cheerleaders, and parents. The crisp night air filled with loud cheering, screaming, and hollering while the drivers of all these cars and busses filled the air with the cacophony of honking horns.

This was one of those surreal moments you recognize even as it unfolds as something you will never forget. I tried with all my might to take it all in, every sight, sound and feeling of all that was happening before me as the visitors' side filled the stadium with sound and energy the likes of which I had never witnessed.

As all of this was happening, I looked over to the shock and disbelief washing over our opposing team and fans.

• • •

That night, more than 25,000 people from all over our corner of Louisiana filled the stands. *Twenty-five thousand people are coming together to watch us play football.* This thought was absolutely electrifying.

"Stretch it out boys! We got work to do," Coach Hedges yelled, snapping us back to reality. "Let's go! Stretch!"

I've always wondered how Coach Hedges must have felt seeing that sight. While I'm sure he was just as moved as we were by such a powerful display of support, I wonder now if it also made him a little nervous, adding a new layer of pressure to the intensity we were already feeling. None of that occurred to us, and it shouldn't have. We were young and strong and wide-eyed — and this show of local support charged our batteries like nothing else in the world.

• • •

We were all pretty sure that that night in Shreveport, Louisiana belonged to us. And then the rains came.

The rain was as much our enemy as Sulphur was. Filling every hole in the field, this deluge was an obstacle our passing team hadn't counted on.

We should have. This was the third time for Woodlawn High School to go to the State finals — and the third time the championship game would be played in monsoon conditions.

Playing behind Terry's great arm, Woodlawn High was a passing team. With this unexpected downpour, our team had to become a running team, and our guys were sliding all over the field.

Our confidence slipped with each skid and skitter, and alongside it tumbled our chance to prove that we were the very best high school football team in the state of Louisiana.

The sound of that final buzzer may have masked the shattering of our hearts and spirits as we left the field in stunned disbelief, completely oblivious to our opposing team as they danced in the rain, hugging, laughing and shooting up their pointer finger toward the heavens, letting the world know that they were, in fact, the winners of that miserable game.

Normally, Barbara waited for me after each game. No matter how long it took me to shower and get outside, even if I took a little extra time to visit with the guys about the game in the locker room, she was always there with a sweet smile on her face when I came out to the parking lot.

This night, however, Barbara knew it was best to leave me alone. She understood me well enough even then to realize I was not going to be in a place to talk or receive condolences for a very long time.

As a team we were crushed. Devastated beyond words. We sat in the locker room for quite a while that night. We needed time to regain our composure, dry our tear-streaked faces, and summon the courage to walk through those locker room doors and somehow return to our families, our school, and our town carrying this enormous disappointment that was, quite literally, too much for our young hearts to bear.

That night as I somehow managed to drag myself through my own front door, the house was dark. My parents had already gone to bed, knowing I would want to be alone. Faint music playing from the radio in my parent's bedroom told me they were still awake, most likely listening to make sure I was home, but the door remained closed.

I crawled into bed, pulled the covers up over me and drew my knees into my chest. I buried my head in them as my heart pounded with grief. Misery washed over me in a wave of nausea as replays of the game swirled around in my head. How? How? How in the world was it possible that we didn't win that game?

At some point, there was a light knock on my door.

I didn't answer. I couldn't answer. My throat was knotted and locked up in way that made speech impossible.

I heard the door open. I glanced up briefly to see who it was, and then stuck my head back down on my kneecaps.

"I'm proud of you son," my dad's voice said.

Somehow I managed to roll my eyes.

As if he saw me, my dad softly laughed. "Where's Noah when you need him, huh?" he said.

I didn't really see the humor in this comment, but I knew he was trying. I said nothing.

After allowing a long pause to hang in the air between us, Dad said, "Tommy, I know that this moment in your young life is really, really painful, but I want you to remember, if you can, what the third chapter of Proverbs tell us about times like these: "Trust in the Lord with all your heart, and do not lean on your own understanding. In all your ways, acknowledge him, and he will make straight your paths."

He paused, letting those words settle around me like a blanket. Then he added, "Your mom and I love you and are as proud of you right now, in this minute, as we have ever been. Tomorrow will be a brand new day. We'll see you then."

The door gently closed, and with my dad's words echoing in my ears, I allowed the first of many tears to break through the dam of my heart that night. My shoulders began to shake, my heart raced, and my tears flooded onto the sheets just as rain had engulfed the championship game that was ours to win. I had just played my last high school game, and it was the first and last time I ever allowed myself to cry over a football game.

Just before I managed to at last drift into troubled sleep, I pondered what Monday at school would be like. I let myself imagine all the sad faces and pitying looks, and I willed myself to face them all, and no matter what they threw at me, I would own and speak the truth: we did our best. Without making any excuses about the rain, I had to say to them that Sulphur won the state championship, fair and square. Period.

• • •

On Monday morning, I steeled myself, ready to give my answer to anyone who questioned our failure. They'd be looking, I assumed before they even asked, for excuses and explanations, anything that would help this devastating defeat make any kind of sense.

The first person to greet me as I walked toward the school building from the parking lot was a kid by the name of Mike Morgan. I had arrived early for school in anticipation of the day's supreme challenge. OK, here we go, I said to myself, taking a deep breath.

Mike was a couple of years behind us in grade level, but on the football field and even at school he always seemed older than his age. A nice guy and a great athlete, Mike was always one of those guys with a smile for everybody, no matter what was going on. Today was no exception.

"Hey, great season, Tommy," he said as soon as he got near enough to hear. "What a ride, huh? One I won't soon forget."

I stopped dead in my tracks, spiraling up from abject dread to pure relief in just under two seconds. It's always been funny to me how simple words of kindness and support from one single person at just the right time can turn your entire outlook around. I knew in that instant that everything was going to be okay. Life was good again.

I revisited this experience many times in my life — any time I found myself grieving over the 'what coulda beens.' It never stopped those useless rascals from making their way into my brain, as they did even then almost every day for an entire month after that game, mind you. But remembering to celebrate the ride rather than the landing — especially the rough ones — would stand me in good stead for years to come.

CHAPTER 11

With our final high school football season behind us, the rest of our senior year flew by in a flurry of special moments, including an unexpected visit from one of everyone's TV heroes, Mr. Michael Landon.

Since that unfortunate incident with Mrs. Bell's school bus, Terry's javelin throwing had just gotten better and better, and as icing on our senior year cake, Terry booked a series of national javelin records and his unbelievable throwing arm garnered such national media attention that Michael Landon paid Woodlawn a visit so that he could meet Terry himself.

"Michael Landon is coming here to meet . . . *me*?" Terry said, with shocked bewilderment on his face that was almost comical. "Why?"

"Good question," I said, "I think I'll ask him why someone so famous has nothing better to do."

The whole school was buzzing with the news of Michael Landon's visit, and once he was on campus, the girls were swooning all over the place.

"Isn't he dreamy," I said in falsetto that made my buddies laugh. The fact was we were all pretty star struck and even more so once we discovered what a genuinely nice and unassuming guy Michael Landon was.

At the end of his visit, Michael presented Terry with an award of recognition for his accomplishments in javelin throwing in front of the whole school during a special called assembly in our auditorium, which was not only a very big deal for Terry, but also for our entire school. Who knew?

• • •

It was right around this time that Penny Clark, Terry's first love, entered his life. After all the time he spent making fun of me for my infatuation with Barbara, it was nice to see my best buddy similarly smitten.

They met in Mrs. Whitaker's English class, and Mrs. Whitaker loved every minute of her front row seat to this budding romance. Terry was happier than he'd ever been and Mrs. Whitaker, obviously a hopeless romantic, allowed the two of them to get by with things nobody else could get away with in her class.

They always sat in the back corner of her room. I sat close, but not too close — he was still my best friend, after all — and they were pretty sickening. I never could quite hear what they were whispering back there with their heads together, but from time to time Penny would giggle.

There's really no telling what he's filling her mind with, I thought to myself as I tried to focus on what Mrs. Whitaker was saying. There was a lot of eye rolling in that class, and from time to time a wave of quiet gagging noises would ripple across the room. Mrs. Whittaker seemed as oblivious to all of this as she was to the giggling and flirting going on in the back corner of her classroom. She'd just smile at that sticky sweet corner of the room and pretend not to notice the disruption — or the pure disgust of the rest of her class.

Penny, bless her heart, seemed to have no clue that any of this was going on. In fact, she didn't seem to notice that there was anyone else even in the room. And Terry, I could tell you with absolute certainty, was having the time of his life entertaining everyone.

When people would glare, sigh, or even mention their discomfort with his romantic antics, Terry would answer with that mischievous grin, a shrug of his shoulders. "What?" He'd ask, looking genuinely concerned. "What'd I do?" Then he'd look at me and wink.

I'll have to say that one of the highlights of our Camelot year as Woodlawn High School Knights did not come on the football field, the baseball diamond, or even the award-winning track and field arenas. Terry and I were in love with the two most beautiful girls at Woodlawn High School, and there wasn't much else that could compare to that.

Penny was sweet, caring, and hung on every word Terry said. Barbara was also sweet and caring, yet independent, stubborn, strong-willed — and did I mention stubborn?

Mrs. Doring's speech class was the last class of the day — and as such was always a time for fidgeting and daydreaming and looking out the windows. On this particular day I was gazing across the school lawn and . . . *Wait! What's going on out there?* I sat bolt upright in the straight-backed school desk, rubbed my eyes a little bit to make sure of what I was seeing.

Yep, there she was, laughing and smiling and talking to . . . *who IS that guy?* For whatever reason Barbara wasn't in class that day; instead, she was standing out there in the quadrangle talking to some guy I had never seen before.

My face pounded, my blood rose toward a boil. *Who in the heck is that guy and why is he talking to my girlfriend?*

Without raising my hand, asking permission or offering any sort of explanation, I picked up my books and shot out the door. I had to get to the bottom of what was going on out there.

"Where are you . . ." Mrs. Doring didn't try to stop me. I can promise you she knew that it was something important and when it came to my relationship with Barbara, well, let's just say she was a fan of us as a couple. A buddy later told me she looked out the window where I had been staring, saw Barbara out there talking to that guy — and then just went on teaching the class.

By the time I got to where they were standing, the bell had already rung and there was no sight of either of them anywhere. I went back to my locker, which was our usual meeting place after school and before practice, and while Terry was there, Barbara was nowhere to be found.

Terry took one look at me and said, "Man, what's the matter with you?"

Before I could answer, Barbara appeared from out of nowhere.

I glanced at her and then turned back to Terry, trying to think of something incredibly important to say.

"Hey, guys," Barbara said, touching me on the arm.

I pulled away and turned toward my locker, as if something in there needed my immediate attention.

Terry looked across at Barbara and said, "Hey Barbara. What's new?" They both turned to me, then, and I just kept rifling through my locker looking for something crucial.

"Tommy, what's wrong?" Barbara asked, moving around beside Terry to look at me straight on.

I looked back at her. "What do you *think* is wrong, *Barbara*?" I said. I said her name with such force she took a step back.

Terry looked at me and then he looked back at Barbara. He shrugged. "Gosh, Barbara, it looks like maybe something must have crawled up his butt."

"Tommy?" She tried again. "I really don't know what's eating you, but you need to tell me what you're so upset about."

"Maybe you'd just better think about it a little bit harder," I said. I turned and walked away, heading straight toward my car.

Barbara looked at Terry, eyebrows raised, and then Terry followed me . . ." Tommy, man, don't be that way," he said. "What's going on?"

"Ask her," I said, climbing into my mean green machine and starting the engine. At least this was a time it did start, which helped the effect of my dramatic exit.

"Tommy!" Barbara had caught up with us by then. "What is it? What in the world is the matter with you!?!?!??"

"I saw you talking to that guy during class," I somehow managed to say over the revving of my engine. I'm not sure whether it was more anger or fear that tightened my throat to the point where I could barely speak. "Who was that guy anyway?"

"Oh Tommy, is that all?" she said, laughing. "Is that why you're acting so ridiculous?"

I could tell by the way she tilted her head and smiled at me that my fury was amusing her. That made me even madder. Or more embarrassed. Or maybe both. *What in the world IS the matter with me?* a small voice in my head whispered. To cover up that emotional conundrum, I pealed out of the parking lot, burning rubber I didn't really have to spare on those balding tires, leaving them both standing there with their mouths open in complete shock.

I drove around town for a little while to try to cool down and get my thoughts in order. Why was I so mad? Barbara was my girlfriend, but did that really mean she wasn't supposed to talk to any other guy . . . ever? Even in my steamed-up state I saw my own ridiculousness. But whatever it was that came over me when I saw her out there laughing and talking and smiling at that guy, well it made me see stars all over again every time I replayed the scene in my mind. Who was that guy anyway — and what was he doing talking to my girl? And what was she doing smiling up at him just like she did at me?

By the time I got back home, Terry was sitting in my driveway. "Man we've got to get over to Barbara's house right now," he said, climbing into my car. "She is maaaaaaaaaaad at you. We've gotta get over there so you two can straighten out what ever this . . ." he waved his hand in exasperation, ". . . is." He turned to me and looked at me with an earnestness that would have been comical if this situation wasn't so serious. "What is the matter with you, man?" he said, peering at me as if he could see inside my brain if he looked hard enough. "I've never seen you act this way before and it's kind of freaking me out."

By the time Old Green chugged into Barbara's driveway I was a little more cooled down, and determined to make things right with Barbara. Terry had said over and over again, all the way to Barbara's house, that this was just a misunderstanding that had gotten way out of hand. He was right. I was almost even thinking about apologizing.

Before either of us could knock, the door opened. The young woman standing there looked like Barbara, except this one had sparks of anger flying out of her eyes. She was, as we say in the South, spitting mad. She was not even attempting the disconnected Southern smile to cover the heat of her pure-dee rage. I had done it now.

"Uh-oh," Terry said. He gave a low whistle. "You've got some work to do here, brother."

"Barbara . . ." I began, . . . She slammed the door.

Terry knocked. I took a step back to consider my options.

The door opened a crack.

"Now Barbara," Terry said in his most persuasive voice, "you need to let Tommy and me in so we can all work this out."

"I am NOT talking to him until he apologizes," came Barbara's voice through the door. Two inches of wood may have muffled the sound, but her icy hot anger was coming through loud and clear.

"He'll apologize," Terry said to the door. Then he turned and looked at me. "Won't you, Tommy?"

"Not until SHE tells me who that guy was and what they were talking about that was so fascinating," I said, arms crossed.

Terry shook his head.

I looked at my best buddy, deciding to take another tack. "Terry, see if you can talk some sense into her," I coaxed. "I just want to know who that guy was and why she was talking to him out there instead of being in class with me where she belongs."

"Where I . . . beeeeelong?" came a shriek through the door. "Terry, you tell him I can talk to whoever I want to!"

"Oh good grief," Terry said. He turned back to the door. "Barbara, please. Open this door. Let's all just calm down, get a Coke, and talk this out." He paused, and then almost whined. "I can't stand to watch the two of you fighting. Please."

The door opened slowly, and Terry and I went through it without another word, and then, just as I was almost past her, Barbara said to me through gritted teeth, "I cannot believe you. You are being impossible."

"I'll tell you what's impossible," I said, hearing my voice get louder with each syllable. "What's impossible is that you won't even tell me who that guy was."

"I don't have to tell you that or anything else, Tommy Spinks!" She yelled. "The NERVE of you acting like I can't even say hello to someone. Who do you think you are????"

"I THINK I'm your boyfriend and I deserve an answer," I shot back at her, doubling the decibels. "If there's nothing going on why won't you tell me who he is?"

Barbara put her fingers in her ears, "I can't hear you," she said at the top of her lungs, "I can't hear you, la la la la la."

By that time Terry was pacing back and forth in the kitchen, wringing his hands. He turned to us and said, "You two. Stop it. You can't do this." He walked over and stood right between us, arms out to each side like a referee. "You don't mean that," he said looking me right in the eye with a sternness I had only seen on the football field. Then he looked at Barbara, "Y'all need to just stop all this yelling and work this out. This is just stupid and you two need to just . . . get along."

We both looked at him, then at each other, then back at him. "Stay out of it!" we said in unison.

Looking dejected, Terry lumbered back to the sofa and plopped down, head in his hands. "I just don't see what you two have to argue about," he said, almost whining. "I know you really, really care about each other, and all this yelling is just so bad for both of you."

Barbara stopped right in the middle of the diatribe she had restarted once he sat down and turned toward Terry. "Terry!" she said, "Stop talking! Why are you even here? This is between Tommy and me! Please! Go away!"

Terry looked at her, then at me, then back at her. With hurt in his eyes he clomped out of her living room and toward the room where Barbara's mom kept all of her sewing stuff — and her typewriter.

Later that evening, with our spat fully resolved and all the kissing and making up over with, Barbara went back to that room to retrieve something and came back with a piece of paper in her hands. "Tommy, look here," she said, laughing and, was that a tear she wiped away?

As I looked over her shoulder, we read together the most horribly typed letter either of us had ever seen, before or since. It was written to Barbara from Terry, professing MY love for her. Pushing his horrible typing skills to their outermost limits, Terry had spent who knows how long back there after we kicked him out of our argument, painstakingly typing out a letter to Barbara urging her to stay with me because he KNEW first-hand how much I loved her:

> This is exactly how it read;
> *Terry bradshaw*
> *Barba loves Tommy Spinks because she told me so, Tommyand Barbra had a fight tonight. Tyey will make upbecause they really love each other*
> *This was written by Tery Bradshaw he wud with Tommy when he came to her house. He's my best friend and theat's why*

I left when I knew that theres was trouble. He loves you Barbra believe me because I wo8ld't lie to you. I know that it means to much to you From here on out I wish you and Tommy all the luck that God can put upon you. May you and Tommy have all the happinest in the wor. If ever you have trouble with him just give me a ring and I can straightened every thing out. He really does care and you must believe me because I know, he's my best friend. Don't be mad at him (please) Next year isgoing to be greatand it can oonly be great if you and Tommy stay togwther. Well that's about all I can say just be great and love Tommy Okey Dokey your friend forever.
Terry Bradshaw "12"

Barbara kept that letter — and later framed it to preserve one of the funniest and sweetest gestures she had ever received from Terry. It still makes her smile every time she looks at it. By that time Terry had become one of her best friends, too, and someone she loved being around almost as much as I did.

• • •

One of the many highlights of our senior year was that Terry and I were once again elected to the Woodlawn High School Accolade Pageant. Although this event always seemed to be a bigger deal to the girls, I would be lying if I didn't admit that I felt completely honored to be elected "King" of this pageant.

"And the Woodlawn High School Accolades Pageant King is . . . Tommy Spinks!" the enthusiastic emcee announced.

Barbara beamed at me as my name was announced, and Terry, standing right there beside me, looked at me with wide eyes and pounded me on the back, clapping and whistling, bringing an abrupt end to any sense of decorum the planners of that ceremony intended.

The haze in which all of this was taking place was made even more dreamlike by what most of the people gathered that night didn't realize. Only Terry, Barbara, and my parents knew I was also secretly battling a high fever, with an undiagnosed case of mono about to make the rest of my senior year pretty much a sleepy blur.

Yes, I probably should have stayed home, but I really didn't want to miss a thing that year — and that was even when I had no idea I was going to be named King of Camelot, and a few weeks later, "Mr. Woodlawn" by my peers.

Being elected "Mr. Woodlawn" was one of those things no one ever expects, and when it happens, you are amazed, humbled, and very surprised. Apparently I wasn't the only one shocked by this honor.

"I can't believe this," my own mother said with a stunned look on her face. "I thought fa shua Terreh would win."

All I could do was laugh. Maybe Terry was on to something all those years ago. Maybe he REALLY WAS my mama's favorite.

• • •

Each year the Woodlawn yearbook shuffled its cover color. One year it would be red; the next year, royal blue; and then, finally, silver. Our yearbook staff devised this genius plan so that by the time we graduated, each of us would have one yearbook in each color to adorn our shelves into our alumni perpetuity.

However, on this particular year . . . the very special year of 1966 . . . things were different — and everybody seemed to sense it. For whatever reason, the yearbook staff proposed and the student body voted that the color of that year's yearbook would be GOLD — the only "golden" yearbook in Woodlawn High School history.

These senior year memories were times I would reflect back on for my entire life.

Camelot.

CHAPTER 12

"So where do you think we want to go?" Terry asked, drilling a pass my way. The warm early spring sunshine on our faces made throwing the football a special delight today. And, although the looming graduation hoopla seemed to be all anyone wanted to talk about, uppermost on our minds was . . . "Then what?"

"I don't know," I said, sending the ball back. It was hard for me to settle on a specific dream in terms of college. All I knew was I wanted to go, I wanted to play football — and while both of us knew the odds were even at best — I hoped that Terry and I would still get to play football together. "You know," I said, expertly catching Terry's next throw, "I think playing wide receiver might be the best decision you've ever made for me."

"That's true," Terry replied, ever humble. He grinned. "But don't take my word for it, Mr. All-city, All-District, All-State. You're a hot commodity. I bet those recruiters are all fighting over you."

I laughed. "We'll see," I said. The truth was I had heard nothing from anyone yet, and I was starting to get anxious about the lack of serious college interest. "We both broke a lot of records this year," I said, sending the ball back a little bit high. "I wonder what they really look at besides our football stats."

Besides my football accolades, I had also set a track record and had a stellar year in baseball. Terry broke his own set of records in football, set a new javelin throwing record, and was already being recruited by some of the largest Universities in the country to play football.

"Oh, who knows," Terry said, reaching up to pluck the ball out of the air before drilling it back my way. "Some of the guys I'm hearing from seem like they've really done their homework. Others have barely read my stats."

"When do you think we'll know something?" I asked the question that wouldn't stop dancing around in my brain.

"Gotta be pretty soon," Terry replied.

"That's good . . . I guess," I said. More than I wanted to get the issue settled, I wanted the news to be good.

• • •

"I'm pretty sure it's going to be LSU," Terry said as we walked to the parking lot after school.

He made this pronouncement in a matter of fact way, as if the choice was ours to make. And for him it might be. But for me, it was a different story. There were no knocks, no letters, no phone calls. Not one single college wanted me.

Deep inside, I knew my capabilities. I knew what I could accomplish on the football field. There was no doubt in my mind that given the opportunity, I would make any school very happy that I was part of their program.

At 6'0 and 170 pounds soaking wet, I wasn't getting anyone's attention as a big guy. What was hard to put onto paper — and to get anyone to consider who hadn't seen me play — was that I was quick, agile and could catch anything thrown to me.

"I'm a little worried that I haven't heard anything," I said, voicing my fear out loud for the first time. Even though Terry didn't share this problem, I knew he understood what I was going through. I was playing it pretty cool, but in truth the fact that recruiters weren't knocking at my door at all was very scary to me. What if no one wants me? I wanted the chance to continue playing this sport I had grown to love. And even though I had more than proven myself over the past four years, those old junior high insecurities began to rear their ugly heads.

I began to question my dreams and myself.

• • •

"Tommy, what do you want to do when you grow up?"

That question had been asked of me ever since I could remember. And, ever since I was 13 years old, my answer usually had something to do with football. Sometimes I said I wanted to be a coach — or even a preacher, like my dad, depending on who the question came from — but deep down I always had the same dream Terry had. I had caught that dream and made it my own.

I saw myself playing college ball. I saw myself playing in the NFL. I saw myself winning a Super Bowl. Because I had caught Terry's infectious lifelong dream, in my mind there was no question that football was my future.

So with the deafening quiet coming from the college recruiters, fear came calling. Quietly at first — it was just a whisper. Then, as the weeks wore on, it got a little louder.

Just about the time Terry became so sure that LSU was his destiny, fear knocked me completely to my knees, and, given my upbringing, all I knew to do was ask God to guide me, to intervene.

"Please, God, help me get a good enough offer so I can play college football," I implored, throwing everything I wanted and needed into one petition. Up to this point in my life, my conversations with God had been frequent and earnest, but never desperate.

Even as a young boy and now a young man, I knew I was blessed. My parents made a practice of reminding me to count my blessings — and count them I did. My life was easy, and things always seemed to be going my way. I was fortunate, and I knew it. So what God usually got from me was a wink, a thumbs up, and a, "Good job, Big Guy."

• • •

"Otis, may I say the blessing tonight?" My mother asked as she walked around the table, spooning the hot fried okra onto each of our plates.

"Of course, Honey," my dad replied.

My sister, Betty, my parents and I were about to have supper, and I could tell by the way my mother held her mouth that she had something important on her mind.

After placing the large serving bowl on the sideboard, my mother sat down and clasped my hand on one side of the table and Betty's hand on the other. On cue, we both reached for Dad's hands at the other end of the table and we all bowed our heads.

After beginning the usual preamble to the blessing of the meal, Mom paused. We all sat there in silence.

I glanced up to see if she was finished and saw Betty Carol peeking, too, likely wondering the same thing. Our eyes met for an instant and then, realizing Mom wasn't finished, we quickly re-bowed our heads. There was obviously more on the way.

"Heavenly Fathah," my mother began in her heavy Southern accent, "I'd like to say a few wuhds about football. We know you have a plan for Tommeh's life . . . and Lawd, we trust in those plans. But Fathah, I think we need for you to step on it. My boy has a natural gift to play football, a talent you gave him, might I add. Don't you remembah he was All-State? Anyway, Tommeh needs to play in college, and we fully expect for you to intervene on his behalf. Amen and Amen."

After finishing strong with the "double 'Amen'," Mom lifted her head and smiled as if nothing was different about that mealtime blessing.

We all smiled at each other, and then passed around the breadbasket like we did every other night.

While nothing was mentioned before or after my mother's football prayer — or the fact that the doorbell wasn't being rung by any colleges, much less Louisiana Tech, I realized that Mom's prayer was to let me know she was talking to God on my behalf — and letting us BOTH know how much she believed in me and my abilities.

My mother always had total faith, even while secretly crossing her fingers behind her back, that things would all work out for the best. And usually, they did.

• • •

I hadn't gotten down on my knees to pray since I was a kid, but the day Terry said "yes" to LSU, I was pretty sure my own football playing days were over. I can't remember exactly what I said in that very particular conversation with God, but I do remember standing up from praying and feeling a sense of relief — a sense that everything was going to be okay, no matter what.

"I don't know, Tommy," Terry said on the way to school the morning after he made his big decision.

"What do you mean, you don't know?" I asked, flabbergasted. Here he had drawn this great offer from LSU of all places. He was this amazing athlete with such a God-given talent that a school like LSU had recognized it and made him an offer — and now he was having second thoughts.

"It's just that, well, I don't know, several things," he said. "I'm a country boy," he began. "I love it here — my home and my family and my friends are all here — and I'm just not sure how much I'll like being in such a big place."

I thought for a moment, trying to put myself in his shoes. "It'll take some getting used to, all right," I said. The truth was I had no idea what to say, but it was clear that my buddy was struggling. Just because I couldn't understand why this was so hard didn't mean I didn't see the angst in his eyes every time he talked about LSU. Something clearly wasn't right with this decision in his own heart and the more he tried to talk himself into it, the less right it felt.

"And what if I get there and I'm not as good as they think I am?" he asked. What always amazed me about Terry was that with all that talent and amazing natural ability, he never saw himself that way.

"You're kidding," I said. "You are better than they think you are." I looked at him with earnestness I hoped he could feel. "Terry, you earned this. You've got so much to offer them — and they're dang lucky to have you. Heck, the one thing I know for sure is that the only reason I set any football records at all was because I had the greatest quarterback I could possibly have throwing to me."

Terry shrugged. "Well I'm pretty sure that if you weren't my receiver who knows what my completion stats would be," he said.

Whaaaat?

Terry clearly had no idea how good he really was. This just goes to prove, I supposed in my complete awe, that even the best of the best sometimes doubt their abilities.

I always knew that Terry truly was a talent like no other. And while you might think that a guy with that kind of talent and ability would be completely full of himself — with a real arrogance over his incredible athleticism and exceptional quarterback skills, the truth was quite the opposite.

Terry was incredibly humble, never seeing what others saw in him. He was always trying to be better, get better, do better, throw harder and become more accurate. I guess that's why he always wanted to throw — and why practicing football consumed his every waking moment.

My best buddy was so dang hard on himself. I hated losing as much as the next guy, but every loss weighed on Terry, ate at him, devastated him. He would think of nothing else for days, re-playing every play in his mind, thinking constantly of how he should have done things differently. Not only were his drive and work ethic unmatched by anyone I had ever known, but his mental tenacity at taking apart each and every loss in order to learn from it was something I couldn't even get my mind around.

"LSU isn't where I need to be," Terry continued to insist every time we talked about it, which was almost daily. Although he had already committed to LSU, his gut told him this school was not where he needed to be.

"So where do you need to be?" I asked him after about the fiftieth time he told me LSU wasn't it.

"I think I want to go to Louisiana Tech," he said.

"Wow," I said. "I'm sure they'd love to have you, but how can you do that when you already committed to LSU?"

"Well, I don't know," he said. "That's the trouble. Those LSU coaches made it sound like they can't live without me, and I guess that just sort of made me feel like I ought to sign." He sighed. "It's a great school. Just not for me."

"And then there's Baylor," I said. Baylor University was also heavily recruiting Terry.

"Yeah, I know," Terry said, kicking at the gravel as we walked across the parking lot. "If my parents had it their way, I'd be a Baylor Bear." Terry's misery was, by now, palpable. "It's like I know what I want, but it's not what everyone else wants for me," he added.

Terry always was a pleaser. In this first big decision of his near-adult life, I could see even then how worried he was about the feelings of everyone besides him. The schools. His parents. His girlfriend. And heck, knowing him as I did, he was probably also worried about me.

"Terry, it's your life and your career," I said. "Do what your gut tells you is right for you."

I hated seeing my buddy so stressed out over what was supposed to be some of the happiest times of our lives. He was so locked in this internal struggle between what he actually wanted and what everyone else wanted for him he was missing out on a lot of the excitement of this time.

"How can I just tell them I've changed my mind," he asked me again and again, the panic rising in his voice with each repetition of this persistent question. His mind was made up; he just couldn't figure out how — or what — to tell them.

• • •

"I've got it!" Terry practically hollered as I jumped into his car. We were on our way to meet the girls and the excitement on his face was a welcome change.

"What?" I asked, beyond curious at what he came up with as solution to the unanswerable dilemma.

"I'm going to fail the ACT!" he said, clearly pleased with the beauty and simplicity of this plan.

"You're going to . . . What?" I asked, not entirely sure I had heard him right.

"See, if I don't pass the ACT, it's not my decision," he embellished. "It's theirs!"

"I don't understand," I said.

"If I don't pass the ACT, it becomes just a circumstantial decision," he attempted to explain the unexplainable. "Then the decision not to attend the university will be made for me! You can't go to LSU unless you make a passing grade on the ACT," he added.

"I understand that part," I said, "But you're a good student — and you have plenty of common sense — so how in the world are you going to fail it?" I thought for a moment. "Besides," I said, "Don't they already have your transcript and know you make good grades?"

Terry heaved a big sigh just as we pulled up to Barbara's house. "Tommy, I'm going to fail it on purpose," he said, speaking those last two words slowly and with emphasis as if I had a learning problem myself.

I was afraid this idea would somehow backfire. And it did, but not in the way either of us could ever have anticipated. Because LSU knew from his academic records that Terry was a good student, when he failed the ACT they had him take it again. Terry took it again — and failed it again. Everyone was up in arms, including Terry, but I know that deep down he knew what he was doing. He had to get out of what just wasn't right for him.

While in my mind those recruiters brought all this on themselves by putting so much pressure on this kid who wasn't really sure, it was also easy to see how frustrating this was for LSU. They were planning on winning seasons with Trey Prather, the Tigers' current standout quarterback, and Terry playing second string to Trey.

This was the same Trey Prather we had looked up to at Woodlawn, the same quarterback Terry started behind in high school. With the taste of starting quarterback leadership at Woodlawn still fresh, Terry didn't want to wait three more years before he held that position again. Who could blame him?

So while Terry's decision and reasoning was completely solid, here's the part that backfired. When Terry failed the ACT, only he and I knew it was on purpose. But those fellas at LSU must have figured it out — after all, Terry's grades and academic records were too good for him to flunk the thing twice — so somewhere along the way they realized he was actually rejecting their offer in the only way he could. I figure that must have made those recruiters hopping mad. Nobody rejects LSU, right? And there wasn't one thing they could do about it. Terry just plain outsmarted them.

The other thing only I understood about this situation was that Terry's decision had nothing whatsoever to do with LSU — and everything to do with what a great big ole' homebody Terry was. Plain and simple, he just didn't want to go to a school 250 miles away from home. He wanted to stay closer to home and family and go to a smaller school and program. But what big stud football player could ever admit that publicly? For all his bluster, Terry was young and scared, smart enough to know what was right for him — and brave enough to do what he had to do to get out of something that he knew just wasn't right.

So when it got mentioned to the press later on that Terry was "too dumb for LSU," it was really the only retaliation those sore recruiters had — and clearly the only way those LSU recruiters knew how to deal with their bruised egos over the fact that a Louisiana stand-out quarterback like Terry — one of the most sought-after athletes in the nation that year — had just walked away from them.

What I've always thought was so unfair was how one ridiculous, vindictive, and completely untrue comment made in anger and frustration somehow attached itself to Terry's persona and followed him for years. Sports journalists and reporters — feeling smart, I'm sure, for digging up the "inside information" about Terry's ACT score and the negative comments made by those frustrated recruiters — would bring this up, even in jest, when speaking about or to Terry. What those reporters and writers neglected to realize was that even if those allegations were true about Terry, it never would have stopped a school like LSU from getting him into their program if he really wanted to go. If those reporters had dug a little deeper they would have realized something was off about those comments — college football always finds a way around academic challenges when an athlete is motivated enough.

And no matter what Terry said or how he — or anyone else — tried to defend his intelligence, that bogus ACT score dogged him his whole career. It became accepted as truth that Terry was not very smart. For those of us who knew Terry best — coaches, teachers, teammates, friends, and family — this was not only maddening to hear, but also it was so far from reality that the only way to cope with it was humor.

Through the years, Terry's gift of using his sense of humor to disarm people stood him in good stead. Any time someone mentioned his ACT score in an interview he'd just make a joke of it and roll with the punches as they came.

Should he have come up with a better solution to get out of going to LSU? Maybe, but he was just a kid, and that "easy" solution was what came to his mind at the time. I just wanted to set the record straight about Terry's intelligence and his brave decision to follow his gut.

And make no mistake: despite all of this, Terry and I both still love LSU. It's hard — if not impossible — to be from Louisiana and not feel the Tiger pride. This is the school that put our state on the map. And to my way of thinking, that makes Terry's decision *not* to go all the more impressive.

One of the reasons I have always admired Terry, during that time and since, was how he handled himself over this situation. Despite the unfairness of what was said about him — and how it spread like wildfire and stuck like glue — I never heard Terry utter an ill word about LSU. Not to me in private or to anyone else. Ever. He also went on to become a huge fan and supporter of the school and their athletic clubs, showing his immense respect for both LSU's athletes and its institution.

• • •

One thing that has always stuck with me most was Terry's decision to go to Tech over LSU. Terry knew in his gut that he was meant to be at Louisiana Tech, and, while his method of following this directive maybe could have been better, he showed me what it looks like to have the courage to follow that deep inner guidance. Listen to your gut.

Looking back now, it's easy to see how history has proven Terry's gut right: Louisiana Tech was where he needed to be for those four years of his life. From the people who came into his life, to how he came to play quarterback, and to the importance of his being able to remain so close to his family and hometown, this turned out to be the decision that set Terry's football career on the road to success.

• • •

"I'm going to Tehhhhhhhhhhhhhch!" Terry bellowed once the confirmation letter arrived. We jumped around like a couple of excited colts running and snorting and whooping and hollering.

The reason this was so exciting was, with Tech so close to home, Terry and I could continue to work out every day and night, like always, right up until school started. We ran sprints and patterns and did drills until well after dark as if we were still in high school, still working toward the dream.

I still had no idea where I was going to go, but the one thing I *did* know was that I wanted to play football, too, so we had to not only stay in shape, but to keep working to get our games to college level.

"I bet Penny's glad about this news," I said as we started throwing the ball to loosen up before starting our practice on the day the letter from Tech came.

"Don't you know it," Terry said, grinning and sending the ball back my way. He didn't have to tell me he was pretty glad about that, too. And not only was his steady girlfriend, Penny, going to Tech, but so was his big brother, Gary. Terry was on top of the world.

"Hey," he added as we began our long slow run before we started the sprints, "did you hear about Coach Hedges?"

"What about him?" I said, settling into our training stride. "Is he OK?" Everything seemed to be changing now. The last thing I wanted to hear was any bad news about our favorite coach.

"I'll say," Terry said. "He just got offered the assistant coach job at Tech!"

"You're kidding!" I said, pondering the implications. "Is he going to take it?"

"Already did!" Terry beamed. "He starts this summer before football, so he'll already be there when I get there!"

• • •

"Coach?" I said, standing once again in the doorway of Coach Hedges' office. Only this time it was his new office at Louisiana Tech, and Coach Hedges, having been on the job for just a couple of weeks, was still settling in to this much bigger place in his career. I had also just learned that Coach A.L. Williams, another of my favorite Woodlawn High School coaches, had joined the Tech football coaching staff with Coach Hedges, and he would be arriving in just a few days.

Since college recruiters weren't coming to me, I had decided to take matters into my own hands and see if I could talk

Coach Hedges and the head coach, Joe Alliet, into letting me try out for the team. It was just one week before the start of pre-season practice, and after watching Terry pack up and head into this new adventure, I knew I had to somehow be part of this team. I supposed if I couldn't get a tryout — or worse, if I did get a tryout and didn't make it, I'd figure out how to do something to be part of the team. Maybe my water boy prediction was going to come true after all.

"Tommy Spinks!" Coach Hedges exclaimed, getting up to come over and clap me on the back, shake my hand, and then do the manly half-hug. "How in the world are you?"

"I'm doing well, sir," I said, suddenly nervous. That's weird, I thought. Why would I feel nervous around Coach Hedges? There was a lot riding on my next question. I cleared my throat. "I came here to ask you a huge favor."

Coach Hedges' face grew serious. "Is everything OK at home, Tommy?" he asked, concern in his eyes and voice that touched my heart.

"Yes!" I said, wanting to allay his worry as quickly as I could. "It's just, well, sir, since nobody has recruited me to play football, it looks like I'm going to be going to Tech to school — and I was wondering . . ." I looked at my feet, suddenly shy. This was so big to me I almost couldn't get the words out. ". . . If maybe you could help me get a tryout for the team." I worked up the nerve to look him in the eyes. "I know you haven't been here very long and this might be too much to ask, but you know me, you know I can play — and you know how hard I'd work if I could get a spot — any spot on this team." I felt the emotion crawling up the back of my throat forming a giant knot that made the next sentence next to impossible, but somehow I squeezed out, "I just have to play football."

Coach Hedges, saying nothing, walked around to the back of his desk and shuffled through a few papers to find his calendar. He flipped through several pages and put his finger on a spot on one page. "Can you be here Tuesday at 1:00?" he said without ceremony. "Tommy, I can't make you any promises, and like you just said, I'm new here, but I'll get you in front of Coach Alliet and let's see what happens." He looked at me for a moment. "Tech, huh?" he said, and then he smiled. "Whatever happens, I'm sure glad you're going to be here. It's a great school and whatever you do, I know you're going to do it with all your heart."

"Yes, sir," I said, finally able to breathe again and trying to keep my quaking insides from showing. "Thank you, sir," I said. "I'll be here Tuesday and bring everything I've got!"

"I know you will, Tommy," he said. "I hope this works out. I'll be pulling for you!"

"Thank you, sir," I said, fighting back tears. "This means a lot. You won't be sorry."

He smiled. "See you Tuesday, son," he said. He sat down in his big leather desk chair and I thanked my lucky stars all the way back home. I couldn't wait to tell Terry — and Mom and Dad — that maybe, just maybe, if everything lined up just right, I was about to become a Bulldog.

• • •

I did a couple of slow laps around the field. No one was there yet, and I had arrived at the Tech practice field very early on purpose, just to jog around a little bit, stretch, and take it all in. It was big — bigger today than it had even looked when I visited last spring with my parents. My parents had insisted we visit Tech "just in case" I didn't get an offer from another school to play football. And, while this was something I refused to even consider as a possibility, I had humored them. Someone was going to come through, right?

And then a few weeks ago, when it became totally obvious no one was coming for me, and with Terry's decision made, it became clear that Tech would be a great place for me to be. I had a lot of friends going here, Barbara would be here, it's close to home, and even if I didn't get to play football, it all felt just right.

And now, with Coach Hedges and Coach Williams there, I had the opportunity to try out for the team. With all the confidence and determination I felt humming in my body, I knew I was going to be able to win some kind of place in this football program. I couldn't stop myself from smiling as I stretched. At that moment, packed with more anticipation than I could get my arms around, my world just couldn't get any better.

"Are you ready, Spinks?" Coach Hedges asked. He had just arrived with clipboard and stopwatch in hand. He then introduced me to Coach Alliet and it was time to get down to business.

Suddenly all nervousness evaporated. All the constant work Terry and I had put in — even though it never felt like work at all — had built such confidence in my conditioning that I knew there was literally nothing they could ask of me that I wouldn't be able to do well.

First I ran some 40-yard sprints, listening for the click of Coach Hedges' stopwatch as I passed the end marker. I glanced over to where the two coaches were standing and I could tell by their body language and expressions, even from a distance, that they were suitably impressed.

Next I did a series of broad jumps, waiting around for a minute or two after each to watch the measurement. I tried not to appear too excited when I jumped even farther than I ever had in practice before. Each time the two coaches stretched the measuring tape between them and noted something on their clipboards, my heart beat a little bit faster.

Coach Alliet peered at me over the top of his sunglasses after my best jump, which came very close to one of my record-breaking personal bests. He said "Son, did I hear that you broke some state records in high school?"

"Yes, sir," I said. I actually broke a few *national* records as well, but I didn't want to brag. I knew Coach Hedges would make sure he had all the stats.

I noticed out of the corner of my eye that some of the other players had begun to arrive. They were watching from a distance, probably wondering what was going on. School started in just a couple of weeks, after all. Who ever heard of a tryout this late in the summer?

Coach Alliet blew his whistle and motioned the players over. "OK, boys, this is Tommy Spinks, here for a late summer tryout," he said.

The boys looked at each other. *What?* You could almost hear their minds exclaiming.

"We're going to run a few drills with Tommy here and see what he's got," he continued, looking over at me. "Spinks, let's first have you run some routes and then let's have some one-on-ones against a defensive back. I need a quarterback," he said as if this just occurred to him. He looked back to where more players had gathered and motioned them over. Terry was among them.

Coach Hedges turned and said something to Coach Alliet.

"Bradshaw!" Coach Alliet barked, "You ready to throw a few to Tommy here to see if he can catch anything?"

Terry grinned. "Yes sir," he said, looking earnest, "I sure am!"

Terry winked at me as we lined up in our all-too-familiar formation — the scenario we had both visualized since that first day in his backyard, our own version of fantasy football was playing out in a way even I could never have imagined.

When I thought Terry was going to go to LSU — and with no recruiters beating down my door — Tech sort of emerged in my mind as the right place for me to go to college. Then, when things worked out for Terry to go to Tech, my reluctant plan solidified, except with the pang of sadness that I would not be playing football. Now, with this sudden opportunity to try out to play for Tech, I thought my mind and heart might explode with gratitude. Who could have dreamed that all our preparation would run smack upside this unbelievable opportunity — and that it would be my best friend and practice partner that would help set my football career?

I was confident. I was in shape. And, above all, I was driven to succeed no matter the cost. Still, you could have knocked me over with a feather when the coaches called me over to the sideline after my tryout concluded.

"Son, what you've done here today was impressive," Coach Alliet began. "And if you think you can keep that up I believe we do have a place for you on the team here."

"Thank you, sir," I managed to say, not even believing my own ears or the words coming out of my mouth. This was surreal, beyond dreams, beyond fantasy, beyond comprehension.

"There's one more thing," Coach Alliet said.

Could he see that I was shaking like a Chihuahua?

"We do have a full scholarship that has just unexpectedly become available," he said. "A kid we had offered a full ride to just got a better offer somewhere else — and he took it."

Whaaaaaaaaaaaaaat? My mind raced. The only worry that was beginning to germinate around the excitement of this tryout opportunity — and the idea of going to Tech, in general — was how I was going to pay for college. We had always assumed I'd get a scholarship, and even though my parents assured me "we'd find a way," I couldn't stand the guilt of putting them into debt because the scholarship had not materialized as predicted.

"So, based on your record, your academics, and what we saw from you today, that scholarship is yours if you'll agree to play for us for all four years of your eligibility," he said.

"Yes, sir!" I exclaimed, fighting back the urge to run up and hug these coaches. I looked from Coach Alliet to Coach Hedges to Coach Williams, and then back to Coach Alliet. "I won't let you down," I said, fighting back tears. "I will give you everything I've got, every single day out there. Thank you. Thank you. Thank you!"

• • •

I don't think my feet touched the ground all the way home, and when I walked in our front door that evening, I headed straight for the kitchen.

"Mom?" I said, trying to wipe the glee from my face to deliver the news deadpan.

"Well, hello there, sweet son" my mother said, not looking up from her meal preparations. "Are you hungry?"

"No, Mom," I said, summoning seriousness, "something just took my appetite away." I hadn't even told her or my dad about the tryout. I didn't want to get their hopes up after the devastating lack of recruiter traffic to my door. Better to let this play out on its own, I had reasoned.

"Oh, dear, what?" she said, looking up at me, alarmed.

"Just a full scholarship playing FOOTBALL FOR LOUISIANA TECH!" I said, letting my excitement gush into those last four words.

Mom threw her arms in the air, threw back her head. "Well, hallelujah and praise the Lawd!" she said, speaking straight up to the Big Guy himself. Then she hugged me so tightly I couldn't breathe. Then she let go suddenly. "I need to sit down," she exclaimed, fanning herself with her dishrag. She then burst into tears, sobbing manic tears of joy into that wadded dishrag. This was a sight and sound I knew I'd remember for the rest of my days.

CHAPTER 13

"Well I have news," my father said at the dinner table one evening a short while after the direction of my life shifted right beneath my feet.

When we say in the South someone looks "like the cat that swallowed the canary," what you need to know is they are describing the look on my mother's face that night at dinner. She clearly knew all about this news of which my father spoke — and was literally about to explode with fluttering excitement.

"I have decided to retire," Dad continued, as if anyone responded to his original pronouncement. I was too busy watching my mother and trying to figure out what had put that silly look on her face.

Then the words sunk in. "Wait . . . What?" I said, whipping my head around the other direction to try to read my father's face. Of all the things Dad loved, he loved being a minister just about as much as anything I knew. And while his time at the church in Shreveport had had its ups and downs, Dad was nowhere near ready to retire. "How can they let you do that?" I asked, totally confused. "You aren't ready to retire!"

Dad laughed. "Well, I'm not retiring completely," he explained. "I am just stepping down from having my own church because I have decided to take another appointment in our conference — as associate pastor at Trinity United Methodist Church."

"Trinity United Methodist . . ." I said, trying to remember where that church even was. "Where the heck is that?" I asked, giving up. It sounded kind of familiar, but I just couldn't place it.

"It's in Ruston!" my mother blurted, unable to keep quiet for another second.

Right. "Wait," I said, looking from Dad to Mom and back to Dad again. "So y'all are moving to Ruston . . . too?" I asked, trying to get my mind around what they were saying.

I mean, it made a certain amount of sense. Betty Carol had just gotten married and she and her new husband, Joey, were already living in Ruston. And, because the town of Ruston was, of course, home to the Louisiana Tech Bulldogs, within days I would be moving there to start the fall semester at Tech.

Now don't misunderstand here, I'm not one of those guys who would be horrified to learn that his parents would be following him to college. Not at all. In fact, it was just the opposite. The only thing I didn't like about going to college was leaving Mom and Dad in Shreveport. Even though it was only an hour or so away, I knew I was going to be one homesick boy. Now the most important parts of home were going to Ruston with me.

"Dad, that's fantastic!" I said, looking first at Dad and then back at Mom, who was positively beaming. "How did all this happen?"

"Well, at Annual Conference last month I found out that a Reverend Douglas McGuire at Trinity United Methodist Church was in need of a new associate pastor," my dad explained. He paused to take a long drink of iced tea. He looked at my mother and shrugged. "I didn't think too much about it at the time," he said, "but then when you found out you'd be playing football at Tech, Tommy, I gave ole' Doug a call to see if he had found anyone." Dad reached for another helping of meatloaf. "When he said he hadn't, I told him I'd like the job if the Bishop will approve the transfer." He looked at my mother. "I didn't say anything because there was a lot of paperwork and finagling involved — we also had to see if we could get my position filled."

I followed suit on the meatloaf and grinned at my mom. "So I guess you'll be making it to some of the Tech games after all to see me play," I teased. Not being able to be at all our games had been one of Mom's great laments once she learned "her boys" would be playing college ball together.

Mom laughed. "Yes, Tommy, I will be there with bells on to see my boys play ball," she said.

Knowing full well what she meant, I said, "But Mom, you know I'm your only son." I gave her the most innocent and charming look I could conjure up.

"Watching you and Terreh play football is one of my life's great joys," she said. "I don't plan to miss a single game."

• • •

What is that horrible smell?" Terry said, plopping down a box of my belongings on the narrow, institutional bed. "Smells like some old lady's armpit."

Caught off guard at this unexpected mental imagery, I spewed into a fit of laughter that nearly caused me to drop the box I was carrying. It was moving-in day for the athletes and he wasn't wrong about the smell. Because I got my football scholarship after the team was already formed and their rooms assigned in the athletic dorms near the baseball field, I didn't get to stay in the same dorms as my teammates.

Instead, I had to stay in Hale Hall, which was the oldest, stuffiest, musty-smellingest, most stifling hot dorm on campus.

Terry opened a window. "Dang, Spinks, I don't know what's worse — the smell or the heat. We gotta get some air in here or you're gonna gag-and-sweat to death."

"It's been closed up all summer," I said, feeling suddenly defensive of my new home away from home. "I'll be fine," I said, trying my best to sound more certain than I felt.

• • •

"This feels a little . . . spooky," Terry said, looking around him, peering into the lengthening shadows as we walked across campus to return to our dorms. Practice ended each evening about dusk, and by the time we changed and headed back to the dorm, it was starting to get dark.

Because the football players were the first to arrive on Tech's campus each fall for football practice, we pretty much had the campus to ourselves. This was great for exploring, which we did, but as the evening shadows fell, the whole place took on the feel of a ghost town, barren and deserted.

I looked around, following Terry's eyes. "Very spooky," I agreed. This seemed like the perfect opportunity to mess with Terry's mind a little bit.

Terry, truth be told, was always very easy to scare. You would think that someone that big wouldn't be afraid of very much. Wrong. My buddy Terry was basically a big fat chicken, and I was the kind of friend who would take the time and trouble to figure out the best way to get him to wet his pants out of shear fear and panic.

We walked in silence for a few steps before I launched my plan. "So," I said, looking straight down at the ground ahead of me so my face wouldn't give me away. "I guess you heard about those kids that were murdered."

Terry stopped in his tracks. "Murdered kids? What are you talking about?"

"Wow, I can't believe you haven't heard yet," I said, turning to face him. "Maybe that's best. There's really no reason to worry you. I know how you worry. We're perfectly fine." I motioned for him to come on.

"Tommy!" he demanded, "You need to tell me right now! What happened?"

"Keep walking and I'll tell you," I said. More than anything else I was hungry and wanted to get back to the dorm before dinnertime was over.

He complied, looking around him as he walked. "Go on," he said. "What happened? What did you hear?"

"Well," I said, taking my good old easy time, pretending I was trying to remember, "I heard that we need to be very careful when we're walking alone on campus because there is someone out there, still on the loose, who murdered some students on campus at the end of summer school. They think he might possibly still be in this area, but I don't really believe that. I'm sure he's long gone. Why would he take that kind of chance?" I shook my head. "There's just no way."

Even in the pitch black that had by now descended on us as we walked, I could actually see the whites of Terry's eyes — they were bugged out like giant light bulbs. He began to walk faster.

Something rustled in the brush off to one side of the sidewalk, and Terry literally jumped straight up in the air. We were coming to the split in the path where I would go to my dorm and he would go to his, so I made the turn and stepped back into the shadow of an overhanging tree. I let him get a few steps along and then I let out a bloodcurdling scream, as if someone was standing there in the shadows with me.

Hearing this, Terry turned, looked wildly around for me, and then he screamed, too. Then he ran backwards a few steps to where I was the last time he saw me, and then he took off running in a zigzag formation, as if he was running for his life but didn't know which way to safety.

I stood there, laughing until I couldn't get my breath at him running around out there like a crazed, headless chicken.

Then I stopped, realizing that I was now completely alone out there. I took off running after him, as he was now lined out and on the way to his dorm. When I finally caught up with him, he whirled around, eyes blazing. "You did that on purpose!" he said. "You ran off and left me being murdered!"

"No sense in both of us getting murdered," he said, finally starting to laugh with me. "And besides, you had it coming."

"You should have seen yourself!" I said, a new wave of laughter coming over me and rendering me speechless. I ran, zig-zagging back and forth, waving my arms and screaming.

I laughed so hard I thought I would be the one to wet my pants.

And then, I had to walk back to my dorm alone.

Life has a way of putting you in your place sometimes, and sometimes, even the best idea can backfire.

• • •

We found a great spot in an equidistant cleared green space between our dorms where we could meet up and throw the football at a moment's notice. Here we'd throw and throw, regardless of the hour, and as far as we knew, not really bothering anyone. Because it wasn't close to any of the dorms or common areas where people liked to hang out, we could pretty much throw there any time of the day or night — whenever we wanted to. It was our go-to place, anytime we needed to let off steam, if we were bored, or if the sun was shining. And sometimes even when it wasn't. This was our refuge, and the hours we spent throwing the football there kept us grounded like nothing else.

College, I quickly discovered, was the greatest thing ever. We could throw the ball all day and all night if we wanted to. Sure, we had to go to class and study, because making our grades meant keeping our scholarships and getting to play football. And football practice and training and games pretty much dominated our lives and schedules from week to week. But hey, when we did have any sort of free time, we could do whatever we wanted to — and we did!

This new taste of freedom was sweet. Intoxicating, actually. We weren't drinkers or partiers — and because we were highly committed athletes, the last thing we'd ever consider was taking any sort of drug — but we exercised this new off-the-leash freedom in all kinds of ways. Some of them were just plain dumb. Others were more on the incredibly immature spectrum. But above all, we knew that these were our glory days — and anything that made us laugh was a thing worth doing. If we didn't want to go home until way after dark, we didn't; if we wanted to eat dessert first, by golly we did. And sometimes we had two of them. And if we didn't feel up to going to church, we didn't.

Well, I take that back, we had to go to church. We were grown men now. But truthfully, we were still very, very immature grown men.

• • •

"Otis! Where in this world have you been?"

My mother rarely scolded my dad, but for about the third afternoon that week, church members had called the house looking for my dad and my mother had not known where to say he was. In fact, she had no idea where to look for either Dad or Rev. McGuire, who also happened to be missing from the church.

This rash of unexplained absences both perturbed and scared her, I think. Not because she thought my dad was off somewhere doing something he shouldn't be. Mom was a worrier by nature, and not knowing where someone was meant something bad could happen to him or her and she wouldn't know. I'm not saying this made any kind of sense, mind you, but that's just how my mother thought.

"Oh Grace, simmer down," he'd say. "The day just got away from us." He'd then go on to tell her the latest news about hospitals and parishioners until she got distracted into forgetting to ask more questions.

When Terry and I were there for these exchanges, we'd try not to make eye contact to keep from busting out laughing. We knew exactly where those two were. From our vantage point on the practice field, we'd look up there on the side where all the trees were and see those two perched on top of their respective cars in their suits, ties, and fedora hats, eating sandwiches and watching us run our practice drills.

Now, I'm not saying they didn't also visit the sick and troubled parishioners; they'd just end their rounds sitting up there watching us practice. They became something of a fixture up there, and the team and coaching staff would often wave in their direction when they arrived. Terry and I, being new, were pretty pleased to be the draw for these two devoted spectators. Besides, it couldn't hurt to have not one but two preachers pulling for you, could it?

• • •

"Otis, I declare," my mother said, hands on hips, as my father came in the front door after another afternoon he went missing.

From the moment we all picked up and moved to Ruston, it had been a time of settling in — Mom and Dad in their new home and me in Hale Hall and getting used to football practice at a whole new level. I stopped by a few times a week, partly to check on them and mostly to see what baked goods my mother might have there waiting, I'm sure, just in case I might come by.

One of the most interesting things for me to observe was how quickly my father and Rev. McGuire had become fast friends, and most particularly, what it was that bonded them.

You see, those two had a secret.

The first time I glanced up at the spot between two shade trees on the hill overlooking the football field and saw the two of them, sitting on their cars and watching practice I had to smile. I didn't know the details, but I did know that they were up there, more afternoons than not, and my dad had never said a word about it.

"Grace, I don't know what's got you so bothered," Dad began, ready, I suppose, to regale her with his afternoon of hospital visits and committee meetings. My dad wasn't one to lie, but he did know how to stretch the truth to its tensile strength.

"Otis Spinks you know EXACTLY what has got me so bothered," Mom huffed. "People have been calling here looking for you all afternoon long." She stamped her dainty foot. "I have no idea what to tell them or how to get hold of you if there's an emergency — and some of these people sounded like they might be just on the verge of emergency." Mom, too, knew how to bend the facts a bit to suit her purpose. She eyed my dad for a moment, waiting for another attempt at response.

"Grace . . ." he began.

And she was off again. "Now don't you start telling me some fiddle-faddle about where you've been." She glared. "I know exactly where you've been and I am worried sick about what's going to happen when Reverend McGuire finds out what you've really been up to all these afternoons." Her voice softened and the real fear seeped through her outrage. "Otis, I'm afraid you're going to lose your job."

Then my dad gathered my mom into his arms and held onto her stiff, angry body for just a moment. "Grace," he whispered, "simmer down now. Who do you think is sitting on top of his car right beside me when we watch the boys practice?"

Somehow I managed to get out of that room before the fit of laughter I had been working so hard to contain burst out of me. But it was a small house, and I didn't fool anyone.

"Tommeh Spinks!" my parents exclaimed in unison.

From the day my dad signed on at Trinity United Methodist Church, my dad and Rev. McGuire became like brothers, and they remained so until the day my father died. He always said he counted Rev. McGuire the greatest friend of his lifetime.

Through the years that followed, Dad and Rev. McGuire had married Barbara and me, Joey and Betty, and Peggy Ann and Glen. Then, years later, he baptized all of our children.

After my dad died in 1987, Rev. McGuire made it part of his life's mission — and his promise to my dad — to carry on my father's legacy in Ruston and in our family. He became the "quasi" patriarch to all of us, and no matter where we lived we traveled back to Ruston so Rev. McGuire could baptize our grandchildren at good ole' Trinity United Methodist Church where he remained one of the most beloved pastors in the entire Parish.

Not only was Rev. McGuire my dad's best friend, he was like a second father to me — and like another grandfather to my children and to their children, as well.

Who could have imagined that all the football decisions and happenstances that put Terry and me at Tech would bring my dad — and my entire family — such a friend?

• • •

One of the things Louisiana Tech was best known for at that time was Louisiana Tech Ice Cream. In Ruston's collective well-considered opinion, the ice cream made right there on campus by our Tech Agriculture department was the best ice cream on the planet. Knowing our special affinity for this amazing ice cream, Rev. McGuire made it his personal business to keep Terry and me well supplied.

There's really no telling how many gallons of the stuff he purchased from the Ag Department on our behalf, and he doled it out to us one touchdown at a time. You see, Rev. McGuire made a promise to us that for every touchdown we made, he would buy us a gallon of whatever flavor of Tech ice cream we wanted. I can tell you without question that this promise was one of the first thoughts to cross my mind every time I crossed that goal line. Somewhere in the touchdown celebration I'd smile and think, *chocolate.*

• • •

"You boys need to tuck in your shirts," my mother stage whispered, coming up behind us as we walked along the street of downtown Ruston. "And stand up straight. You two need to remember that you are always representing Tech Football — not just when you are on that football field."

Terry and I looked at each other and grinned. And then we tucked in our shirts. And stood up a little straighter. If anyone lived for football as much as we did, it would be my parents.

"Hey, Mrs. Spinks," someone we didn't even know called from across the street.

"See?" Mom said, validated. "Everyone in this town knows who we are."

Behind her back and where only I could see him, Terry made a big-eyed face, and I couldn't keep from cracking up. Mom spun around, catching him red-handed. "Terry, I'm serious," she chided.

"Yes, ma'am, I know you are," Terry said.

It went without saying that my parents were our biggest fans, on and off the field. And they loved living in Ruston. No matter where they went in town, people were always talking football — and they always recognized my parents even when they weren't sporting their "I'm the proud mom of #43" and "I'm the proud dad of #43" buttons they wore to every single game.

"Tommy, Mr. (insert name) wanted me to tell you that (insert advice)," was a common dinnertime conversation starter in our family. With that much football talk going on, pointers and accolades came our way in a constant stream. And more often than not, my parents were the recipients and carriers for these messages and advice.

Generally, I'd just roll my eyes, say "thank you," and go on about my business.

This annoyed Mom. "Tommy, you need to speak to Mr. (insert name) about this. Remembah, his family is very supportive of Tech football, and you'd be smart to listen and appreciate what he has to say."

Dad usually kept quiet during these exchanges, but often he'd nod his agreement. It was clear to me that Mom and Dad felt like some kind of Tech royalty, and it was the people of Ruston who made them feel that way. As much as I pretended to be bothered by all this attention and advice, I secretly enjoyed it — and I particularly enjoyed how special that whole town made my parents feel. They were happy everywhere they ever lived, but Ruston was home for the rest of their lives.

• • •

One of the things that makes college life great is that almost everyone in college is poor, so you are literally forced to learn how to have fun with little or no money to spend. No matter who we were or where we came from, for that single period in time, we were all the same. For me, Terry, and all our other football buddies, new and old, this was a time of working hard on the field, having fun together, making our grades, and making memories that would be with us for life.

"Wow! Would you look at these!" Terry exclaimed, peering into an open box.

When it came to Terry, that sort of invitation could mean almost anything. "What is it?"

"Just come look!" he said.

We had been sent by the coaches to the back office of the field house on an errand — to find some boxes of forms we were all about to have to fill out. The office supplies area of the field house was the kind of jumble you might expect. Football players — and especially football coaches — have never been known for their attention to organizational skills.

So for the past hour and a half we had been pawing through boxes and folders, looking for what Coach was certain was "in a big grey box" stacked somewhere in this chaotic mess.

I made my way over to the precarious stack Terry was working his way through and peered into the box of interest. This was a box filled to the brim with staple guns.

He looked up and laughed at my puzzled expression.

Why is there a giant box filled to the brim with staple guns? Why is this so fascinating?

In answer to my unvoiced questions, Terry picked up a staple gun and stapled my sweatshirt to my arm.

"OW!!!" I shrieked, picking up a staple gun and returning the favor.

They were tiny staples, and most of them didn't really penetrate the fabric enough to draw much blood, but a few of them did. But after a few rounds of this good old-fashioned staple gun fight, we mutually decided to return the guns to their box and resume our search.

If Coach noticed the spots of blood on us when we returned with the forms, he didn't mention it. I'm sure if he had any idea what caused them he'd have forgone the lecture anyhow. The lesson itself was painful enough to stand on its own merit. And some things are just too stupid to waste your time discussing. To this day I can't look at a staple gun without remembering this and some of our other crazy antics. Anything for a laugh and a story to tell.

CHAPTER 14

"Anybody up for Ray's PeGe?" Terry posed the question to the bunch of us standing around the locker room. Our scrimmage had run long, dinnertime in the dorms was over, and since visiting hours were also over, seeing the girls was out of the question.

"Sure!" I and a few others agreed. I pulled out my wallet and examined the contents. Yep. Just enough to cover a burger and fries. "I'm in!"

We piled into a few cars and headed toward our favorite burger joint in the whole world, just about 30 minutes down the road in Monroe. Ray's PeGe, a greasy-but-spectacular diner was everyone's favorite place to get a burger and some unbelievable homemade onion rings. My mouth still waters at the thought of those onion rings.

We got there just in the nick of time, one of the last orders to get placed for the day. In Ruston, a bunch of Tech football players showing up to eat this late in an evening would keep the doors open. But this was Monroe, and while there were still plenty of Tech fans here, they felt no obligation to feed us any time we showed up, and usually not on the house. But, because the Ruston restaurants were all closed, this was our next best option.

We laughed, we told stories on one another, we talked football, stats, and made predictions for the upcoming NFL and AFL season — and we ate an enormous amount of food. Finally, when it was just about time to head back to Ruston, I excused myself to go to the restroom. Those six giant glasses of sweet tea would not tolerate the drive home.

When I came out of the restroom and headed back to the table, my buddies had disappeared. A tired looking young woman was clearing the table, loading our dishes in a grey plastic tub. Our check was laying right out there in the center of the table. There might as well have been a spotlight on it.

In an instant I knew what was up. "Did you see which way they went?" I asked, trying to keep the panic out of my voice. No sense alarming this woman who looked like her sense of humor had gone home at 5:00.

"They left," she said, not looking up from her loading.

"Oh no they didn't," I said, turning to look through the plate glass windows that covered the entire front of the restaurant. The parking lot, it appeared, was deserted.

So I had two problems on my hands. First, how to pay the bill on just enough cash to cover my own meal. And second, how to get back to Ruston if they had, indeed, left me here. Oh wait. And the third problem was how I was going to hide all those bodies once I caught up with them.

"So are you going to be taking care of this?" the waitress asked, reaching over to pick up the check from the tabletop.

"Um. Sure," I said, searching for what in the heck I was going to do. "You see, well, my friends, they left me here as a joke . . . I think . . ."

"Some friends," she said. "That doesn't sound like a very good joke to me."

"Oh, believe me, they're not going to be laughing once I catch them," I said with more confidence than I felt. How was I going to get out of this current jam and on to the next one?

"Look," I said, "I can give you right now every cent I have on me . . ." I dumped my wallet out on the table and pushed the meager stack of bills toward her. Then I reached into my pockets and produced a few coins on one side — and nothing but lint from my wrong-side-out pocket on the other.

She took the bills and the coins, counted them, and then looked back at me, one eyebrow raised like my mother used to do when I was trying to put one over on her.

"Ok, look . . ." I said, scrambling for an idea and landing on one. I took the pen and pad from her apron pocket. "Here. Let me give you my name, address, and phone number. I go to Tech and I live in Ruston. In fact, my parents live in Ruston, too. So here's what I'm going to do. I'm going to give you everyone's names and phone numbers — and I will personally guarantee that this bill will get paid in 24 hours."

"I can't . . ." she began.

"Listen, I know this is a big favor to ask," I said, speaking fast as if that might help convince her of my earnestness. "I just hope you will help me." I gave her my most charming smile and guileless eyes. "You've got to know that this is just a stupid prank my knucklehead buddies are playing on me. I'm paying you for my own food, see, with a very generous tip."

She looked at the money in her hands. Again the eyebrow.

"I'm in college!" I said. "It's a pretty good tip!"

"I'll make sure you get the rest," I said, sensing that she was weakening. "Plus double tip for your trouble." I had no idea how I was going to enforce this promise. Everyone else was as broke as I was, but there had to be some penalty for being a bunch of jerks.

I paused, looking around me at the deserted restaurant. "Or I could stay and wash dishes," I said. "Or sweep and mop this place for you."

"Oh, hell no," she said. "I need to go home. I've been here since 6:00 this morning and have to be back at the same time tomorrow."

"Also," I said, "Can I borrow your phone? I need to call someone to come and get me."

She was just about to answer when the whole bunch of those losers came barging back through the door, laughing their butts off like they had just witnessed the funniest episode ever of Candid Camera.

"You idiots need to pay your dang bill and apologize to this woman," I said.

It really is a wonder I didn't kill each and every one of them in their sleep.

• • •

From our very first practice I knew that something special was in store for the Tech football program. It was a unique situation for sure. By the time school started we had a pretty big piece of our old Woodlawn team back together. Several players made their decision to come to Tech once Terry and I had both committed. With Coach Hedges now on board at Tech as an assistant coach, it was great for so many of us to be back together again — and this time, on a much larger stage.

When we first arrived on the Louisiana Tech football scene in 1966, a cloud of media frenzy surrounded my buddy Terry, who was being heralded as the "Sensation from Shreveport." The town was elated over Terry's choosing their community as his home away from home for the next four years, and I was happy to see that a little bit of that excitement was spilling over in my direction. Someone had to be fast and savvy enough to catch those amazing long passes, right?

Terry's nickname, the Blonde Bomber, was bestowed almost upon arrival by a guy named Phil Robertson, the Tech starting quarterback who was just beginning his junior year. It was odd to imagine, especially with all the hoopla, that Terry would play behind anyone, but after just a few practices watching Phil work, I was dazzled into acceptance.

Watching Phil's utter presence in the pocket, I was mesmerized. Tall and wiry, 6-foot-2, 195 pounds, not only did he have a good arm, but also he was just so settled. There was always something in his manner that fascinated me — he was so calm and deliberate in his movements, and yet had the fastest release I had ever seen. Phil always knew exactly where he was and what he was doing back there — and man, could that booger chuck a football.

"Man, where did you learn to throw like that?" Terry asked Phil after one of our early scrimmages and first exposure to Phil's talent. We were hanging out in the locker room after practice, just kind of soaking it all up and getting our bearings. Mostly, Terry and I were trying to get to know this enigma that was Phil Robertson.

Phil looked up from tying his shoe. He examined Terry's expression for a moment, as if to assess whether the question was genuine or just banter — or bait. He paused, and then turned his attention back to his shoelaces. "Bomber," he said, standing up, "a good arm is just something you're born with or not." He looked at Terry with the gentle intensity he was so well known for. "Ever since I was a little kid, I could always throw farther than all the other kids. I don't know why or how. That's not something that can really be learned — it's either there or it's not." He picked up his bag to leave. "You know what I'm saying, Bomber. You have it too."

Terry stood there, quiet for a moment, then said, "I never really thought about it until now. I've always loved to throw — and I guess from the very beginning been able to throw long. It's just always been . . . there."

"I saw that the first day you came on," Phil said. "And every day since. And you need to know that you've definitely got me on distance."

"What do you mean?" Terry asked, puzzled.

"I'm about a 65-yard man, tops, Bomber. I've seen you going 70-plus. Consistently."

"Yeah, well I may have the distance, but you still have the fastest release I've ever seen," Terry said. "How in the world do you do that? Is that natural, too? Or something you learned and developed?"

Phil laughed. "I don't know. I think I just worked it out somehow, somewhere along the way. He thought for a moment as if this was the first time he really considered this. "I don't come back too far, I think," he said. "It's all from about the ear, doncha know . . ." He demonstrated using a wadded up towel, ". . . From . . . right there — forward."

He made it sound so simple, but what he was talking about was far from it. Watching Phil's timing and release of the ball was pure poetry in motion. Standing there, watching those two talk like that, I wondered how all this was going to go. Phil was two years ahead of us with a four-year-scholarship. I wasn't sure how Terry was going to like playing behind anyone, but it was really hard not to like this guy.

Terry paused, then he grinned. "Ever chuck a javelin?"

Phil laughed, "Yeah, I did, actually . . . and pitched a little baseball . . . I've always liked pretty much anything that involved throwing."

"Me too!" Terry said, beaming.

We later learned that Robertson had been all-state in football, baseball, and track and field, all of which afforded him the opportunity to attend Tech on a football scholarship. There was no question that he was an extremely talented athlete. The other thing we soon learned about Phil was that as much as he liked football, there was something he actually loved much more.

The first time he showed up for practice with blood on his shirt, Terry punched me and whispered, "Looka there. I wonder what the other guy looks like."

I grinned. We had both heard tales of Phil's love of hunting. This was just the first time we actually saw the evidence of it.

"Been hunting, Phil?" Terry asked.

Phil stopped in his tracks, startled. "Yes," he said, peering at Terry as if trying to read his motive for asking, then giving up. "Why?"

"Man, you've got blood . . . and feathers stuck all over your shirt . . . and . . . is that a squirrel tail hanging out of your pocket?"

Phil grinned. "Yeah, maybe," he said, stuffing the squirrel tail back in his pocket. "But I made it here in time, didn't I?"

Rumor had it that Coach Aillet made Phil come over and spend the night at his house before games to keep him from getting up at 4:00 am to go duck hunting on game days. It was his weak attempt to keep Phil's mind on the ballgame instead of hunting and fishing — if only for just one day a week.

We all just came to accept that anytime we saw Phil, whether on campus, entering the field house or on his way to class, he had most likely just gutted a deer on his kitchen table, picked a bunch of ducks in his sink, skinned a few squirrels on his porch, or filleted some fish on the counter of his small apartment. The guy was obsessed with hunting, fishing, and anything to do with being in the woods, in nature, and living off the land. He was a hunter of whatever wildlife roamed the backwoods countryside he loved to explore.

The other thing Phil loved besides football, hunting, and his family was holding court. You really couldn't help but like him — he was such a country boy who, by his own admission, was most likely born in the wrong era. He was funny, he was smart, he was insightful — and he told a story in a way that kept all of us riveted. Whenever Phil spoke, we listened. And not only did he know how to tell a story, but he also knew how to tailor any conversation to his audience. Watching Phil's interaction with his teammates, coaches and others, I learned what leadership looked like.

One of my favorite memories from that first year at Tech is standing around the locker room after practice, listening to Phil's latest tale. One of my all-time favorites was about the time the Dean of Men called Phil into his office. "When you go to the Dean of Men you had messed up somehow," Phil told us. He paused, looking around to let our imaginations take hold of this story.

"So, what he said was," Phil continued, assuming the voice of the Dean, completely free of his usual rural southern Louisiana dialect, 'Mr. Robertson, do you realize the name of that street you live on? Would you give me the name of that street?'"

Phil looked around the circle of us and shrugged. "And I'm thinking, 'what the heck is it?' And then the Dean said, 'Let me help you out. It's called Scholar Drive. You live on Scholar Drive.'"

"As luck would have it," Phil said, "when the president of the University invited some dignitaries over for a visit, he was showing them around — bragging on Louisiana Tech's housing facilities." He grinned, resuming the voice of the Dean, "'Mr. Robertson, I've got to tell you, when we got to your house there were nets. There were duck feathers. And blood on the sidewalk. There was an old deer hide and antlers and a bunch of old junk piled up on your porch.'

"And I said, 'Dean Lewis, that old junk is my *equipment*.'

"So he said, 'I want you to get out there and get that stuff out of sight because . . . it's just not real scholarly, Mr. Robertson.'"

I still laugh as I imagine that exchange — and then I smile when I remember my first glimpse of Phil's honesty — and his courage to stay true to his passion in the face of pressure to do otherwise. There was never any put-on about Phil. No matter what the circumstances, Phil stayed true to Phil.

• • •

Even in lives completely focused on football — football practice, football games, thinking about football, reading about football, and dreaming about football — it was still a major priority for Terry and me to find any extra time we could to simply throw the thing some more.

We started throwing one evening just after visiting hours were over and I had said goodnight to Barbara on the steps of the girls' dorm. Between my football practices and the archaic hours of the girls' dorms, it was very hard to see each other. Only a few months into the school year and already this was getting old.

So with nothing else to do but study, Terry and I agreed to meet in that open space where we loved to throw for a while before we buckled down to our studies. But by the time we got there and were just getting loosened up, darkness won. Even with the ambient light of the streetlights dotting the campus, it was just a matter of time till one of us got nailed in the face.

"We need more light," Terry said, motioning me forward.

I looked toward the street. Too much traffic.

Then Terry's eyes widened as only a truly great idea could cause them to do. "I've got an idea," he said. "Follow me!"

Of course, I did.

We jogged across campus in the direction of the stadium, and as we approached, I began to suspect that this idea might not be so great.

"What are you doing?" I asked as he scaled the chain-link gate that was closed and locked for the day. Presumably to keep people out.

"C'mon Spinks, try to keep up!" he called over his shoulder as he disappeared into the shadows under the bleachers.

For a bonafide scaredy cat he was displaying an unusual amount of courage. I'm not sure what made me follow him. Might have been curiosity, might have been not wanting to be left alone there in the dark. I may have been braver than Terry, but that's not saying much.

When I finally caught up with him, Terry was standing inside the stadium at the top of the bleachers, looking up a light pole as if making some sort of mental calculations.

Already I did not like the way this was looking.

"You know you can turn these things on manually from the top," he said, taking off his shoes and stuffing his socks into them.

"Oh, is that so?" I said, trying not to think about what he was about to do. And ask me to do.

As if on cue he said, "You go get that one and I'll get this one. That should be plenty if we stay on this side of the field."

"Oh yeah, and nobody can see these things from, say, ANYWHERE ON CAMPUS," I said, heading toward the other pole.

The light was glorious, as was having the whole stadium to ourselves. We threw the ball for about an hour before the security guards came.

"What are you boys doing out here?" one of them asked.

"We're just getting in some extra practice time, sir," Terry called, sending a perfect deep spiral to me as he did.

The guards both watched the trajectory of the ball in silent admiration.

"How did you turn on the lights?" the other one asked.

"We climbed up there and turned them on manually," Terry said.

"You know that's dangerous, boys," the older one said. "We're going to have to ask you not to ever do that again."

"Yes, sir," Terry said. "We won't."

Fully expecting to get written up, scolded, fined — whatever they do to trespassers, I threw the ball one last time to Terry and then turned to walk toward the security guards — only to see them going up the steps. I looked at Terry, who grinned, shrugged, and sent the ball back my way.

Those guards sat there in the stands for another 45 minutes or so, just watching us throw the ball.

"Time to call it a night, boys," they finally said, standing to walk us to the gate. "Y'all be careful going home, now," they said as they locked the gate behind us. "And don't let us catch you over here doing this again."

"OK, sir, thank you, sir," we said in unison, both of us somewhat stunned at this most unusual display of Ruston love for its Tech football team.

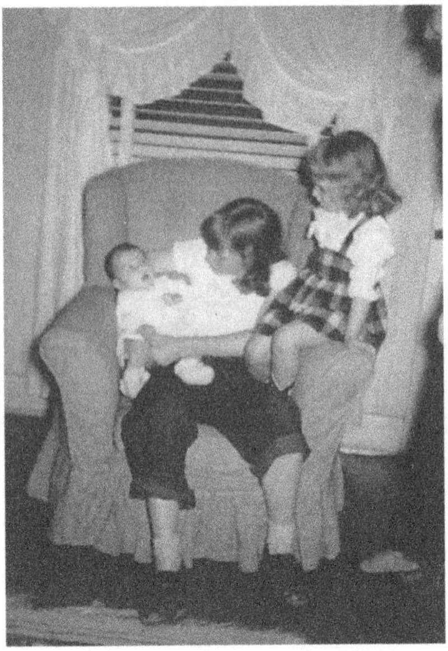

Tommy, Peggy Ann, and Betty Carol Spinks, 1948

Photo courtesy of Spinks family

Grace and Otis Spinks

Photo courtesy of Spinks family

Barbara Lindsay's Woodlawn High School Senior picture

Drummond's House of Photography, Inc. | Photo courtesy of Woodlawn High School

Tommy Spinks' Woodlawn High School Senior picture

Drummond's House of Photography, Inc | Photo courtesy of Woodlawn High School

Terry and Tommy, Woodlawn High School football

Photo courtesy of Woodlawn High School

Tommy, Woodlawn pole vaulting

Photo courtesy of Woodlawn High School

Terry, Woodlawn javelin

Photo courtesy of Woodlawn High School

Accolade Pageant, where Tommy met Barbara

Photo courtesy of Woodlawn High School

Tommy's Senior year, Mr. Woodlawn High School

Photo courtesy of Woodlawn High School

Terry, Woodlawn High School quarterback

Photo courtesy of Woodlawn High School

Tommy, Woodlawn High School baseball

Photo courtesy of Woodlawn High School

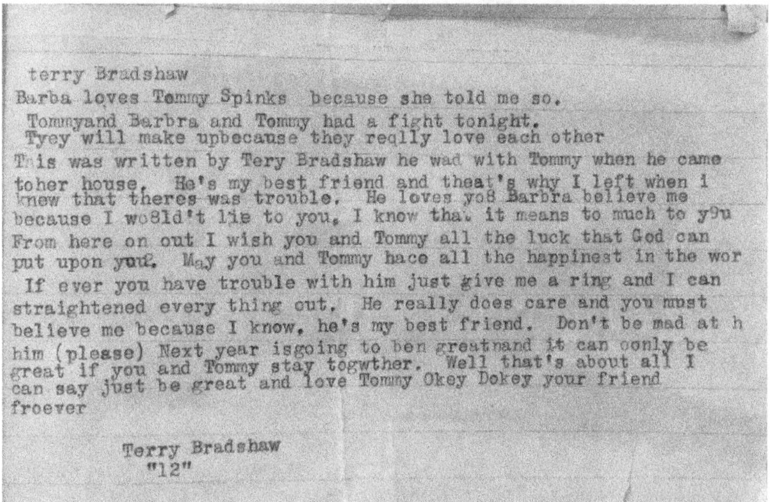

terry Bradshaw
Barba loves Tommy Spinks because she told me so.
Tommyand Barbra and Tommy had a fight tonight.
Tyey will make upbecause they reqlly love each other
This was written by Tery Bradshaw he wad with Tommy when he came
toher house. He's my best friend and theat's why I left when i
knew that theres was trouble. He loves yo8 Barbra believe me
because I wo8ld't lie to you, I know that it means to much to y9u
From here on out I wish you and Tommy all the luck that God can
put upon you. May you and Tommy hace all the happinest in the wor
If ever you have trouble with him just give me a ring and I can
straightened every thing out. He really does care and you must
believe me because I know, he's my best friend. Don't be mad at h
him (please) Next year isgoing to ben greatnand it can oonly be
great if you and Tommy stay togwther. Well that's about all I
can say just be great and love Tommy Okey Dokey your friend
froever

Terry Bradshaw
"12"

The letter Terry typed to squelch an argument between Tommy and Barbara

Photo courtesy of Spinks family

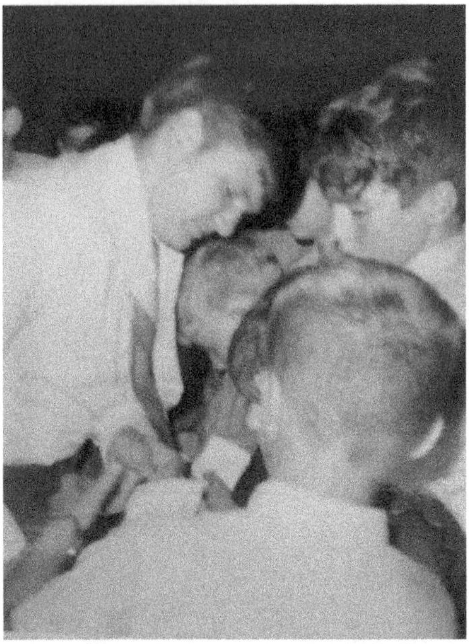

Tommy, signing autographs
Photo courtesy of Spinks family

Barbara, senior homecoming court
Photo courtesy of Woodlawn High School

Barbara, captain, Woodlawn High School pep squad

Photo courtesy of Woodlawn High School

Woodlawn High School football team

Photo taken by Clell Baker | Photo courtesy of Woodlawn High School

Terry, Senior Knight, court of the Accolade Pageant
Photo courtesy of Woodlawn High School

Tommy, King of the Accolade Pageant
Photo courtesy of Woodlawn High School

Signs Grant-in-Aid

Spinks In Fold At Tech

LEE HEDGES (left), former Woodlawn High School head coach who is now offensive backfield mentor at Louisiana Tech, looks over blueprints of Tech's new football stadium with Tommy Spinks, All-State end at Woodlawn who has just signed a grant-in-aid with the Ruston school. They'll enlist in the Bulldog cause this fall along with ex-Knight quarterback Terry Bradshaw.

RUSTON — Louisiana's top triple-A passing combination of 1965 appeared to be safe in the Louisiana Tech fold today as Tommy Spinks, former All-State end from Shreveport's Woodlawn High School, signed a grant-in-aid agreement with the local school.

He was signed by his former prep coach, Lee Hedges, who became a Bulldog assistant during the current summer.

The pitching half of the ex-Knight aerial combo, quarterback Terry Bradshaw, had signed with Tech some months ago and is expected to report for fall drills Sept. 1, although he has been courted heavily by several other colleges right through the summer.

Last season, while Hedges' Knights were rolling into the state playoffs, Spinks caught 22 of Bradshaw's tosses good for 11 touchdowns. He was a cornerback on defense, as well as a pole vaulter in track and a shortstop on the Woodlawn baseball team.

Spinks' father, Rev. Otis Spinks, is a retired Methodist minister who was formerly pastor at Shreveport's Summer Grove Methodist Church. The family has moved to Ruston since Tommy's graduation.

Head Coach Joe Aillet said that the six-foot, 165-pound newcomer will probably fit into Tech's pro offense as a flankerback.

"He's a little light, it's true," Coach Aillet conceded, "but he's blessed with a fine pair of hands and speed enough, as well as the requisite toughness to play college ball. He'll be following in a great Woodlawn tradition here at Tech, too."

Quarterback Billy Laird and end Wayne Davis, who formed a record-smashing aerial combination for the past several seasons, hailed from Woodlawn High, as does Ken Liberto, one of the returning lettermen at the flankerback position.

Lee Hedges, head football coach, Woodlawn High School accepted coaching position at Louisiana Tech University and helped Tommy get the tryout that paved the way for his successful college football career.

Photo courtesy of the Shreveport Times

Penny Clark, Terry's high school sweetheart

Photo courtesy of Spinks family

Rev. Otis Spinks doing what he loved most, watching his son play football

Photo courtesy of Spinks family

Maxi Lambright, new head football coach, Louisiana Tech University, Terry and Tommy's sophomore year

Photo courtesy of Louisiana Tech University

Tommy making a play in the Grantland Rice Bowl football game

Photo courtesy of Morris Edwards Studio

Tommy being introduced at the Grantland Rice Bowl

Photo courtesy of Spinks family

Catching footballs before players wore sticky gloves

Photo courtesy of Louisiana Tech University

Spinks Wedding party, 1967

Photo courtesy of Spinks family

Tommy and Barbara Spinks

Photo courtesy of Spinks family

The new car borrowed from Joey Bales, Tommy's brother-in-law, used as honeymoon getaway car with strict instructions that no shoe polish, only posters, be used to decorate it

Photo courtesy of Spinks family

Rev. Doug McGuire with Kimberly at her christening

Photo courtesy of Spinks family

Tommy's Louisiana Tech football program photo

Photo courtesy of Louisiana Tech University

Coach Mickey Slaughter, former Tech great and ex-Denver Bronco, with Tech's quarterbacks and receivers

Photo courtesy of Louisiana Tech University

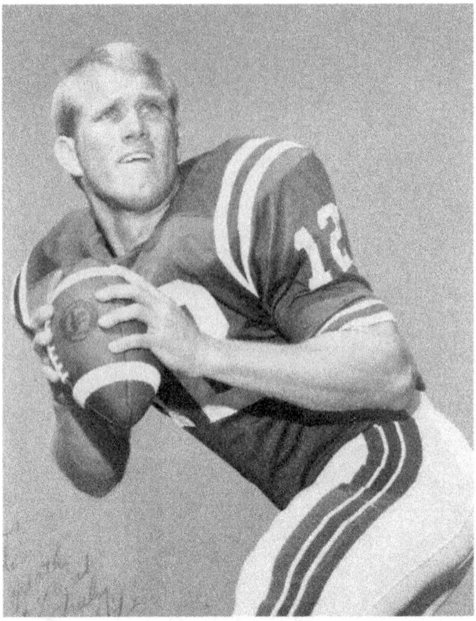

Terry's Tech football program photo

Photo courtesy of Louisiana Tech University

The Tech photo used to make the bronzed plaque that hangs in the Louisiana Tech Hall of Fame

Photo courtesy of Louisiana Tech University

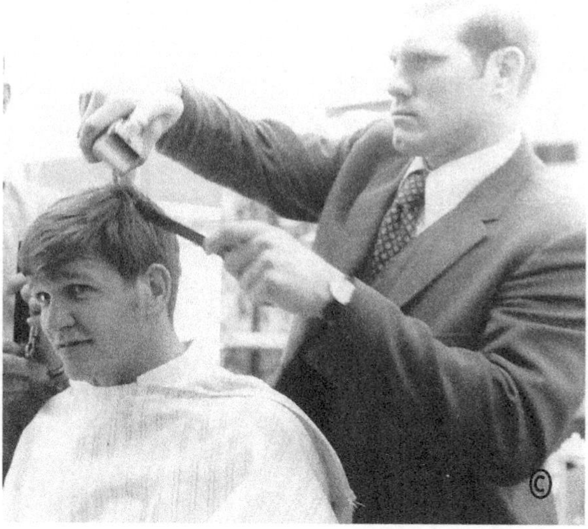

Terry giving Tommy a haircut before their trip to Washington, D.C. to meet President Nixon

Photo credit, R.E. Voll | Photo courtesy of Louisiana Tech University

Ken Liberto, Tommy, and Terry waiting to board the plane to Washington, D.C.

Photo courtesy of Spinks family

President Richard Nixon said he was, "impressed that a school the size of Louisiana Tech would have three of its football graduates drafted to the pros."

Photo courtesy of Louisiana Tech University

Joey, Betty Carol, and Beth Bales

Photo courtesy of Spinks family

Dr. Hall, family friend and OB/GYN specialist, credited with getting Tommy the care he needed to recover from his bout with the deadly amoeba, Naegleria fowleri

Photo courtesy of Spinks family

Tommy boarding the plane to Minnesota for Vikings training camp

Photo courtesy of Spinks family

Tommy graduates from Louisiana Tech University

Photo courtesy of Louisiana Tech University

1971 Pittsburgh Steelers, Terry #12, and Tommy #86, with some of the players who were later inducted into the NFL Hall of Fame: #34 Andy Russell, #47 Mel Blount, #59 Jack Hamm, #75 "Mean" Joe Greene, and #20 Rocky Blier, a Vietnam Veteran whose life story was later made into a movie

Photo courtesy of the Pittsburgh Steelers

The Rooneys, Pittsburgh Steeler owners

Photo courtesy of the Pittsburgh Steelers

Terry waiting to be introduced on national TV

Photo credit, Bob Griffin

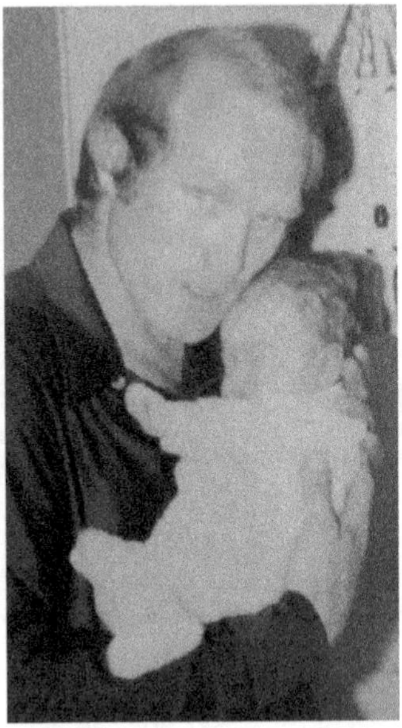

Terry, visiting Tommy and Barbara after the birth of their youngest daughter, Lindsay

Photo courtesy of Spinks family

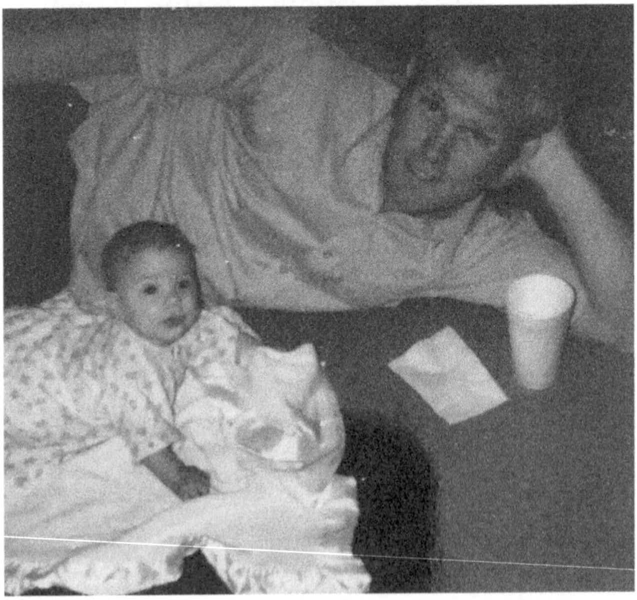

Terry with his namesake, Teri Ann Spinks

Photo courtesy of Spinks family

Family fun at the Bradshaw farmhouse in Shreveport, Louisiana; Terry with Teri and Lindsay Spinks

Photo courtesy of Spinks family

Tommy and Terry at Terry's farm in Shreveport, Louisiana

Photo courtesy of Spinks family

The Spinks Christmas photo in Pittsburgh

Photo courtesy of Spinks family

Tommy and Grace Spinks at Tommy's Louisiana Tech Hall of Fame induction ceremony

Photo courtesy of Spinks family

Tommy with close friends, Benny Thornell and infamous Louisiana sports writer, Buddy Davis, at Tommy's Hall of Fame Induction

Photo courtesy of Spinks family

Terry and Tommy at the Terry Bradshaw Golf Classic in Shreveport, Louisiana

Photo courtesy of Spinks family

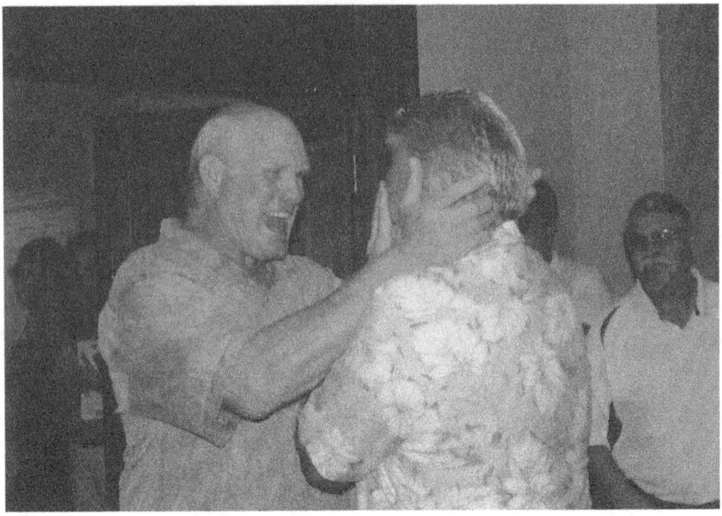

Emotional reunion when Tommy surprised Terry by showing up at one of Terry's public speaking engagements.

Photo courtesy of Spinks family

A.L. Williams, one of Tommy's High School and then college coaches who became a mentor and close family friend for the rest of Tommy's life, quoted as saying, "If Tommy can get to the ball, he'll catch it. He's got tremendous hands."

Photo courtesy of Spinks family

Tommy and Barbara, 1991

Photo courtesy of Spinks family

Anytime Terry and Tommy got together later in life, it always involved playing golf. Benny Thornell, Terry, Mike Newsom, and Joey Bales.

Photo courtesy of Spinks family

Spinks siblings, Betty Carol, Tommy, and Peggy Ann

Photo courtesy of Spinks family

Joey and Tommy were more like brothers than in-laws. They played golf together as often as they could — and argued constantly about how the other played.

Photo courtesy of Spinks family

Two months after Tommy died, the Louisiana Tech football team paid tribute to his legacy. Barbara, wearing Tommy's old football jersey, was honored by walking with the team captains and tossing the coin in the coin toss.

Photo courtesy of Spinks family

Tommy and Barbara with their grandkids at the Spinks annual 4th of July celebration

Photo courtesy of Spinks family

Thomas Allen Spinks
October 29, 1948 – August 26, 2007
Photo courtesy of Spinks family

Barbara with her kids, Teri, Kimberly, Lindsay, and Jason, standing in front of Tommy's bronzed plaque in the Louisiana Tech Hall of Fame
Photo courtesy of Spinks family

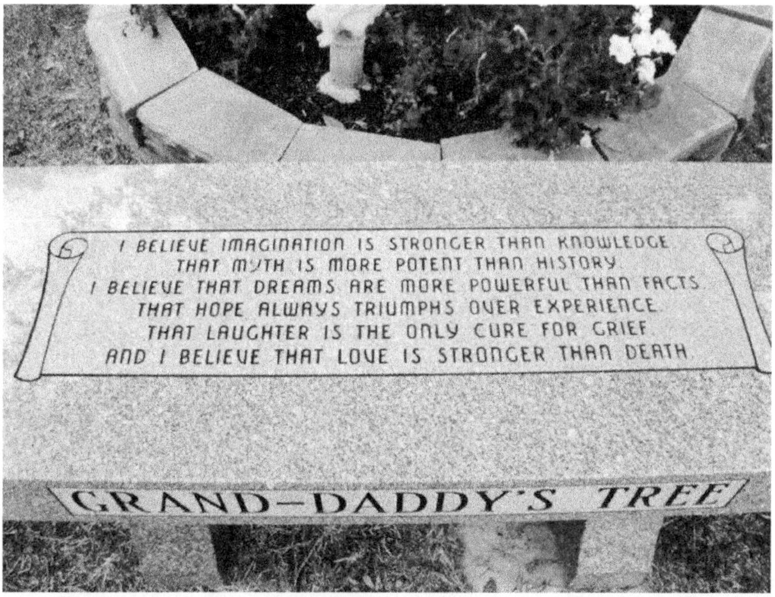
I BELIEVE IMAGINATION IS STRONGER THAN KNOWLEDGE
THAT MYTH IS MORE POTENT THAN HISTORY
I BELIEVE THAT DREAMS ARE MORE POWERFUL THAN FACTS
THAT HOPE ALWAYS TRIUMPHS OVER EXPERIENCE
THAT LAUGHTER IS THE ONLY CURE FOR GRIEF
AND I BELIEVE THAT LOVE IS STRONGER THAN DEATH
GRAND-DADDY'S TREE

The bench that sits under the oak tree planted in Tommy's memory with his grandkids surrounding the bench

Photos courtesy of Spinks family

CHAPTER 15

It didn't take long for Terry and me to start making our mark on the football program at Tech. We were doing what we loved and what we did best, throwing and catching and being thrilled to be a part of the program.

Taking the field against Bear Bryant's Alabama Crimson Tide in our freshman year, I'll have to admit was as humbling as it was inspiring. Of course, they beat us like drums, 34-0, but that, to me was just background to the really big deal — Coach Bryant being quoted in the paper the next day saying, "That young man over there on the Tech sideline, that quarterback, he has one heck of an arm. He's a great prospect. He's one of the best prospects I've seen." That young prospect was Terry, and that kind of affirmation was all we needed to fuel our hard work and our dreams.

Nevertheless, that game was a beating of the highest order, nothing like I had ever witnessed before. I'll never forget watching Phil stand in the pocket, facing down the most efficient charge I had ever seen, never flinching as those big hooligans came at him relentlessly, play after play.

"What's it like to stand back there trying to throw the ball with all those great big guys all over you all the time?" I asked him in the locker room after the game, breathless, wanting to absorb every detail. I also couldn't quite believe he was still standing after the beating he took in that game. In those days, back when head-butts and violence were perfectly legal — and even encouraged — in college football, it really is a wonder any of us survived at all.

"Well, Spinks," Phil said, winding up to hold court as everyone gathered around to hear, "I'll tellya what. Those Alabama boys showed up. They chewed my tail up and I mean good."

"You got some good completions, though," Terry said, thoughtful and taking it all in — wondering, I knew, how he would have measured up, given a chance to play. He hadn't said as much, but I knew him well enough to know that Terry was already tired of being a "prospect" and itching to get into the game.

"I did, Bomber," he said. "They may have picked me off three or four times, but I slashed 'em up pretty good."

When our local reporters asked Phil after the game what it was like playing Bear Bryant and the Crimson Tide, he said, "When the ball was snapped it sounded like a clap of thunder."

We didn't disagree.

All through our first season, even though we weren't winning games, we knew we were building something. As the season progressed, in most games Phil and Terry played equal time as quarterback, and Ken Liberto, Larry Brewer and I were the primary receivers. We were jelling quickly as a team, and the level of talent on the team was obvious. We ended our first season with a 1-9 record but it didn't diminish our optimism. We knew we were on our way.

• • •

"Hiya." I said, approaching the bench where Barbara sat. We usually met in this spot between classes whenever we could — just to see each other and to spend a few minutes before we had to go to our next class.

As I got closer I noticed her arms were crossed and she stared straight ahead without responding to my greeting. Not a good sign.

"What's up?" I asked, scooting her stack of books over so I could sit down right beside her.

She turned to me. "Well how would I know?" she said, eyes blazing.

Huh? I wracked my brain for the thing I might have messed up, didn't do, or just plain forgot. Nothing. "Barbara?" I began, touching her shoulder. "I can see you're mad at me, but for the life of me — and I'm sorry — but I can't figure out why. What have I done, Sweetheart?"

She jerked her shoulder away from my touch. Then she turned back to face me, full on. "Oh, Tommy I don't even know why I'm so mad, but I am," she wailed, eyes brimming with tears. "And I'm not really mad at you — but I am mad that it just seems like everything is keeping us apart these days." She waved her arms at the campus around us. "From school to stupid dorm rules to . . . football, football, football . . . I just don't know anything anymore. I do love you but how can we even be together when we can't ever be together?"

Football, football, football? "Now wait just a minute," I said, my own ire rising now. "Are you trying to say that I'm supposed to choose between seeing you and playing football?"

"Oh, no," she said, "of course not!" She looked down at her hands, fingers laced tightly together in her lap.

Her knuckles looked a little bit white, so I knew we were far from through with this conversation.

"I'm just not sure what I'm supposed to do," she said quietly. "I go to class, I study, I wait for you to come by, but if you don't make it by 8:00 the stupid dorm is closed and I have to wait another day to see you." She looked straight into my eyes with that look that made me want to do anything in the world to make her happy again. "If all we're ever going to have is Saturday night dates and maybe a little bit of time together on Sundays, is that supposed to be enough?" She dabbed her eyes with a tissue she produced from her clasped hands. "Is that enough for you?"

"Barbara," I said, reaching out to touch her arm. This time she didn't pull away. "I know it's hard, baby, but we just have to figure out how to make the best of it. I have to play football — for all kinds of reasons. And I have to have you in my life. Forever."

"Forever?" she said, eyes softening. "You mean . . . forever, forever?"

I laughed, pulling her into my arms. "Yes, my sweet, sweet Barbara, forever forever forever and even longer than that." I kissed her. "So try to remember that whenever you start to feel lonely — and remember that this is just college. We're going to have forever."

"Well, I suppose forever is something," she said, standing to gather her things. "But it sure doesn't make right now very fun." She looked at me. "Like, here we are, having this important moment, but guess what? Important moment now over — we have to stop right here and run like mad to make it to class on time. And unless we happen to cross paths here again, it might be days before we see each other again!"

She had a point. Trouble was, there was really nothing I could do about it. From the night I asked her to go steady back in high school, Barbara and I both knew we were going to get married someday, but we never really considered when that might be. And even though we had tossed around the idea of marriage — and talked about forever enough to make it feel like a certainty — we really had no plan. And now, with our schedules making it all but impossible to see each other, a strain was growing in our relationship.

• • •

I threw open the door to my dorm room and slammed my books down on my bed.

Terry, sitting backwards in my desk chair and talking to another teammate who had stopped by to shoot the breeze, looked up, startled. "What the heck is the matter with you?" he asked, puzzle mixing with concern on his big goofy face.

"I just don't know what to do anymore!" I exclaimed, louder than I intended. Barbara's frustration had clearly rubbed off on me — and gained momentum on my walk back to the dorm. Ever since that day we had our heart-to-heart on the bench in front of the Ad building — and I thought everything was OK — the petty arguments had continued. Lately, what little time we had together was getting eaten up with continuous snipping and snapping between us that, quite frankly, was wearing me out. Today was no different, except that it had escalated into a full-blown argument — over nothing.

"Barbara and I had another fight," I said, plopping down on my bed beside my books. "It just seems like we don't ever get along anymore."

Terry's eyes got big. "Do you think you're going to break up?" he asked. "I hope not! If you two can't make it, nobody can!"

"Well, wait a minute," the other buddy said, chiming in without invitation.

I looked at him with what I hoped was the most withering of glances, saying without words, *Who the hell are you to be commenting on my love life?* I barely knew this guy, but he was on the team and liked hanging out with Terry.

Terry snickered, getting my message.

Oblivious, the guy continued, "Ya know, Spinks, there are countless girls in love with you! I can always fix you up with any one of them."

Well no sense taking my irritation with Barbara out on this innocent bystander, right? "Sure," I said, "fix me up."

"Tommy! You don't mean that!" Terry interjected. From the look on his face you'd think I had just kicked his puppy.

"Well what am I supposed to do, Terry?" I said. "Barbara's clearly not happy — and I can't fix this. And when she's not happy, it makes me really unhappy. Maybe it's just time for us to see other people."

"I don't think so," Terry said under his breath, untangling his long legs from the backward chair. He looked at me and started to say something else, but seeing the glower still rising, thought the better of it. "I'm going down to dinner," he said instead and headed out the door without giving me a second glance.

"Good idea," I said, following him — and slamming the door behind me.

• • •

"Spinks, I have that date set up with you like we talked about," he said, running up to me like a dog with a dead squirrel. He thrust a piece of paper toward me, "Here's her name and number. She's waiting for your call!"

What?!?!?!??? I looked from him to the piece of paper now in my hand and back again.

"You gave me the green light yesterday, doncha remember?" he said, breathless and wide-eyed. "She is out of her mind that Tommy Spinks is going to take her out on a date. Brother, you're a hot commodity! I bet I can get you a different date every Saturday from now on. Play the field, man! Isn't that what college is for?"

"I'm a hot . . . what?" I said, head suddenly spinning. "Wait a minute! You really called this girl and told her I wanted to ask her out on a date?" I dropped that piece of paper on the floor like it had just burst into flames.

"You betcha!" he said, clearly pleased with himself. "And she's over the moon about it! You lucky dog. You're gonna score with her for sure. She's a fox, too!"

"Oh no!" I heard myself say, like a disembodied voice. "Oh . . . no, no no no no!" I began pawing frantically through my desk drawer looking for a piece of paper. And then a pencil. Then I sat down and scrawled a quick message to this girl saying that I would most definitely not be going on a date with her — and how sorry I was for the mix-up.

I folded this note and shoved it into the hand of the gape-mouthed young man standing in my doorway looking like a bucket of ice water had just been dumped on his head.

"You take this to her right now," I said, closing his fingers over the note and turning him around and shoving him back through the doorway. "Right now! And hurry!" I called after him.

"Well, that's more like it," came a wry voice from the other corner of the room. Terry looked up from his biology book and grinned. "I was hoping you'd come to your senses so I wouldn't have to lock you up in the equipment room over the weekend."

I grinned and threw a football at Terry's big head. "I've got a big picture of that happening," I said.

"Just think," Terry said, drilling the ball back into the center of my chest, "now there's going to be a senior high school girl out there tonight, getting all swoony from getting a personal letter from Tommy Spinks. By tomorrow she'll be taking it to school and telling everybody she got a letter from Tommy Spinks, without, of course, revealing the contents of the letter."

"She's in high school?" I said, lobbing the ball back. "Did I know that?"

"Yep," Terry said, returning it. "You were too mad to hear much detail, I think." He paused, growing serious. "Tommy, I couldn't believe my ears when you told him to fix you up with her."

"I was so mad I couldn't see straight," I said tossing the ball underhand. "But that was just plain stupid, even for me." I looked across the room at Terry as I felt the color draining from my face as the reality of what I had done hit me full force. "Terry, Barbara can never find out about this," I said.

"Mum's the word," Terry said, placing the ball back in its home on the shelf above his bed. "Let's go eat."

• • •

"You are never going to believe the silly rumor I heard last weekend when I was back home," Barbara said as we walked across campus between afternoon classes. I always loved seeing her face up in the stadium, especially on the road, but since I traveled with the team and there was a lot of down time, unless there was a group of kids going it just made more sense for her to stay in Ruston. Or go home and see her family.

I laughed. "As big as it is, Shreveport is such a small town," I said. "So what's going on now?"

"Well," Barbara said, winding up as she always did to tell a good story, "some silly girl that goes to Haughton High was going around telling EVERYBODY that she was being fixed up on a blind date with Tommy Spinks, and that he even wrote her a letter! Can you believe the nerve of people who make up such lies? Of course, all those stupid little high school girls back home just drool whenever they hear your name, but really, can you believe she thought anyone would believe that ridiculous lie — or that you could possibly be interested in someone like that?"

"Wow," was all I could manage to say. It had been about two weeks since the misunderstanding began, and I had put the whole thing completely out of my mind — until now.

Barbara turned to look at me. Have you ever actually *felt* the blood drain out of your face? Well I did, and she saw it happen. I swallowed hard and opened my mouth to speak — but nothing came out. Not a sound.

She stopped walking, dropped the books she was carrying and covered her mouth with both hands. Above those hands I watched her eyes grow wide, then fill with tears.

"Barbara . . . It was all a . . ." Just as I was able to get some words out, I was speaking to empty space. Barbara turned and took off running back to her dorm, leaving her books right where they fell.

I stood there for a moment, watching her go, knowing I could catch her, but not knowing what I would say when I did. I picked up her books and followed her tracks to her dorm. I was numb with dread and fear. What had I done?

• • •

When William Congreve, the English playwright and poet, penned the phrase, "Hell hath no fury like a woman scorned," what he really needed to illustrate that turn of phrase with was a picture of Barbara's face when she finally came downstairs to meet me in the lobby of her dorm. I still wasn't sure why she had agreed to see me so suddenly — she had hung up on me — slammed down the phone, actually — each and every one of the 30-something times I had called her from the house phone downstairs. Then, on that last time I called, she said, in a voice colder than Antarctica in a blizzard, "I'll be down in just a minute."

"Barbara . . ." I began, moving toward her as soon as she cleared the last stair step.

She put up a hand, palm out, stopping me where I stood. "Stop. Right. There. Don't. You. Even. Say. A. Single. Word." She spat each word of that sentence like a molten nail.

"Baby, please let me explain this whole thing to you . . ." I tried again, keeping my feet planted and despising the whine that had somehow crept into my voice. My heart pounded in my throat and nausea overtook me. I needed to sit down. I didn't dare move.

"There is nothing about any of this you can explain to me, Tommy Spinks," she said, eyes blazing. "The only reason I came over here right now is to let you know that you can go ahead and go on your date with that girl this weekend because my mother will be here within the hour to pick me up. I am going home."

"Home?" I repeated the only word from that verbiage flurry that my mind could latch onto.

"Yes, home," Barbara said. "I am out of here. O.U.T. Out," she said.

"Out?" I repeated. For some strange reason, I had become incapable of anything other than one-syllable responses to this angry, angry woman.

"If you think for one minute I'm going to stay around here and let you make a fool of me and carry on like some idiot with high school . . . groupies . . . well you'd better think again, Tommy Spinks."

I hated it when she used both of my names. *Think, Tommy,* I screamed inwardly. *What can I say right now to talk her out of walking out of my life forever?* Everything in me knew that once her mother arrived and she got in that car back to Shreveport, there would be no stopping her. I didn't doubt for a second that she was completely serious.

"Tommy? Are you even listening to me?"

Barbara had been talking while my mind raced, and I realized that, indeed, I hadn't been listening at all. It was as if my ears closed up and sealed over once I heard the word "home." So caught up in trying to figure out what to say and do to stop her, I had completely drifted away.

"Oh. Yes. I am listening," I said. "I'm just. Well. Barbara, I love you and that was all a big mix-up. I'm not ever going out with anyone but you — ever!"

"Well I guess you should have thought about that before you authorized your little matchmaker to set you up with some high school girl," she said. "The very idea!" She gave a dramatic shrug. "But you know what? It really doesn't matter anyway, because I'm leaving you, Tommy Spinks."

With that, Barbara Ann Lindsay turned and walked up the stairs and out of my life.

I just stood there, dumbfounded, watching her leave, wondering what in the world I could say or do to make things right with her and stop this from happening.

CHAPTER 16

I'll never forget the look on Terry's face when I told him what happened. He just grabbed his jacket and keys and said, "Come on, dumbass! We've got to stop her!"

I'm not at all sure how it happened, but somehow Terry and I managed to flag Barbara's mom down at the exit ramp from I20. She looked a little panicked when I asked her to roll down the window, but as soon as I told her my side of the story she smiled. Apparently Barbara hadn't told her mother *why* she wanted to come home. She nodded and rolled up the window and pulled slowly away. With no idea what was going to happen next, we jumped back into Terry's car and roared into the parking lot of Barbara's dorm. Terry slammed on the brakes, screeching to a halt in front of Katherine Lindsay's running car just as Barbara was hurrying toward it.

Terry shoved me, hard. "Go!" he ordered.

I felt my feet moving toward Barbara. Even though I had no idea what I was going to say I knew I had to get to her. Talk to her. Somehow get her to listen to me. I waved my arms to get her mom's attention. If I had to I was going to beg her mom not to drive away with the love of my life in that car.

"Barbara," I began softly, trying to get her to look my way.

She kept walking. It had started to rain, so she was trying to shield the load of clothes and books she carried as she hurried toward the car. Behind the windshield, I could see Barbara's mom watching us. This gave me some measure of relief because from the look on her face I could tell she wasn't going anywhere.

"Barbara?" I began again, a little louder this time.

She continued to ignore me as she piled her belongings into the back of the car.

"Barbara, please don't do this," I said, reaching the car at last. I stood across the car, looking at her for what might well be the last time. "Please, *please* forgive me for being so stupid," I said. My misery poured into every last word and I realized that I really didn't know what I would do without Barbara in my life. All our dreams. All our plans. That beautiful future with the house and the kids — all that was slipping away just as surely as those raindrops slid off her mother's windshield.

Barbara stood straight up then and looked at me over the roof of the car. She didn't say a word.

"Please, Barbara," I begged. "Please don't go." I felt the tears welling up and was now quite grateful for the rain to camouflage the raw emotion dripping down my face and off my chin.

Still, she stood there. Her face was completely unreadable; her eyes expressionless.

I turned, defeated, to walk back to Terry's car. It was over. There was no getting through to her. No way to make her understand. I felt numb and nauseated and completely lost in my own misery.

"Tommy," Barbara said, so softly I didn't hear her.

I kept walking. Head down, trying to get my mind around what was happening. Devastated beyond words.

"TOMMY!" This time it was Katherine, Barbara's mom, doing the talking — or yelling, as it were. Then I heard her say something to Barbara, but the only words I could make out was "biggest mistake of your life."

I turned, puzzled. Why was Katherine yelling at me? Was the mistake she spoke of to stay with me or let me go?

Then something amazing happened. Barbara began walking toward me.

I took a few tentative steps toward her, and then we both began to run until we were close enough to grab one another, sobbing wordlessly in one of those sappy love story embraces that, until right that minute, I always thought were completely made-up and bogus. We just stood there holding on to each other for dear life in the pouring down rain while Terry hooted in the background.

We set a wedding date soon after that.

We figured out that if Barbara got a full-time job and we lived in marital housing on campus, we could make ends meet and still finish college. Nothing, we vowed, was ever going to keep us apart again.

Later, I learned that when Barbara had called her mother to come get her, Katherine had tried her best to talk her through and out of this angry decision, but Barbara wouldn't listen. What made her giggle for years was that in her frenzy of packing to go get her daughter, Katherine had packed a little suitcase with one duster and 4 pair of slippers. This story became a family favorite and made my children howl with laughter to see their mother get mad all over again every time she recounted the tale of my unwitting indiscretion.

• • •

Both families gathered at our house to decide on the menu for the rehearsal dinner, which would be at Barbara's mom's house with my mom and dad providing the meal.

"I think we should have fried chicken," Terry said, draping himself backward in the dining room chair at the end of our living room. Whenever there was a lull in the excited exchange of ideas between Barbara's mother and mine, Terry took it as an opportunity to pipe up with what he wanted to eat.

Barbara and I were sitting together on one side of the table. We held hands, taking it all in, processing all that was happening.

In answer to Terry's suggestion about the fried chicken, my mother rose from her seat, took a cookie from the beautiful polished silver tray she had loaded with goodies for this momentous occasion, and shoved it in Terry's mouth. Then she returned to her seat without a word.

Terry winked at us and munched on his cookie. Message received.

"Grace, I think you're absolutely right about the ham," Katherine said. "It would be filling and tasty and easy to prepare ahead." She looked across the table at my mother with a genuine affection that warmed my heart. "There's just no sense in having you scurrying around any more than I know you will trying to do something fancy and complicated. I think a simple meal of your beautiful baked ham with salad and bread would be delightful — and perfect!" She beamed.

There was a lot of discussion about the rehearsal dinner that I neither wanted nor needed to follow. Something about place settings, tablecloths, centerpieces . . . I just looked at Barbara and thanked my lucky stars we were here and about to be married and that as soon as we got through with all this wedding hullabaloo, our life together could really begin for real. Married. While that word might have been a little scary to some guys, it gave me a sense of peace and joy — it represented everything I wanted and knew would happen since that day at the picnic when Barbara Ann Lindsay stole my heart.

Mom looked around the table to make sure everyone agreed with this assessment. Satisfied, she nodded. "Then ham it will be!" she said. She looked around the table again, flashing a sudden, giant smile at the group gathered. "This is such a wonderful, wonderful day and I just want to thank God for each and every one of you and for His blessing on each of us as we prepare for the wedding of Tommy and my sweet Barbara." She got up and went around to where Barbara was sitting and squeezed her shoulders as she pressed her cheek to Barbara's. "I am just so thankful for you, honey. I couldn't have made a better choice for my Tommeh myself!"

Barbara, not one to enjoy being the center of attention, blushed and patted Mom's hand. Then she looked up at my mom, eyes brimming, "Thank you, Mrs. Spinks," she said, as soon as she could speak.

I nodded my agreement. No words could describe the parade of thoughts and emotions tromping around in my heart and head.

Then Barbara, finding her voice, surprised me by continuing, "I am thankful, as well, to get to join this beautiful family." She looked at her own mom then. "For all of us to get to become one big family, well, my heart is just so full of gratitude for you all — for everything you're doing and about to do to make our wedding so perfect and beautiful." Now it was her turn to look all around the table, from face to face. "Thank you, everyone, for being here and being so happy and supportive of us and our wedding — and our marriage. It really means the world to me." She squeezed my hand. "To both of us. We are so blessed."

What a lady. What a gift to us all. But most especially, to me.

• • •

The preparations for the wedding, by all accounts, went pretty much without a hitch. Our mothers were busy working through every detail, calling each other at least once a day and talking through the merits of this or that — a constant barrage of details and preparations that truly illustrated the Southern principle of simplicity and beauty that required tremendous effort in order to look effortless. While most of this was going on, Barbara and I were finishing our school year. Once we arrived home for the summer, the finishing details were being put into place for our June 3 wedding. My instructions were pretty much to just show up. Barbara's only request was that her flowers would be daisies.

"I got a dress this weekend," Barbara said to me in our nightly phone call after she returned to Tech after a weekend at home.

"That's good," I said, not really knowing what else to say. There was a lot of hoopla I really didn't understand around Barbara's wedding dress and bridesmaid dresses — the two mothers and Barbara had been preoccupied with these details from the very beginning. I feigned interest, but the truth was what those girls wore made very little difference to me — and Barbara was going to be beautiful no matter what she wore, so I really didn't understand the fuss. Still, from her tone I knew something important had happened. I also knew that I wasn't supposed to ask many questions about her dress — or, God forbid, see it before the wedding. It was a confusing dance and I was doing my best. "So are you happy with it?" I asked, thinking this a safe question.

"Oh yes!" Barbara said. "It's just perfect. And even though mother was going to make my dress and we were just trying to get an idea of style, I tried this one on and it just fit like a glove and I just loved it. So when I came out of the dressing room my mother had bought it for me. Oh, Tommy I couldn't believe it and we both cried and well I know she can't afford such a thing but she had already made up her mind. I . . . I just can't believe it."

Cried? Over a dress? Both of them? "Well I'm glad you love it so much. It must be really great. I'm . . . Well, I can't wait to see it!"

"Oh, yes, you *will* wait, Mister," she teased. "It has to be a total surprise!"

"Oh," I said. "Right. Well good. Good that you got that done."

"Well, she's still going to make all the bridesmaid dresses," she said. "And adorable little pillbox hats and shoes dyed to match."

"That does sound *adorable*," I said. How much longer could we possibly talk about this? But she was so excited and happy I just loved to hear the sound of her voice bubbling over the phone. I was just out of ideas about what to say next.

"Are you making fun?" Barbara said, her tone changing to the opposite of bubbly.

"No!" I said, my earnestness surging through the phone line. "I just don't know much about dresses and stuff." I paused as inspiration struck. "What's a pillbox hat?" I asked.

"Oh it's just a little flat hat that sits right up on top of your head, usually sort of tilted to the back," she said. "Mother's going to use the tops of oatmeal boxes to make them!"

"Well that ought to be something to see," I said. And I meant it.

• • •

Before we knew it, a whirlwind of showers and parties ensued to herald the upcoming wedding. In the South, even though our families weren't wealthy, these events were lavish — in our case this meant lavish in enthusiasm and participation by all our extended family and overlapping circles of friends, even though they were quite simple in detail and concept. Barbara had three showers, a lingerie shower given by her best friend Jane's Aunt Pansy, a kitchen shower given by my sister, Betty, and a miscellaneous shower given by Betty Hyde, who was a close friend of her family. All I knew was every time we talked about these showers, all I had was a mental image of Barbara sitting in the middle of a big circle of women while underwear, nightgowns, kitchen utensils, and sheets and towels rained down on top of her head. I, of course, did not mention this highly amusing mental imagery to her. Also, the stuff we got was pretty good.

I'm not sure reality had even begun to set in when we arrived for the wedding rehearsal at King's Highway Christian Church. Terry and I arrived just as people were filing into the church. We just sat there for a moment, watching. Terry gave a low whistle, "Wow," he said. "Would you look at all those people? And this is just people who are in this thing." He looked at me and grinned. "Tommy, are you sure you're ready for this?"

"I'm ready to get it over with!" I said, glad that no one heard me say that. I didn't want to seem ungrateful because I knew all the work our mothers and entire families had put into making our wedding one of the most special days of our lives — and I had no doubt that it would be. But all this pressure and fuss was getting old. I just wanted to get in whatever car they decided we were supposed to get in with Barbara and drive away married — ready to start our life together. I was beyond ready to stop juggling schedules in order to see each other and to get to come home to her every day instead of that stinky dorm room and only a phone call to say goodnight.

Ever since that rainy day in the parking lot outside Barbara's dorm when we decided to get married, the trouble and bickering over our schedule conflicts and not getting to see enough of each other had settled down. But that didn't mean the reality of it had changed. Tomorrow, all that would come to an end, and as far as I was concerned it couldn't get here fast enough. We just had this one detail of the wedding to get through.

"Let's do this thing!" I said, jumping out of the car and taking the church steps two at a time to get into the doors before they closed behind the last people in. Terry was right beside me, and as we entered the church I'll have to say I was glad to see that he had tucked our dorm room football inside his jacket and under his arm, just in case things got slow at the rehearsal. Odds were, they would.

It wasn't but a few minutes into the instructions part of the rehearsal — we had been standing around for longer than was tolerable and the wedding coordinator was going on and on and on, telling the girls way too much about what kinds of steps they were supposed to take as they came in and proceeded down the aisle.

I stifled a yawn, politely covering my mouth with my hand, when out of the corner of my eye I saw an underhanded spiral coming my way, hidden from view between the group of groomsmen standing in the aisle along the right side of the sanctuary and the side wall of the church. Instinctively, I reached out to catch it and then, glancing around the room to make sure no one noticed, I sent it back.

The other groomsmen, trying not to react, struggled to keep straight faces. In between throws and catches, Terry and I tried to out-do each other with our expressions of attentiveness to what was being said. The other groomsmen were struggling desperately to maintain cover, and I could feel them just about to crack up when out of nowhere, a sudden tap on my arm told me we were cooked.

"Tommeh Spinks, my heavenly lands," my fully incensed mother said through the clenched teeth of that Southern fake smile I knew all too well. "Have you two boys lost your everlovin' minds???"

"I . . . We . . ." I struggled for something to say and came up with absolutely nothing.

"Give me that ball right this instant," she said. "We do NOT throw a football in the Lawd's house."

Fortunately, the ball, at that moment, happened to be in Terry's possession. "We'll stop, Mom, I promise," I said, holding a flat palm up to Terry to warn him not to throw. In all her petiteness, my mother was most likely out of his view. "And besides, it's Terry's ball, anyhow."

"I don't care if it's Vince Lombardi's ball, you will not be throwing it in *heah* again," my mother huffed. "The very idea." She turned to walk away. And then, when she got about three steps away from us — and yet still out of earshot of the rest of the rehearsal party — she turned back to us and added in a stage whisper, "and anyway, you boys need to tighten up that spiral.

Those low ones can't afford to be sloppy." Satisfied she had handled all aspects of the situation, she turned and waltzed back to her assigned place, seemingly oblivious to the uncontrollable snickering of the groomsmen no longer able to contain themselves.

• • •

"Y'all be careful, Tommy," Barbara said as we stood on the front porch of her mother's house after the rehearsal dinner had ended. "Don't get hurt — or stupid." She squeezed my hand. "I love you!"

"Us? Stupid?" Terry chimed in from behind me, butting into our moment as only he could.

I reached out behind me and put a flat palm over his face. "Go away, Terry, this is a private conversation."

Ignoring me — and my hand on his face — Terry kept talking, "Don't worry, Barbara, I'll take really good care of him — and I'll make sure he gets to the church tomorrow on time and in one piece."

Barbara looked past me and smiled. "Thank you, Terry. I'm going to hold you to that." She looked back at me, dismissing Terry and turning her full attention and beautiful eyes on me. "Just think, Tommy, this time tomorrow we'll be married!"

I held her face in my hands and kissed her. "I can't wait." I meant it.

"Well just one more night apart and you won't have to!" she said, mischief twinkling in her eyes.

"Ok, that's enough, now," Terry said, pushing us apart like a referee separating linemen. "We have a bachelor party to get on with and you, dear lady," he took Barbara by the elbow and guided her back in the direction of her front door, "you have to get your beauty sleep."

"I beg your pardon?" she teased.

"You know what I mean," Terry said, backing up. "You don't need it, of course, but isn't that what people say to brides? You're plenty beautiful already!" Terry flailed. "What I meant was . . ."

"Um, I think you'd better just put down the shovel and walk away," I said, enjoying watching my buddy try to squirm out of his lack of forethought. "You're just digging yourself in deeper."

"Right," Terry said. "G'night, Barbara. I'll see you tomorrow!"

Barbara laughed — that wonderful sound I now knew I would actually get to hear for the rest of my life. "Good night, you two. Be safe and have fun!" She blew a kiss to the two of us and I caught mine with my heart.

"Good night!" we said in unison, and then looked at each other and laughed. And then we were off.

Terry had been trying to help plan my bachelor party ever since the day we got engaged. Despite the many ideas he came up with, some pretty good and some that would be asking for trouble in capital letters, I just kept telling him, "Let's keep it simple and fun — but nothing too wild."

"I know . . ." he finally replied one afternoon in complete exasperation, "how about if we just order a bunch of pizza and Cokes and invite all the guys on the team over to my house and we'll just play football and eat pizza and drink Coca-Cola all night." He clearly meant this offer as sarcastic. Apparently he had something much more risqué in mind.

"You know what?" I replied, "That would be just perfect!"

"Oh," Terry said. "Well. OK. If that's what you want."

"That is everything I want," I assured him. It really was. My best friends, my favorite food and beverage — and the whole night spent playing football . . . What could be a better last day of bachelorhood than that?

So that's exactly what we did. Only instead of having the party at Terry's house, he secured his parents' friends' weekend house. It was out and away and had plenty of room to run and play football without disturbing any neighbors. It was perfect. We played and laughed and ate and drank with no regard whatsoever for what time it was or what anyone thought of our silliness. And then, sometime in the wee hours — after the food and cola ran out — we fell asleep where we lay and stayed there, sleeping that mind-numbing deep sleep of puppies and babies that is completely oblivious to the passage of time.

• • •

"Oh . . . Noooooooooooo!" I yelled, jumping to my feet from my place half-on and half-off a beanbag chair where I had slept through the rest of the night and most of the day. I could tell by the angle of the sun and the brightness of the room that we were well into the afternoon. And the house was way too quiet. Where is everyone? I thought. Why didn't anyone wake us up?

My heart pounded as I struggled to see the alarm clock. Why didn't we set an alarm?

3:40. "Oh no. Oh no. Oh no," I said, running around the room, pawing through the pile of my tumbled belongings for my clean clothes. Because my parents were coming in from Ruston for the wedding, I had packed a bag and planned to stay with Terry for the entire two days before the wedding. The day before, following the timetable Barbara gave me from our mothers, I had picked up our tuxedos and Joey's car, which we would be borrowing for our getaway car and honeymoon. So fortunately for me, everything was fairly well organized when we came back to Terry's after the bachelor party.

I was in and out of the shower in two minutes flat. When I came out, Terry was sitting up on his bed, rubbing his eyes and shaking his head.

"Terry, we gotta hurry, man," I said, pulling on my tuxedo pants, buttoning and tucking in my shirt and then rifling through the attached bag for my tie, socks, and shoes. "We are so late."

"What time were we supposed to be there?" he said, still groggy, clearly not getting the sense of urgency I had been so desperately trying to convey.

"An hour ago!" I yelled. "The dang wedding is going to start in about 15 minutes!"

"Oh, man! We've gotta hurry!" he echoed, springing out of bed and sprinting toward the shower.

I was still trying to tie my tie when Terry, showered and dressed, grabbed his jacket and headed out the door. "I'm going to go ahead and go!" he yelled over his shoulder. "I have to take my car, anyway — I'm supposed to light the candles before the ceremony!"

Crap. I glanced at the clock, gave my tie one last yank and grabbed my jacket and followed Terry. With my hair still wet and sticking up everywhere, I screeched into the parking lot just as the last wedding guests were climbing the steps.

We were met at the back of the fellowship hall where we were supposed to enter by BOTH of our mothers, wearing the exact same expression. "Good lands, you boys need to get in there and fast," Grace instructed. She looked at us, affection creeping in alongside her irritation. "You two never cease to amaze me," she said. She didn't even ask where we were or what we were doing to be so late. No time for that. I felt pretty sure we'd be reliving this story for years to come. I wasn't wrong.

I entered the hallway that led up to the sanctuary door on the "groom's side" where we were supposed to wait. Dad was standing there in his robe, along with the other groomsmen, and he looked at me over the top of his glasses, eyebrows raised, but way too much of a gentleman and man of God to say what he was probably thinking.

He opened the sanctuary door and then turned to us, all business. "OK, gentlemen," he said. "Are we ready?"

As we entered the sanctuary, the first thing I saw was Terry, lighting the candles with all the carefulness of an altar boy — with his 3/4-length white tuxedo dinner jacket sleeves exposing the entire bottom half of his forearm. When I saw him out there looking like Lurch on the *Addams Family*, my heart stopped for a second.

I looked down at my own sleeves then to discover that they extended beyond the tips of my fingers by several inches. Somehow we had gotten our jackets switched and there was absolutely no way to correct this gaffe without screwing up the whole ceremony.

I cringed. *What will Barbara say when she sees this?* My thoughts raced. And soon on the heels of that worry came another, bigger concern: *What will my mother say?*

Mom, of course, would be worried about the opinions and observations of nearly every man, woman, and child present. In the South we are big on propriety, and this unfortunate distraction, although not meant to be comical, was going to make it hard to take any part of this wedding seriously. I tried to catch Terry's eye, but he was concentrating on his candles. Then, with seconds to spare, Terry and I did a quick change of jackets just as the music signaling the beginning of the ceremony began.

Abject dread joined the butterflies in my stomach, as I noticed that all eyes were on me when we lined up in the front of the small sanctuary. This was way different from a stadium filled with noisy fans. *Maybe it's just because they're so quiet that's getting to me,* I silently reasoned with my rising fear. I sincerely hoped this new combination wouldn't make me barf, especially atop all the pizza we consumed the night before.

The music changed its timbre and they began to seat the grandparents. I glanced down at my watch to find that, miracle of all miracles, it was straight-up four o'clock! "Thank you," I murmured, turning my eyes upward for just an instant to the Man Upstairs. I was pretty sure the Big Guy had a hand in getting us there on time. I guess He didn't want our carelessness to spoil an otherwise perfect day.

Once the girls started coming in, taking their perfect steps in their beautiful yellow dresses, everything else was a blur. I tried not to remember that their perfect yellow pillbox hats with dainty white veils were once lids to oatmeal. I tried to look at the packed congregation gathered and was overcome with the thought that all these people from both our lives had stopped whatever they were doing to come to our wedding.

Then my eyes found Barbara, standing at the back of the church on the arm of her brother. Her radiant beauty was enough to give any angel a run for her money. I tried to smile, and was surprised to feel tears well up as I watched them make their way up the aisle, especially at that moment when it was finally time to take her hand.

We faced Dad as he said the preamble to the ceremony, and then he asked us to face each other and bow our heads for prayer. As the first soloist began to sing, we all focused our attention on our friend, Anne Whalen, who was singing "I Love You Truly." (Anne would marry Ronnie Brown that same summer.) Next, Beth Taylor, Barbara's college roommate, sang "The Lord's Prayer." Then Dad stepped up and performed the ceremony. There is a sacredness to all wedding ceremonies, of course, but the added layer of having your own father utter those important words and admonitions, well, it struck a very special chord deep in my soul. What an amazing thing.

It was a perfect day. I was marrying my first love, my best friends were standing beside me, and my dad was officiating the wedding. I knew we were young, but ever since our first date, that April picnic when we were juniors in high school, I knew I was going to marry Barbara Ann Lindsay. I knew from the start that she was perfect for me. I was right.

Years later, Barbara would tell me that when we were announced as husband and wife and began to make our way back down the aisle, she saw her own deceased father standing at the back of the church, just smiling at her. She said she smiled back with tears in her eyes. She said she had seen him once before — on her graduation day — with that same proud smile. Barbara didn't tell many people about that. She thought people might think she was crazy. I know better. The special people in our lives are always with us, even once they leave this life for the next — and they do come back to let us know they are with us when we need them most.

• • •

After a simple reception in the church fellowship hall, we emerged to find Joey standing guard by his car as the crowd gathered to pelt us with rice and see us off in a flurry of cheers, applause, and well wishes. Joey's aim was to make sure no one shoe polished his new car. "It'll ruin the paint!" he'd tell anyone who tried to talk him out of this rule. Especially Terry. Terry was sure he could change Joey's mind, but at last, realizing time was running out, acquiesced and made a poster. Following his rule of "posters only," posters of all sizes and shapes were taped to the car's windows, nearly completely obstructing our view. *This can't be safe,* I thought as we settled into our seats and I peeled back a few of them to give myself a window to see through at least until we got a few blocks from the church when I could remove them all. *Who wants to draw that much attention to themselves as newlyweds,* I wondered.

As we pulled away from the church we noticed that Ronnie Brown's familiar brown Corvette and Donny Baughman's ageless, legendary — and nearly rusted out — "beater" car were accompanying us, each with a bunch of my buddies piled inside. Their plan, they shouted through rolled-down windows at the next stoplight, was to "escort us." Hearing this I couldn't help but wonder if they were planning to "escort us" all the way to Little Rock. I decided against asking that question out loud.

Then Barbara asked a much more practical question: "You *do* know how to get to Little Rock, right?"

I looked at her and smiled. "I have absolutely no idea," I said.

As we approached the next stoplight, I allowed Ronnie to pull right alongside us again. I rolled down the window and said, trying not to appear as sheepish as I felt, "Um, do any of you know how to get to Hot Springs?"

The car beside me roared with laughter and I saw Barbara trying not to laugh with them.

Then Donnie said, "Follow me!" As they guided us to the highway we needed to be on, I again wondered if my earlier prediction was about to come true. But instead, once they led us onto the Interstate they flashed their lights, honked, and hollered as they took the next exit to return to Shreveport. I knew right then that this would be featured regularly among the favorite stories they'd tell on me for the rest of my life.

• • •

When we arrived at the hotel in Little Rock, we sat there in the driveway for a while, silent. We were both so nervous and self-conscious — I had even removed all signs of "newlyweds" from our car at our first stop for gas and a Coke.

"I'm nervous," Barbara said, putting into words my exact thoughts.

"Oh, don't be nervous, baby," I said, taking her hand. "It'll be OK," I was offering her reassurance I didn't exactly feel. "We'll figure it out."

"Not that, silly," she said, laughing. "I'm just thinking about all those people in there who will see us checking in at 18 years old and saying we're Mr. And Mrs. They're going to know we're about to have sex!"

I laughed. She wasn't wrong and that was only part of the anxiety I was feeling. I had no idea how all this was going to go and had really pretty much put it out of my mind — until now. "Let's drive around a little," I said, buying a little bit of time. We made a few stops around town — I bought a few sports magazines and tried not to notice the amused twinkle in Barbara's eyes. She, of course, knew that the last thing on my mind right now was sports.

We finally worked up our nerve to go into the hotel — and to our surprise there was absolutely no one there besides the tired old clerk behind the desk. He didn't even look up when I said Mr. and Mrs. — he just handed me the keys and told me which way to the elevator. I didn't dare look at Barbara until we were safely inside the elevator with the doors closed. Then we broke out laughing like we hadn't in months.

About two hours later, Barbara was still in the bathroom. What was she doing in there?

"Are you OK?" I asked. "Are you ever going to come out of there? What are you doing in there?"

"Just a few more minutes," she's say each time I asked.

When she finally came out, I suddenly lost all interest in the magazine I was reading — and in sports in general. Barbara would later tell me that she had spent that two hours in there just sitting on the other side of the door, trying to work up her nerve to come out. She didn't even have a magazine.

We figured it out.

CHAPTER 17

A scream rang out in the darkened theatre. A section of the big, heavy curtains that ran alongside the soaring theatre walls moved just a little.

It was Terry.

Hiding behind the thick curtains during the scariest part of the movie, Terry peeked out with just one eye — and kept the other one covered. As if that would make the scene on the screen just half as scary. Dork.

I loved going to scary movies with Terry and the two girls — Barbara and Penny, Terry's longtime girlfriend. The three of us were always more entertained at watching that curtain — and Terry getting scared behind it — than by the movie itself. In fact, we rarely even knew what was happening in the actual movie.

"Spinks, why'd you make me go to that horrible thing?" He'd always wail as we walked back to campus. "There wasn't even any story to it. It was just . . . all about being . . . scary."

It was the beginning of our sophomore year, and Barbara and I had moved to a house on North Minden Road. Terry was living a couple of miles away in a little house behind Trinity United Methodist Church. Truth be told, Terry didn't actually spend very many nights in that house, because he was usually sleeping on our couch.

When he did stay in his own house, Terry always slept with a knife under his pillow. I have no idea what he thought he would do with that knife, should the Boogeyman arrive in the dark of night, as only the Boogeyman would do. More than likely, neither did he.

Knowing how easily Terry spooked, it became my goal to scare him at any opportunity possible. In the story I am about to tell you, however, I had absolutely nothing to do with his pure, unadulterated terror when, late one night, after Barbara and I had settled in and were just drifting off to sleep, Terry burst through our front door.

Barbara and I both sat upright in bed, terrified.

"Bradshaw!" I said, once I could make sound come out of my mouth, and as soon as I recognized the gasping-for-breath person standing in the doorway of our bedroom. "What in the world are you doing?"

"Thhhhhhere . . . is . . . a . . . hoooooooo bo . . . in my HOUSE!" he hollered, loud enough to unsettle our whole housing complex — and probably half of Ruston. My buddy was wound up tighter than a three-day clock and shaking like a leaf.

"A hobo?" Barbara said, translating.

Apparently Terry had come home to find a transient in his home — a real hobo — and without sticking around to ask any questions, he had just bolted. To our house.

So as any true friend would do, I grabbed my baseball bat and we got in my car to head back to his house to investigate.

Once we got to Terry's house, we walked right in. We didn't see anyone — or any evidence anyone was there, but with my bat poised to take out the knees of any intruder, we combed the house. Room by room, we looked under furniture, checked all the windows and locks, peered behind drapes, and threw open every closet door with the intent to maim anyone who jumped out at us.

And yet, no one did.

As we walked all around the house, we talked very loudly with our tough-man voices, just in case the hobo was listening.

"BETTER PUT THAT GUN AWAY, TERRY," I cautioned, lifting back the edge of a curtain. "WE DON'T WANT TO KILL ANYONE . . . AGAINNNNNN."

"YOU'RE RIGHT, TOMMY," he answered, working up his nerve to lean way over and peer beneath the sofa. "BUT I SURE DO FEEL LIKE MESSIN' SOMEONE UP. I NEED A FACE TO USE FOR MY PUNCHING BAG."

This set me off. I started to laugh — just couldn't help it any longer — and Terry shoots me a look that tells me he is certain the hobo murderer is listening.

"Stop laughing!" he hissed. "We can't show any sign of weakness."

"Right," I said, covering my mouth with my hand and trying not to let any more sound escape.

Once we finished checking everything out and made sure everything was locked up, I assured Terry that he was safe. "Just lock the door behind me when I leave," I said, "and try to get some sleep."

I then left his house to drive to my house, just down the street.

When I walked in the front door, the very first thing I saw was Terry, lying on our couch. The second thing I saw was Barbara, handing him a blanket and pillow.

"What the heck are you doing?" I said, trying not to yell and wake up the neighbors — again. "And how in the world did you get here faster than I did?"

Terry looked at me like I was the stupidest person he had ever laid eyes on. "Did you really think I was going to stay there?" he said. He looked straight at me. "TOMMY. THERE WAS A HO. BO. MURDERER IN MY HOUSE."

I stared at him, still trying to process what just happened.

"I am just fine right here," Terry said, punching up his pillow to make it just right for his big, goofy, scaredy-cat head. "And I would appreciate it," he added, closing his eyes, "if you would please turn that light off so I can get some sleep."

• • •

"Spinks, I don't know if all this is going to work out after all," Terry said, out of the blue, one day after practice. It was still early in our sophomore season, and Terry was frustrated, both by having to share the quarterback position with Phil, and by the rumors that Coach Lambright was going to want to stick primarily with a ground game.

"All . . . What?" I asked, trying to appear confused, even though I wasn't. I had just had a great practice, and most of all I just wanted to play football and for everything to stay the same and be OK.

Clearly, it wasn't.

"I think I'm going to ask around," Terry said. "See what else might be out there."

My heart stopped for a second. "Bradshaw, you don't want to do that. You love Tech. You love playing for Tech. You love Ruston. Why would you want to go anywhere else?"

"Because I want to play, Tommy. And here I only get to play half of the time, at best. And if Lambright isn't going to want to throw, I may never get to throw the ball." He looked at me with earnestness that reminded me of that very first day I met him. "I have to throw, Tommy."

"I understand," I said. And I did. And while I wanted the best for my friend, it was hard not to want the best for me, too. The idea that he was about to cut our playing time together short wasn't something I could let myself think about.

I promise I had nothing to do with it, but I did breathe a big sigh of relief when the news of Terry's "checking around" got back to the coaching staff — and somehow they convinced him to stay. In return, they promised to support Terry's passing game and ensured both playing time and more opportunities to do what he did best — throw the football.

Along about that same time, and completely unrelated as far as I ever knew, Phil decided to quit football. I'm not sure of his reason for quitting — I suspect it was somewhat complicated. Phil was married, and he and his wife, Kay, had their oldest son, Alan, when they first got to Tech. And, having grown up in a family who pretty much lived off the land in the backcountry of Northwest Louisiana, some of his love for hunting was about the sport of it — and much of it was providing for his family.

"Playing football is a game, boys," he liked to say. "Hunting is my lifestyle."

As a full time student as well, it probably just made sense to him at that point to bow out and let Terry have his spot as quarterback. "Now y'all got somebody here," he was reported to have told the coaches, "so let me get out of the way and I'm gonna do my thing, you do yours. It's just that simple."

This, of course, meant Terry would be playing the whole game as the quarterback, and as much as we all hated to see Phil go, I was happy for Terry. This was the opportunity he had been hoping for — and a chance to live up to all the excitement around his signing. For me, it was like coming home. I could stay focused on what came so naturally — and even though I had gotten better at receiving for Phil, catching what Terry threw was like breathing.

Terry took to this new leadership role immediately, and things settled into a fine new rhythm. Then, out of nowhere, just before the Delta game, Phil showed up to play.

What we had not realized was that all the time Terry was settling in as the full-time quarterback, the Tech coaching staff was trying to persuade Phil to come back and finish his eligibility — and then to return to the woods and his beloved lifestyle. "You've got the rest of your life to hunt and fish," they reportedly told him. "You only have right now to play college football."

I'm not sure why this was so important to the coaches. Terry clearly had it covered. I think they just hated losing Phil and that extra dimension he brought to their strategies. When they finally got Phil to agree, he was immediately reinstated and put back on the team.

Learning of this, I dreaded the thought of what Terry might do now. This was bound to be a blow and a disappointment to him — and especially after that same coaching staff had promised him the moon to keep him at Tech. I didn't know all the ins and outs of it, but it sure seemed like unnecessary roughness to me.

But Terry surprised me. Whatever his private thoughts were on the subject, he kept them to himself. He was looking at the bigger picture, I think. I was always amazed at Terry's ability to compartmentalize his frustrations and commit to the game in front of him.

Now that's not to say he liked it. "Playing two quarterbacks in a game just isn't a good system for building a winning team," he told me through a mouthful of pizza after that first game with Phil back in the picture. "That's just not how you win games."

Terry hated to lose games more than anything in the world. Because of this trait, along with the decisiveness and aggression that had already earned the team's trust, we had somehow managed to pull out a win in the Delta game, but only after Coach Lambright pulled Phil out of the game and put Terry in. Phil had struggled with the start, but Terry went in with flawless execution that led to winning the game.

In the next game, however, things were different. Coach Lambright started Terry as quarterback, and this time it was Terry's turn to struggle, so they pulled him out of the game and gave Phil another shot. Phil turned it on and had an amazing game. It was back and forth like this all season, which made for a crazy, unsettled time for all of us in Tech football.

And, although we only won three games that season, Terry and I, along with some of our teammates, were breaking school and conference records all season long. Chief among these broken records was Phil's school-record 302-yard passing game against Southeastern Louisiana.

We may have lost the game on a bobbled reception, but we were proud of that 302-yard passing record, which was an exceptional passing game back then.

• • •

"Tommy?"

I could hear the excitement bubbling over in Barbara's voice before she was through the front door of our little house. I was home early on a rare day when practice didn't run long — and had already showered and changed and was about to see if I could find some leftovers for dinner while I waited for Barbara to get home from work.

She had started interviewing as soon as we got back from our honeymoon and soon landed her new job at T.L. James, a very prominent Ruston-based heavy construction company in its prime, building roads and highways all over the South. She was working as secretary to the data processing manager, and just as we calculated, finances were close every month, but it was enough to make it with a few odd jobs sprinkled in for me in the off season.

"What is it?" I asked, coming to meet her with a hug and a kiss.

She looked up at me, giddy with excitement.

"This must be big," I said.

"It is!" She squealed.

"What?!?!?!?"

"Come sit and I'll tell you the whole thing," she said, dragging me by the hand to our sofa.

This was her story. We sat.

"Do you remember me telling you how at T.L.James there is this thing where when it's time for one of the top executives at the company to get a new car, the old car becomes available to the next in line for a very small price — and they're usually nearly new — less than two years old!"

"Yes?" I said, trying to figure out where this was going. Barbara was neither a top exec nor a next-in-line one, so I couldn't imagine what this was going to have to do with her.

"Well . . .," she said, winding up.

I've always loved how much Barbara enjoys setting up a story. Sometimes, however, I love it less, especially when the point seems in danger of being irretrievably lost. Still, I waited patiently and with faith that this wasn't going to be one of those times.

"I have no idea how Jimmy Love knew that we needed a car," she said, "but today when he got his new car, do you know what he did?"

"No clue," I said.

"He offered it to us!"

I sat there for a second, as if someone had bonked me on the head with a 2x4. "Wait," I said as the words slowly registered. "Do you mean to say that Jimmy is going to let us buy his old car . . . And we can afford it?"

Speechless, Barbara bobbed her head rapidly, beaming and teary.

I grabbed her and squeezed — and then stopped, sat back, held her by the shoulders and looked at her. "Really?" I asked her again.

"Really really!" she said, laughing at me as her tears flowed freely now. "Can you believe he would do such a thing? That's just so nice. So amazing. So sweet. How did he even know?" She paused. "And we figured out what the payments will be, and I think if we're careful we can totally do it."

I shook my head in utter disbelief. "I have to call him," I said, jumping up and heading toward the phone. Then I stopped.

"Oh. Wait. I don't have his number. Why would I have his number? He's one of the top execs at T.L. James. It's not like he's someone I just call all the time. Or ever." I realized I was making no sense, but it's not every day someone helps you get a car, right? I turned and looked at my gorgeous wife. "Barbara! We're going to have a car!"

"I know!" she said, laughing as I picked her up and twirled her around the room.

• • •

"Mr. Spinks? Are you listening?"

Mrs. Lambright's sweet Southern drawl had a way of lulling me right into daydreams of catching game-winning touchdown passes, roaring crowds, and championship rings. And, more often than not, she caught me there and brought me back with an unceremonious thud.

"Yes, ma'am," I said, sitting up a little bit straighter and giving her my most earnest and studious face.

"Then what did I just say?"

Is this college algebra or third grade math? The smart-mouth in my mind retorted. "I have no idea, ma'am," I said, ducking my head with a sheepish grin. "I'm listening now. I promise."

Mrs. Lambright was Coach Lambright's wife. I had already failed college algebra twice, fall and spring of my freshman year, and this was my third attempt. Even though Coach Lambright was new, it didn't take a rocket scientist for him to see if he didn't figure out how to help me pass this course he was going to be out one charming wide receiver.

Enter Mrs. Lambright on a special mission called Save Tommy Spinks. Mrs. Lambright enjoyed a great command over her classroom, and both her students and her peers revered her. Tall and svelte, she was very easy for a Southern boy to listen to — her voice was thick like honey, and words seemed to swirl from her mouth like soft serve ice cream into a cone — even when all she was talking about was math, which she obviously had a great love for. Go figure.

And make no mistake. As soft and genteel as Mrs. Lambright seemed, she was also quite the taskmaster. She expected her students to come prepared for class, to sit up and listen, and to ask thoughtful questions. She also expected her struggling students to come to her daily tutoring sessions and to actually study for her tests. This was where what I lacked in dedication I had to make up for with charm.

And charm, as it turned out, was the winning ticket to keeping Mrs. Lambright's interest in helping me in spite of my lack of motivation. Now don't get me wrong, Mrs. Lambright was no dummy. And neither was I. I just happened to hate math and we both knew that wasn't going to change.

Another factor in Mrs. Lambright's willingness to go the extra mile to help me was that she and my mother were church friends — cut very much from the same cloth, actually, which explained both why I got away with very little — and why the very same charm that got me out of trouble with mom worked pretty much the same way with Mrs. Lambright. Outside of the classroom she treated me like the son she never had; inside those walls I was just like any other student. Sort of. Mrs. Lambright had definite expectations of each of her students, and as far as I knew no one had lived to tell what might happen to someone who didn't meet them.

"Tommy, my lands, yoah test grade is in the tahlit. You're going to need to come in for tutoring every single day next week if you want to get yoahself into passing range. Can you come by my office after class today so we can set something up?"

Chortles and snickers behind me told me my classmates didn't really appreciate this blatant preferential treatment, but what are you going to do? Was it my fault I was clearly her favorite project?

"Yes, ma'am," I replied. "I'll be there . . . for sure!" I flashed her my most charming, most dimple-optimized grin.

"See that you do," she said, turning her attention back to the board. I realized above all things with Mrs. Lambright that I could push her just so far — then no further. By all calculations, I was right at that line, and there I usually made it my practice to stay.

Keeping a watchful eye on my average and nudging me toward tutoring whenever that slope grew slippery — and then spending whatever extra time it took to help me understand those basic-but-elusive concepts of algebra at least well enough to pass her tests, Mrs. Lambright somehow got me through college algebra.

This was partly due, I realize now, to her commitment to her husband to keep me in the passing zone, partly due to her friendship with Mom, and partly due to whatever she saw in me that made her want to keep trying. With Mrs. Lambright as both champion and irritant, I managed to pull a C in her algebra class, which we both knew was just about as good as I could ever hope or want to get. And, to the best of my knowledge, I haven't touched the stuff since.

Not a bad trade.

CHAPTER 18

The field stretched out, silent and green ahead of us as Phil, Terry, and I walked out there early for a look around. It was the fall of 1967, just before the last game of our sophomore season. It was also the last game of Phil's college career. Rumors were already starting to fly about where he'd land in the NFL.

Phil looked around, and as always, scanned the sky above. He whistled, long and low as a gaggle of geese flew over. "Boy they pretty, ain't they?" he said. "Blues and snow geese, comin' down from Canada," he added, as if we asked or cared. "They call it the 'grand passage.'"

Terry and I looked at each other and then at Phil as he just sort of fell into a trance, watching those dang birds fly.

Then Phil looked straight at Terry and said, "Bomber, I'm done with football."

"You're not!" Terry said, startled. "Why? What are you gonna do?"

"You go for the bucks, Bomber. I'm going for the ducks," Phil said, clearly pleased with his poetic delivery of this shocking news.

"What do you mean?" Terry asked him, still trying to comprehend what Phil was really saying.

"What I mean is, you go be the NFL star, Bradshaw," he said, pointing a forefinger at Terry. He paused, and then turned that finger back toward his own chest. "I'm going to be out there with the ducks."

"What? How can you throw away everything you've worked for?" Terry couldn't stop the obvious question. Watching Phil just walk away from it all was incomprehensible to both of us.

All of that talent, wasted on . . . ducks? I thought. I knew better than to speak my thoughts aloud.

"Why would you quit now?" Terry called after him, dumbfounded beyond words. "You've got so much talent. With an arm like yours you're a shoo-in for the NFL!"

"Bradshaw, I love the game and throwing touchdown passes is fun," he said, "but what really gives me the adrenaline rush, my man, is big bunches of mallard ducks raining down through the trees. That's what does it for me — it's just that simple."

His mind was made up. This time there was no talking him out of it.

"I can't believe you're really quitting, man," I said to him as he packed up his gear and emptied his locker after the game.

"You know, Spinks, there's just really nothing like being one with nature," he said. "I'm just a country boy — and I just don't see any good in wasting any more of my time on something that doesn't do it for me as much as hunting and fishing."

Now, I'm a fan of nature as much as the next person, but I was and always have been a city boy through and through, so I really had no concept of how any kind of love of nature could make someone walk away from such a promising football career, for heaven's sake. Still, I couldn't help but admire Phil for choosing what he loved over what others thought he should do. That takes a rare kind of courage that few people really have.

We later learned that Phil had, shortly after that day, passed up the opportunity to be drafted straight into the NFL, flatly refusing Paul Harvey's attempt to recruit him to play for the Washington Redskins. And then, when another offer came a few years later to play for the Redskins as a "walk on" for a reported salary of $60,000 — which in those days was big bucks — Phil again declined because football season, as it turns out, always falls in direct conflict with duck season.

"Looks like to me," he said in an interview with ESPN many years later, "the choice always came down to me in the woods hunting ducks, or getting in a situation — a lifestyle — whereby large, violent men are paid huge sums of money to do one thing, and that's stomp me into the dirt. You know, I just thought it would be less stressful to go after ducks."

As it turned out, this decision that seemed so odd to all of us at the time was prophetic testament to following your passion. For Phil, football was only about keeping his scholarship long enough to finish school. And, following his heart back into the woods led to Phil's eventual "Duck Dynasty" multimillion dollar empire and fame beyond anyone's wildest imagination. After finding wealth as the inventor of the Duck Commander duck calls and then fame as the patriarch of a clan of Louisiana duck hunters on A&E's *Duck Dynasty* reality series, our buddy Phil proved to the world what Terry and I already knew all too well. Phil Robertson is no backwoods bumpkin. In addition to becoming a multi-millionaire entrepreneur with a master's degree in education, he's also perhaps the best athlete ever to come out of the little town of Vivian, Louisiana.

Phil's decision to chase after ducks marked the beginning of Bradshaw's season in the sun as Tech's legendary starting quarterback. With our junior and senior years now stretching out in front of us, and a solid foundation earned through those grueling first two years, we were ready to move into our destiny.

For so many reasons, the town of Ruston always reminded me of the fictitious town of Mayberry from TV's old Andy Griffith Show. Not only did everyone seem to know everyone, but also the people who lived there really looked out for one another. Beyond that, they knew and supported each other's interests, goals, and dreams. It was an inspiring time in an amazing place.

• • •

The bell clanged as I entered, and before my eyes could fully adjust from the bright outside sunlight, Mr. Rogers came hurrying toward me, beaming. "Tommy Spinks!" he said, grabbing my hand and pumping it up and down in unbridled enthusiasm. "What brings you in today?" He paused. "Do you and Barbara need a little something for the house?" He eyed me for a moment. "You're not in the market for a baby bed, are you?"

"Oh gosh no, nothing like that," I said, blushing a little bit. I still wasn't quite used to people's knowledge and assumption that Barbara and I were having sex. I had come to Rogers Furniture on a specific fact-finding mission.

"Well come in, then!" He said, motioning me toward a grouping of chairs that was a little bit to the right of the main path into his sprawling furniture store. Bill Rogers was a member of Trinity United Methodist Church who poured his time and money into helping people like nothing I had ever seen before. Rumor had it that every time he went into any of our local drug stores, he'd go up to the counter and anonymously pre-pay for a candy bar for every kid who happened to be in there, with their mothers' permission of course, until the money ran out. This guy was doing the fast-food-drive-thru-pay-it-forward thing long before it came into vogue.

"No, Mr. Rogers, I didn't come here for furniture," I said, sitting down and then leaning forward in the overstuffed chair I really wanted to sprawl out in. "I came to ask you a few questions."

Mr. Rogers looked at me for a moment, as if trying to gauge the seriousness of these incoming questions. "Of course, Tommy, anything you need," he said, sitting down in the matching overstuffed chair across from me. "What do you want to know, son?"

"I want to know more about why you do all the stuff you do," I said, feeling awkward giving voice and words to this enigma the whole town knew about and talked about in hushed tones.

"What stuff?" Mr. Rogers asked, puzzled. "I don't know what you mean."

I squirmed a little, but my curiosity and determination kept me focused on my mission. Something in me knew that this was one of the most important conversations I would ever have. "Everyone knows how much you help people here in Ruston — throwing in an extra piece of furniture here, giving someone something for cost there, helping kids with tuition, "hiring" Tech kids to help deliver furniture or do odd jobs to help them make ends meet — heck, when Barbara and I came home from our honeymoon there was a nice lamp on our table with a personal note from you on it wishing us 'the best life has to offer.'" I paused, catching my breath. "All of that has gotten me thinking, Mr. Rogers," I said. "What makes you do all that? What do you get out of it?"

Mr. Rogers thought for a moment, clearly caught off guard. Then he spoke the words that shaped me for the rest of my life: "Tommy, I'm just a firm believer in using my life and all I've been blessed with to make the lives of those around me better, nicer, and easier — any way I can."

I sat there for a moment, letting these words and the energy behind them sink in.

"And you love Tech and Tech students," I added, urging him onto more familiar ground. Clearly he had never really articulated any of this before. Most likely because no one had ever asked him to.

"And especially Tech Football!" he said, his eyes lighting up. "Never miss a game!"

Ah, there's the football connection, I thought. Amazing. "So tell me," I said, "how do you know what to *do* to help people? How do you decide who to help and how to help them?"

He shrugged. "I just watch," he said, "and I listen. I get to know people and learn about what's important to them, what their struggles are, what makes them tick." He looked out the plate glass storefront windows, remembering, I could tell, some of these observations.

He looked straight at me then and continued, "So when I see a young bride eyeing a piece of furniture, or hear about a kid struggling to pay his tuition or make his grades, or I have a long-time, loyal customer who just can't afford something he or she really needs, I just do whatever I can to help. Sometimes it's just a small thing, sometimes it's something bigger — it just depends on the situation and what I can manage." There was a look in Mr. Rogers' eyes then I'll never forget. "Tommy, when I do all I can, and I use all I have to help people who need it, it blesses me far more than it does them." He stood up to go and greet a new customer coming in the door, but before he did he turned and looked straight at me. "When you invest yourself in others' lives, Tommy, you'll always be a rich man in every way that counts."

There's a saying that is always attributed to John Wesley — even though no one is sure whether Wesley actually said it, or just *would* have said it if he'd have thought of it: "Do all the good you can. By all the means you can. In all the ways you can. In all the places you can. At all the times you can. To all the people you can. As long as ever you can."

If ever there was a man who lived this advice with his whole being, it was Bill Rogers. I knew right then and there I had found the role model for my own life. Just as surely as football brought me to Ruston, I have no doubt that God brought Bill Rogers into my life at the precise time when I was deciding what kind of man I wanted to be, the kind of man that does for people, helping and inspiring them in all the ways I can.

During our very impressionable years in Ruston, one of the things that has stuck with me is the old adage, "You reap what you sow," which I have come to know as Universal Law. We thought we were in college to play football but unbeknownst to us, there was much more taking shape within us during this time. Our experiences and the people of Ruston were shaping our character and drive to help others. This would play out in both of our lives in very different ways, rooted in the nurturing we found in Ruston.

CHAPTER 19

I could almost feel the winds of change shifting as I laced up my shoes for our very first pre-season workout the summer before our junior year.

"I have complete confidence in Bradshaw as team leader and number one quarterback," Coach Lambright had said in our first team meeting of the year, just before the workout began. We had an experienced and dedicated coach in Lambright and his coaching staff, guys from all over the state of Louisiana coming to Tech with proven records. They knew how to get the job done.

Terry looked around the room, grinning. "I've got some good help," he said. He whistled. "Who'd have ever thought we'd have 10 former Woodlawn Knights on our team?"

Instinctively, I think we knew that this coming season was exactly what we had been building toward for the past two years. Our time was now. We knew it, our coaches knew it, and best of all, none of our competitors had yet begun to realize it — until the season began.

• • •

Our first game was against Mississippi State. Knowing that Tech had been picked to finish last in the Gulf States Conference, I'm pretty sure when those Mississippi State Bulldogs rolled into town they were pretty confident they were going to get an easy win to help jumpstart their tough upcoming season and boost the confidence of their players.

They couldn't have been more wrong.

As we stood waiting for the signal to make our way onto the field, Terry looked across the tunnel at me with an expression only I immediately understood.

I nodded. This, we knew, was going to be our time to shine. We also knew we were about to shock our opponents out of their socks.

We took an early lead with a 3-point field goal with 4:11 left to go in the first quarter. In the second quarter, Mississippi scored from the one yard line, making it 3-7.

Soon after, Richie Golmon broke through the right tackle for a 67-yard scoring drive to make it 10-7 at the half. During the second half, Mississippi scored on an 86 yard drive in 13 plays, making it 10-13.

Throughout the game, and much to the Bulldogs' chagrin, our defensive line was like a brick wall. Cutchins, Lanius, Brown and Causey weren't letting anything get past them, and Bradshaw's arm was absolutely on fire.

On offense, Golman, Liberto and I were all over the place, gaining yards with every play. After another successful field goal and a pass interception, we knew we had control of the game.

With the game tied 13-13 and 2:21 on the clock, we were at fourth and ten when Terry dropped back and found me on a curl pattern. I cut to the opposite side of the field where Terry hurled that ball to me for a 37-yard completion. I caught it, broke one tackle, and ran untouched for the winning touchdown.

This was a true upset for Mississippi State. Terry threw the ball for 201 yards that game, and I brought in five of those passes myself for 95 yards.

And best of all, we knew this was just the beginning.

• • •

Every time I looked up in the stands, there they were. Man, my parents loved watching me play. It didn't matter if it was pouring down rain, freezing cold or hotter than the fourth of July. They'd be there, decked head to toe in Tech colors, sporting, of course, my number #43 in all the ways you can imagine. And some you can't. Just in case anyone on the planet didn't know it, those were MY parents. And, even though this would have been the same no matter what our win-loss record — we could've had a losing season and they would still be there, proud to come watch me play the sport they had grown to love — even more than baseball!

Mom, of course, committed every second of every season to her infamous scrapbooks, a very elaborate obsession she had that drew quite a bit of ribbing from the family. Nevertheless, she persevered.

I was thinking about those scrapbooks — especially the old baseball ones she had created back in Alexandria — and how I had used those scrapbooks as exhibits in my case against moving to Shreveport — as I entered Mom and Dad's new home in Ruston.

Sure enough, there she sat at that same old dining room table where she always worked on her scrapbooks, always ready to sweep the whole mess up into a couple of decorative baskets that lived under the sideboard whenever it came time to clear the table for a family meal.

I leaned over to kiss her on the cheek. "How's it going?" I asked, looking over the table littered with newspaper clippings, photographs, printed programs from our games — you name it. "How in the world do you get all this stuff?" I asked, as puzzled as I was amazed.

She laughed. "Oh, I just pick up a little here and a little there," she drawled. "You know, if I see something I think I can use, I just slip it in my purse!"

"Yikes," I said. "I'll have to remember to tell the guys not to stand still too long or they might end up spray-mounted into one of your scrapbooks!"

"Now Tommeh, that's just *silly*," she said, laughing. "But don't I wish I could!" She studied me for a moment. "You hungry?"

"Of course!" I said.

We gave mom quite a bit to scrapbook that phenomenal 1968 season. Phil's "Blonde Bomber" nickname somehow became known to the press and became part of almost every headline about Tech football. Also among the dozens of articles and photographs mom clipped, many of those headlines also touted the Bradshaw/Spinks duo.

Mom would pull out that giant, overstuffed old scrapbook decades later when my children were old enough to read. "Rememba when you gave me such a hawd time bout keepin' this ole scrapbook?" she said, smiling triumphantly at me as she extended her trademark sweeping arm gesture toward my kids crowded around this archive, utterly enthralled. "That's why."

• • •

Beating most of the teams we played, really good teams, by large margins, became the norm as the season went on.

"Ok, guys, good game," were the words Terry and I came to dread as Coach Lambright decided to pull us out, once the margin in each game got big enough to give our younger players some game experience without cost.

"Oh, maaaan," Terry would say as we filled a cup with water from the cooler before taking our place on the bench.

"I know," I'd mutter out of the side of my mouth, plopping down on the bench beside him. "Can you imagine what the score might have been — and what records we might break — if we could stay in there to the end?"

This was good coaching and we got it. Giving those guys behind us some experience and plenty of playing time was good for our depth and the future of Tech football, but I'll always wonder what kinds of numbers Terry and I might have put up during that spectacular "turnaround" season if we had been able to finish all those games.

• • •

"Boys, we're in!" Coach Lambright hollered, waving the piece of paper that confirmed Tech's first ever bowl bid. The fifth annual Grantland Rice Bowl game in Murfreesboro, Tennessee on December 13, 1968 would be the game to determine who the Collegiate Division National Champions would be. And we were going to be one of those teams. It was going to be a climactic end to the season.

Of all the whooping and hollering and jumping around I've ever witnessed — that kind of excitement that just couldn't be contained with both feet on the ground — this is a moment that will forever be one of my favorites.

Snow was falling on the day of the game, and it was a frigid 25 degrees, but with all the adrenalin coursing through this team of Louisiana boys, I don't think we even noticed much that we couldn't feel our fingers or our toes. We were playing against Akron, a tough team with a winning tradition.

We didn't pay much attention to that, either.

By the end of the first quarter we had scored three touchdowns. Terry ran the first one in for a 16-yarder, and Buster Herren scored the second one on a two-yard burst. The third was a 36-yard pass to me. By the end of the game, I had set a new bowl record by catching 12 passes for 167 yards.

But that wasn't the biggest thing that happened in that game. What lived on in all our minds was the six-yard pass thrown to Larry Brewer in the fourth period.

Terry was rushed and hit pretty quick, just seconds after dropping back to find his target. He pushed that first guy off with one hand, and then got hit again. He kicked that second guy off and worked himself free, and then three Akron players hit him from all angles. He had one of them around each leg and the third bear hugging him around his torso.

Then something crazy happened. Terry stood straight up, saw Larry standing in the end zone, and threw that bullet straight into Larry's hands for the touchdown. It was beautiful beyond words.

It was that kind of fight from start to finish. With the entire team following Terry's leadership and single-minded focus, we won that Grantland Rice Bowl game with a final score of 33-13. I guess it goes without saying that Terry was a shoo-in as MVP, completing 19 of 33 passes for 261 yards.

• • •

My mother was sitting at the kitchen table with her head down, wiping away tears. Behind her, my father stood with his hands on both of her shoulders. He was looking down, too, clearly fighting back tears.

"What happened?" I said, hurrying into the kitchen. Barbara and I had just stopped by for a quick visit a couple of days after the bowl game.

Stretched out in front of them on the kitchen table was the Shreveport Times. Coming closer, I fully expected to see the paper opened to the obituary section.

But it wasn't.

Dad looked up at our concerned faces with tears in his eyes, yes, but also the biggest grin on his face I had ever seen. Then Mom stood up and they both began hugging me. I looked over the top of my mother's head at Barbara, who was looking just as confused as I was.

When I finally saw what they were looking at, I had to laugh, partly from relief and partly because, well, it felt pretty good to be noticed. The newspaper article that had gotten them all verklempt was about . . . Guess who?

The headline of this particular Shreveport Times article by Jim McLain touted, "Louisiana Tech's Ex-Knight No Longer 'Unknown Soldier,'" and went on to say:

> *Louisiana Tech's All-Gulf States Conference split end Tommy Spinks must have wondered if he were gargling with the right mouthwash or using the wrong underarm deodorant during the winter and spring of 1966.*
>
> *The Woodlawn High School ace made the All-District, All-City. All-State teams and played in the All-Star game in Baton Rouge after helping pace the Knights to the state Triple-A football finals in 1965. That fall he caught 32 passes for 702 yards and 10 touchdowns.*
>
> *But while other city gridders were being ardently wooed by college grid scouts, the 155-pound Spinks couldn't get a tumble. "Too small," said some. "Too slow," said others.*
>
> *Tommy felt about as unwanted as a Russian in the Pentagon and by the time school was out he'd made up his mind to go to Louisiana Tech where he had been promised a "tryout." Athletic Director Aillet must wish one like Tommy would come along every autumn.*
>
> *In his three seasons at Tech Spinks has grabbed 148 passes for 2,135 yards and 10 touchdowns. He led the GSC in receiving the last two campaigns and was named to the All-GSC squad both years.*
>
> *With one season still to play Tommy is already the all-time Tech leader in receiving and yards gained on receptions with 136 for 1,968 yards. Bowl games do not count in school records.*

The so-called Post Pattern in which the receiver races straight at a defender, then veers off to the right or left, is the route Tommy runs best. GSC defensive backs are said to have recurring nightmares about it.

Tech Head Coach Maxie Lambright, speaking of Tommy's lack of popularity with college recruiters in 1966, says "We're glad he didn't have too many offers." Lambright, who guided the Techsters to an 8-2 regular season record in his second year at the school, said, "I think Tommy is exceptional."

How did this spindly-legged youngster prove the experts wrong? A.L. Williams, Woodlawn head mentor who helped coach Tommy in high school, says, "His greatest asset is his desire to catch the football. He'll catch a ball other boys won't even try for. He'll make an effort to get it whether it's in a crowd, low or high, he'll come up with it most of the time."

Another factor in Tommy's favor was the presence on the Tech squad of hard throwing ex-Knight quarterback Terry Bradshaw. Tommy and Terry were the state's premier prep aerial team in 1965 and had worn the grass off several lawns throwing together when they were neighbors in the Southern Hills suburb of Shreveport.

Tommy says his secret is concentration. "You've got to concentrate on catching the ball and block everything else out, even though you know you're going to be hit as soon as you catch it."

Spinks, now up to 175, has concentrated on catching the ball so well that in 1967 he set a GSC single game record with 15 grabs for 211 yards against Southeastern and this year equaled the mark with 15 catches against Southwestern.

Earlier this month Tommy cracked a Grantland Rice Bowl record by hauling in 12 of Bradshaw's tosses on a 33-13 victory over Akron. Most of the Rice Bowl catches came against All-America defensive back Tony Pallija of the Zips.

Summer workouts with former Cleveland Browns great Dub Jones, a Ruston resident, have also been a big help. "He taught me some of the moves they used at Cleveland and it really helped me," said the six-foot end. Although he caught eight less passes this season (54) than he did in 1967, they went for 74 more yards (885) and five more touchdowns (7).

Warnings of Spinks' breakaway speed by the Rice Bowl TV commentary team brought howls of glee from Tech gridders when the game was rebroadcast in Ruston recently and signaled the start of some good-natured ribbing for Tommy. But opponents might not think it was so funny, Tommy caught one for 61 yards against New Mexico State and also a 38 yard touchdown pass against the Aggies. He also caught a 38-yard TD toss from Bradshaw, now known as the Blonde Bomber, against Mississippi State.

"Tommy's faster than most people think," said Lambright. "He's fast enough that we're going to try to get him behind people."

Some grid buffs contend that Terry and Tommy have worked together for so long and know each other's moves so well that it's almost like mental telepathy.

In Tech's 35-7 win over Southeastern in Ruston this season, Tech had the ball on the Lions' 11-yard line. Terry dropped back and drilled what looked from the stands like a bad pass. It was low and apparently off target. Tommy, about two yards deep in the end zone, made a leap to his left and grabbed it about two feet off the ground for a touchdown.

Tommy's leaping catches have become commonplace to Tech fans, but opponents must sometimes think they are seeing a rerun of the Olympic diving competition. Williams credits pole-vaulting experience in high school with Tommy's relaxed method of reeling in Bradshaw's bullet passes. Some football fanatics contend that Bradshaw's bombs arrive with such velocity that the light weight Spinks gets a free three or four yard ride off of them.

Tommy showed enough promise in 1966 to earn the Outstanding Freshman award at the Tech grid banquet and last year he was named the Most Outstanding Lineman. Asked what was his biggest thrill, Tommy, whose ambition is to be a coach, said he guessed it was catching seven passes against Southeastern in Tech's only win of the 1966 season. His biggest thrill this year, said the former Knight, was, "seeing Liberto going down the sidelines against Northwestern."

The play Spinks was referring to was Ken's fantastic catch and run with a Bradshaw aerial that gave Tech a touchdown and a 42-39 victory over arch rival Northwestern in the annual State Fair game. The play covered 82 yards and came with but 25 seconds remaining in the game.

His goal for next fall, the Bulldog end said, is for Tech to win the conference crown. "I think we're going to have just a great team. We'll have just about everyone coming back."

Lambright says he doesn't have to worry about whether Terry and Tommy are working out during the summer. "The only thing we have to worry about is how many footballs they're going to wear out," the football mentor stated.

As my dad was pounding me on the back, my mom was hugging me, still weepy, saying, "Tommeh, isn't this just the most wonderful article? I'm jus so, so proud of ya, son!"

At the time I didn't really understand why that article touched them the way that it did. In fact, I only sort of remembered talking to that reporter, Jim McLain, but it really wasn't that big a deal to me. But clearly it was to them. They were astonished and grateful that this reporter held me up for all the Tech football world with the recognition they believed I deserved. It wasn't until I was a parent myself that I fully understood.

This single reporter's take on my career gave me a lift I didn't realize I needed and a sort of redemption I didn't even know I was looking for.

And then, when this one article began to get picked up by other papers in other cities, with headlines that read, 'Like the Sun, Tommy Spinks is Taken for Granted,' I felt a little self-conscious, as I always did when things were written about me, but I will admit, it felt pretty good.

CHAPTER 20

"Barbara, you are *not* going to believe the latest," I said, coming in the house and sweeping her up into a hug and kiss. It was just two weeks after the Grantland Rice Bowl game, and every day brought more attention from not only the press, but NFL scouts.

"Try me," she said, smiling up at me.

"Terry had another guy call him this afternoon and really put the pressure on him about playing for the NFL." I put my hands to my head. "It's like, every single day there's someone out there who wants Terry — and sometimes me — to just up and go. Like . . . now!" I began pacing back and forth in our small living room, waving my arms in the air as I talked. "I mean it's exciting — and flattering as all heck — but geeeez! We have one more year to play college ball!"

"That's right, you do," Barbara said, watching me pace with an amused smile. And there was something else behind that smile, but in my agitated state I couldn't really put my finger on it.

"And on the other hand, what if we get hurt next year? What then? If we want to play pro ball, shouldn't we jump on these chances? And are they really bonafide opportunities, or just some scout making promises, trying to be a hero?" I looked at Barbara. "Right? We need to finish college and then see what happens, right? It would be stupid to quit school to play ball if we can get the same or better offer next year, right?"

"Right," Barbara said.

I stopped pacing and turned toward her. "But how do we know?" I said. "How do we know this time next year there'll even be offers or interest or people calling us every single day asking us what we want to do?" He paused. "We just won the freakin'

Grantland Rice Bowl! Is this our shot? Do we need to make the most of this thing now — ride this success — instead of waiting?"

"Nobody knows, Sweetheart," Barbara said. "But I do know one thing for sure."

"You do?" I asked. "What's that?" I asked, wondering how in the world she could know anything for sure when I didn't.

She put her arms around my neck and looked up at me adoringly. "I know that this time next year . . ."

She trailed off, cutting her pretty eyes upward and to the right as if trying to see exactly into one year from that very moment.

"What?" I kidded, playing along with her game, "do you see happening exactly one year from today?"

"Exactly one year from today, Tommy Spinks," she began, "I can't say which team will be coming after you, but I do know one thing for sure."

"And what's that?"

"That whoever comes calling and wanting you to play football on their team this time next year will discover that you," she said, pointing a dainty finger into the center of my chest, "are a brand new daddy."

"A . . . What?" Did I just hear her right? Weren't we talking about football?

Barbara nodded her head vigorously. "I wasn't sure until today, but the doctor confirmed it."

Speechless, I hugged her tight.

"Are you . . . Is this . . . Tommy, say something!" she said, worry creeping into her voice.

"Barbara," I began in my most serious voice. I paused. *For effect*, as my mother would say. Then I was no longer able to suppress the biggest grin that had ever crossed my face. "I think this is the very best news I could possibly hear — and I've just been part of a team that won its first bowl game and I've been talking to NFL scouts! Are you kidding me? Barbara! This is fantastic!!!!" I seriously began to wonder if any one had ever actually exploded from joy.

And as excited as I was about this news that made all NFL scouting calls pale by comparison, my buddy Terry was maybe even more excited than we were. His continuous questions ("Where will it sleep?") and hopes ("God, I hope it looks like Barbara!") and predictions ("Spinks, this is going to be one heck of a smart, good looking athlete — especially if it takes after its mother.") kept us laughing, dreaming, and planning all spring and into the summer as we waited eagerly together for this little miracle to arrive.

• • •

There's nothing I know of to make you think about being a grown-up adult more than the impending birth of your first child. Realizing the need for maturity and perspective that only comes with age and experience, Terry and I decided it was time to grow up and get focused on being pillars of society in our new hometown of Ruston.

To help this plan along, and largely due to our recent Bowl Game victory, we found ourselves constantly being asked to be somewhere for a grand opening, a ribbon cutting, or a photograph holding a football. It seemed like everywhere, all of the time, schools, stores, and local charities were discovering that having our ugly mugs on their ads or posters or life-sized cardboard cutouts tended to help them with all kinds of things from selling shoes and clothing to getting people to come out for an event or demonstration of a new product or piece of equipment.

To our surprise — and sometimes outright terror — we were also being asked to speak at local chapter club meetings, and we even received a Kiwanis award with some of our teammates in recognition of our winning season.

While all of this both humbled and amused us, we also felt a sense of obligation and responsibility to give back to this town that had already done so very much for us. That was probably our first real step toward that grown-up adult status we were looking for.

• • •

"Tommy, this is perfect!" Barbara declared, turning herself 'round and 'round in the living room of the little frame house across the street from the James Mansion.

Hearing that we had a little one on the way — and after their last child moved out of their "extra house," the James family offered us this beautiful little place just across the street from their home for as long as we needed it. Each of their own kids — and a few nieces and nephews along the way — had used this house as their "starter home." We would be the first people not named James to live there, making this both a huge honor and a responsibility we would need to take very seriously.

Taking in the details of this place, I couldn't imagine a better place to bring our baby home to — and to live until that fuzzy day somewhere on the horizon when we'd have to leave the sweet fold of Ruston, where people like the James family went out of their way to help Tech students and little families get a good start.

We had been casually looking for a bigger place to live since Betty and Joey and little Beth moved to Monroe back in February. Joey took a job with Ellington Mayflower and decided to finish school at Northeast, and while Betty still worked in Ruston, the biggest reason for us to stay in Tech married housing was gone. Even then I understood that when an opportunity like this one presents itself, seemingly out of nowhere, you take it.

"It is," I agreed, looking in cabinets and closets and checking out the back yard through the ruffle-curtained window. "Let's tell them we'll take it!"

We loved that house from the day we moved in, but it was not without its quirks. For one thing, the kitchen sink was way too far from the cupboard where we kept our dishes.

"Tommy," Barbara said, looking exhausted one night after she got the dishes washed after dinner. "Will you please put the dishes away so I can sit down?"

She was doing well with the pregnancy, but after working all day and cooking dinner, she was done. It was also very important to my sweet wife that household duties would be divided evenly. Always.

"I know," I said, ever the problem solver. "Why don't you just toss them to me from the sink and I'll catch them and put them away."

"Because I like these dishes and don't want to break them," she said, clearly not convinced of the pure genius of this plan. "Plus I want to sit down."

"C'mon, let's give it a try," I coaxed. "It won't take a minute and I promise I won't let anything get broken. It'll be fun! And besides, it will give me a little extra practice catching things gently but firmly. That's what makes for good hands, doncha know."

"You already have great hands, Sweetie. Everyone says so. Especially me," she flirted. But she was still standing next to the stack of clean dishes, so I knew she was considering it.

"Let me prove it to you," I said, waggling my fingers in her direction.

"Ok," she said, still dubious, "we'll try it. But the first dish that gets broken, we're done."

Tucking the dishtowel into the front of my pants like a quarterback's towel, I wiped my hands, just for good measure, cracked my knuckles and smiled. "Let's see what you've got, Lindsay," I said. "Hut!"

"It's SPINKS," she said, sailing a dinner plate right into my breadbasket. "And don't you forget it!"

This became our nightly game, almost all the days we lived there. And we never dropped a dish.

Another nice quality of the James house was it had the perfect configuration for indoor catch. Just enough open floor space with immovable obstacles in all the right places. One of my favorite drills was "wild throws" — catching balls thrown low, wide, high, and hard — to hone my reflexes.

So of course, it only made sense to me that unless Terry moved in with us, Barbara would have to be the one to throw these balls to me.

"OK," I said, handing her the ball. "What I want you to do is throw it as hard as you can, and mix up the directions — low one time, wide one time . . . and be sure to move it around."

She took the ball and put her fingers on the laces just as I taught her to do, with her dainty pinky stretched back as far as she could to help steady the spiral. Still, there was doubt in her eyes as she made the first throw.

"Pretty good!" I said snagging the ball out of the air high and to my left. "Now again — and the other direction. And a little bit harder, if you can."

Saying nothing, she chunked it low and to the right.

"Not bad!" I said, flipping it back to her. "Now just mix them up. And throw it as hard as you can."

She hit all the directions and was doing a pretty good job, so I decided to add one tiny critique. "Now, honey, check your grip on the ball. You need to tighten up that spiral if you can. And can you throw it a little harder?"

This was a mistake.

Winding up, Barbara hurled what was, indeed, a perfect spiral — right into the center of my gonads. Fortunately for me — and for my future dynasty of offspring — my reflexes were good enough to catch it.

"I'm NOT Terry!" she shrieked, frustration she'd been containing all evening apparently reaching the point of combustion. "I'm going to bed . . . alone!" With that, she turned and stomped out of the room and slammed our bedroom door.

• • •

Terry and I stood in an impromptu circle of young boys, each clamoring to be heard over the rest, all of them stretching out their autograph books, ball caps, footballs, or whatever else they wanted us to sign, there was a single moment in which time just seemed to slow down.

And in this slo-mo moment, I took a mental step back from where we were and noticed a single small thing that whopped me between the eyes with responsibility like nothing else ever could have. Almost all of these boys were wearing terry cloth wristbands, the kind people were starting to wear to keep sweat from running down their arms and onto their hands to make them slippery. The kind some people used to wipe sweat from their foreheads to keep the salty stuff out of their eyes.

There wasn't a day in my life that I didn't pull on a pair of sweatbands as part of my normal daily wear. Growing up in Louisiana, sweating was something everyone became accustomed to, pretty much year 'round. And because if Terry and I weren't throwing the football, we were about to throw the football, we had just finished throwing the football — or we were at practice — sweatbands were as essential to me as shoes. Maybe more so. I could still catch the ball barefoot, but not if my hands were sweaty. Come to think of it, the only time I didn't wear sweatbands on my wrists was when I was asleep.

So looking at these boys and noticing their wristbands as if a spotlight had somehow been shone upon them, it dawned on me as never before that every single thing we did was scrutinized, analyzed, and emulated by young fellas we might never even see or know. Riding alongside this realization was a sudden new awareness of the opportunity Terry and I had to make a positive difference by setting examples these boys could internalize and use to reach for their own crazy dreams and aspirations.

Also, I never washed my sweatbands. It was a superstition of mine, maybe silly and positively unsanitary. But something about keeping — and wearing every day all of the sweat I put into my sport somehow made me feel . . . invincible. I guess it's probably for the best that those little guys couldn't have known that.

It was this kind of interaction with kids that made us realize how closely we were being watched and observed — on the football field and off. It was about this time that we both made a conscious decision to try our very best to be the kind of role models that the people of Ruston could be proud of — and the kind of people these young kids could look up to.

• • •

"Terry! Wake up! Time to go!" I banged on Terry's door to get him moving. I had arrived a little bit early on the serious likelihood that he would be, as he now appeared to be, still asleep.

We were due to speak in Sunday school at another small church in a parish just about 30 miles down the road. And unless the big goof turned on the speed, we were going to be late. Being a preacher's kid had its advantages. I was conditioned to getting up and getting ready on Sunday mornings — as my father always said it was his most important workday of the week. Sleeping in or moving slowly on Sunday mornings in the Spinks household was simply not an option. That was very different, I later learned, from those who just get up and go to church. There is just a lot more pressure when you are with someone who is in charge of doing church.

To our surprise, another offshoot of our Ruston football celebrity was being asked to speak almost every week at some area church. Because it was well documented that Terry and I had a strong Christian faith and strong Christian values, not to mention my father was a Methodist preacher, which I guess meant I was just one generation from the pulpit, we were quite the hot ticket in the church world that surrounded Ruston.

The biggest challenge I had discovered in making these Sunday morning events happen was, in fact, waking Terry up and getting him to a church at the appointed time. When the church happened to be in a neighboring town, this was quite the feat indeed.

The other thing that tended to panic me about these gigs was that it usually wasn't until we were driving to the church that we would start trying to figure out what we were going to speak about once we got there. This bothered me much more than it did my buddy Terry.

He'd just smile that cheesy grin of his and say in his fakeest Southern preacher voice, "Tommy, the Lawd Gawd will give us the words that He wanteth us to speaketh to the congragationeth! There is noeth reasoneth to feareth, my child…eth."

I think it was this sort of statement that helped me hyper-ventilate a little as we walked into the church from its packed parking lot. How could we not look stupid?

And yet, Terry was always right. Thinking back on these times now — and completely unable to remember what it was we said in those talks — I'm certain that God was using us to share whatever he wanted shared at the time. And it must have been what people wanted or needed to hear, because we kept getting invited back. During that stretch of our junior and senior years at Tech, we spoke to so many church congregations it sometimes felt like we were turning into a preaching duo instead of a football duo.

Nevertheless, and according to the elders of the churches we visited, we were making a positive impact with every talk we gave, especially on the young kids who came to hear us. Parents of these kids would often stop us in the hallways of the churches where we spoke — as well as on the streets of Ruston — just to let us know how happy they were that their children had us to look up to.

As goofy as we both were, this was both humbling and amazing to us, and we took this new responsibility God gave us very seriously. Before too long, we actually began looking for opportunities to continue making that positive impact on our community.

And just like that, we were on the road to becoming the pillars of the community that we had set out, half in jest, to be.

CHAPTER 21

"Good lands, I am so glad you're here! Come on in here!" said Evelyn James as we entered the home she shared with her husband, Billy, five rambunctious boys and an infant daughter.

It was toward the end of the 1969 school year, and with a baby on the way I was hoping to make some money over the summer. I had just begun looking for a job when Terry, Barbara, and I got an invitation to dinner at the James house.

"Thank you for having us!" I said as I stepped through the massive doorway of their rambling, beautiful home.

Billy and Evelyn James were church members of Trinity Methodist Church, and some of the nicest and most laid-back people I had ever been around. While Mr. Billy was soft spoken, kind and generous — the kind of guy who just sort of faded into the backdrop of any situation and liked it that way. His wife, on the other hand, was nothing short of exceptional in every way.

Quick witted, always with a smile on her face that made her eyes sparkle, Mrs. Evelyn spoke with the same deep Southern drawl as my mom did, except (and this was hard for even me to imagine) Evelyn drew her words out even longer. Evelyn James was also a person who wouldn't take "no" for an answer. And, to be honest, you never would want to say no to her anyway, even if you could.

"So do you boys have any plans for yoah summah?" Mrs. Evelyn asked, handing us each a tall glass of sweet tea from the tray she had just brought into the living room with her.

Terry and I looked at her. Then at each other.

Terry shrugged. "I don't know yet," he said.

"I'm looking for a job!" I said.

"Good!" she said, clapping her hands together and looking

pleased. "I want to ask the two of you to be Youth Leaders for the church this summah!" Then she looked at me. "And if the two of you boys would be willin', Billy and I also need some help takin' care of things out at Toma Lodge. If y'all could come out in the mornings and help us get a few projects done out there — and then come to the church to be our Youth Leaders on Sunday mornings and evenings — we can see to it that you will both have a paycheck all summah long!"

Toma Lodge was a family retreat that the James family owned. While we had no idea what kinds of "projects" she was even talking about — or what being a "Youth Leader" entailed — the idea of a paycheck was just too good to pass up.

"OK!" Terry and I said in unison.

Just as we were about to ask Mrs. Evelyn for a few more details, we all heard a sound from the dining room that brought all conversation to a screeching halt. 'King', the James' very affectionate and large German shepherd, was standing in the middle of their long, gorgeous dining table, helping himself to the appetizers Evelyn had put out just before answering the door.

In true Mrs. Evelyn James fashion, she looked at King for a full moment, and then, in her slow, soft, southern drawl, she said, "Kaaaaang. Kaaaaaang, you betta get dowen from thayah, you silla, silla dawg." She stood there, watching as King first looked at her, looked at the bowl of dip he had all but emptied, and then complied with her request. She shook her head and muttered, "Well, it looks like I need to make some mo-ah appetizers."

Mrs. Evelyn then turned her attention back to us. "So it's all set then? You boys can start out at Toma Lodge the day after school lets out, and on Sunday mornings and evenings as soon as you're ready and able!"

"Yes, ma'am," I said, looking at Barbara and then back at Evelyn. "That's going to be a really big help to us. I really appreciate the opportunity because . . ." I pointed at Barbara, who by now was very clearly showing, "we're going to have a baby at the end of the summer!"

Mrs. Evelyn laughed. "Yes, son, I know!" she said, her wide blue eyes reflecting her vivacity as only hers could. "We're so very excited for the both of you, and we really do want to help out all we can. In fact . . ." She paused, wondering, I realize now, if she was just about to push it too far. "I'm also wondering if the two of you might like to earn a little extra money — and get a little bit of hands-on parenting practice this summer by babysitting our children from time to time when we need a sitter."

I looked at Barbara and shrugged. "I guess so," I said. To be truthful, I was a little bit unsure. There were six of them, after all.

"Sure!" Barbara said, eyes dancing. "I'd love to! Thank you so much for all of this," she added. "We are so blessed!"

"Darlin' ya might want to wait to thank me until you've spent some actual time in the trenches with my little angels," Evelyn said, then laughed. "They can be a handful!"

She wasn't wrong. But we'll get to that a little bit later.

• • •

"Now what, Mrs. Evelyn?" I said, trying to catch my breath after running up the hill to the house.

Terry and I had arrived at our appointed time that morning, ready to do some work. Mrs. Evelyn had stood there on the porch, shading her eyes with one hand as she looked out to the left and then the right, as if trying to think of something, anything, for us to do.

"How about if we rake those pine needles over there," I had suggested, as this was usually one of my jobs at home.

"Or we could clean the lodge . . ." Terry had proposed, grabbing a broom. "And to start with, I'll sweep this porch!"

Mrs. Evelyn had laughed, and agreed to those things, plus restacking some logs that had fallen from the big pile at the bottom of the hill.

And now we were back. Terry came up behind me, also winded from sprinting up the hill. "Now what?" he echoed.

Mrs. Evelyn waved her slender hand in the direction of a sunny clearing about 30 yards away. "Why don't yawl boys go ova there an throw the footbawl awhile," she said. "I can't think of anything else for y'all to do right now, but if I need ya, I'll call ya." She yawned, covering her dainty mouth with her hand. "Now if yawl need anything at all, just call fa me, I'll be inside restin'."

So for the rest of the summer, Terry and I would show up for our "work day," and if there was something we saw or thought of to do, we did it. The rest of the time we spent in that beautiful clearing, doing what we loved best — throwing the football. From time to time, Mrs. Evelyn would step out onto her porch and holler down to us to ask us if we needed any 'sweet teeee' or 'watta.'

I don't remember what we were paid that summer, but I do remember feeling — and still feel — grateful for this strange and wonderful help from the James family. Now I understand that although they wanted to help us, they also wanted to give us at least the illusion of a paying job. I also suspect they were trying to offset the real work we'd be doing at the church without pay.

• • •

Stepping to one side of the huge rock fireplace, I found my receiver downfield and fired the ball into the waiting arms of Mark James, the middle brother among the five boys and one girl of the James family.

"Tommy!" Barbara said as Mark and his brother Jeff took out a lamp somewhere during the tackle.

"What?" I said. "I didn't do anything! *They* did!"

"*You* threw the ball, Tommy Spinks!" She glowered. "This is not a football field! This is a LIVING ROOM!"

I looked at the huge expanse of real estate of the massive living room in the James home. Working around that big rock fireplace in the center of the room, the available space was easily half the size of a football field.

Which is exactly how we saw it.

While the James parents were out of town the care of their six children was left to Barbara and me — and Terry usually joined us to help me corral the five boys while Barbara took care of Ginger, the James' baby girl.

Babysitting what we affectionately called "The James Gang" was quite a job, as it turned out, because true to Mrs. Evelyn's word, those boys were a handful. An energetic bunch, they were always moving, wrestling, jumping, racing, and competing with each other. Terry and I often remarked that they had more energy in their thumbs than we had in our entire bodies.

The James kids were stair-stepped in age, just a little over a year apart, from Billy, to David, to Mark, to Bob, to Jeff, and finally Ginger, the only girl. It was easy to love Mr. Billy and Mrs. Evelyn — and easier still to love their kids.

When the three of us came to "babysit," what that actually meant was that Barbara would keep every one of the kids in line, fed, and in bed at a descent hour. Our job, as we saw it, was to play. While Barbara took care of Ginger, the baby, Terry and I were "in charge of the boys," which meant we were throwing the ball in the house, off the roof, over the hills, through the woods, off the balcony, and even sometimes through the fireplace.

"We're just here to have fun!" we'd moan when our rough-housing pushed Barbara over the edge and maybe scared her a little bit for all our safety. In truth we were having as much fun as any of those boys.

"No, you're here to create chaos!" Barbara would say, hands on hips in that don't-you-dare-go-one-step-further-with-this stance I'd come to know, love, and above all, respect in the years to come. At that point we'd meekly comply with whatever job she'd then assign us to do, because we had "created our limit of chaos" for the evening.

• • •

When we agreed to be Youth Leaders at Trinity United Methodist Church, we had no idea what we were agreeing to — or what a Youth Leader even did.

"So, um, Mrs. Evelyn," I said, shortly after we arrived for duty on that first Sunday, "what exactly are we supposed to *do* as Youth Leaders?" If this gig was anything like Toma Lodge — and even babysitting the James kids — we were in for a whole new batch of fun.

Well, that wasn't completely untrue. It was just a different *kind* of hardworking fun than we had ever before experienced.

"Well first of all," Mrs. Evelyn said (I've later learned that in the South when a woman starts any sentence with "Well, first of all . . ." you're in for trouble.) ". . . Your main job for Sunday evenings," she said, "is creating all kinds of fun activities for the kids."

Besides football? we wondered — but didn't ask aloud. I'm pretty sure it was in unison.

"Y'all are also in charge," Mrs. Evelyn continued, "of finding a guest speaker to come to the church and speak every Sunday night."

This wasn't going to be easy, we knew immediately. Our entire circle of friends consisted of a bunch of goofballs, only a few of which were marginally mature enough to handle a responsibility like this. So that's mostly who we called on.

Among these friends was a very quiet, somewhat shy fella named Cecil Marr. Cecil was a friend of ours who sincerely believed he had been called into the ministry, so asking him to speak at a church on a Sunday evening seemed to be a perfect solution.

Although we were pretty confident that Cecil had what it took to be an effective speaker for our youth group, we weren't sure at all how he would do in the pulpit in front of a large congregation. Cecil was shy, remember? And reserved.

So on that Sunday night, Cecil showed up early, dressed in a suit. He was beyond serious, and nervous beyond words.

"Are we going to have to carry him outta here?" Terry wondered, watching Cecil pace back and forth. From where we stood we could almost hear his heart pounding.

"Cecil you're going to do fine," I said, trying to lighten things up with some pleasantries. "Nice suit, by the way."

"Thank you," Cecil said. His normal jovial self had been abducted by its stoic and focused twin.

Finally, it was time.

"Here goes . . . something . . . I hope," I whispered to Terry out of the side of my mouth.

"I've never seen anyone so freaked out," Terry said, watching Cecil make his way to the front of the church.

As he passed the third pew, a little lady whispered to him, in a loud enough voice for all to hear, "Be sure and keep it short sonny, the boys are landing on the moon tonight."

"Oh sweet Jesus," Terry said as we took our seats in the back pew and Terry pulled out his Bible with his Sports Illustrated magazine hidden in the middle of it. "That was about the last thing ole' Cecil needed to hear."

I nodded, looking heavenward and asking for strength for my buddy Cecil. What had we done? Why had we put this poor guy in this awful position? "He might not ever get over this, Terry," I said.

Terry was too engrossed by then, in his "Bible Study" to respond. So I fixed my eyes on Cecil and hoped for the best.

We all sat back, then, prepared to suffer with poor Cecil through a nice, quiet, halting little superficial sermon when suddenly we were jolted to attention by the spectacle now coming to life in the pulpit. From out of nowhere, it was as if Cecil was channeling Billy Graham himself. Every word, every gesture, every pause commanded the undivided attention of every single soul in that room.

If anyone had been planning to doze through this guest speaker, they weren't anymore. Even Terry looked up from the Sports Illustrated Bible, eyes bugging out, and then hastily closed his Bible, all eyes and ears on our buddy Cecil.

Cecil was animated and impassioned as he implored our congregation to live the life God intended us to live. His voice was loud and powerful. His words were strong and sure. His face was red with passion. His arms were waving every single righteous point he made into our collective consciousness.

Old women were clinging to their Bibles, now held close to their hearts. Whether the response I saw in that congregation was shock, fear, or divine intervention, I'll never know. But what I do know is that Cecil's words and energy were moving them in ways I had never seen this group moved before. Of that, I was certain.

Wide-eyed, Terry and I looked at each other in stunned silence, mouths hanging open. Then Terry made a goofy 'What the hell just happened' face at me and it was all over. In the next split-second we were doubled-over, fighting to muffle laughter that could not be contained. The harder we tried to stifle our laugher, the more powerful the impulse became.

We were in shock. We were beyond stunned. Who knew that our good friend — the perpetually quiet, kind and gentle Cecil Marr — had a steroid-laced religious soul just yearning to be set free?

After Cecil finished his sermon, the rest of the service was a blur. Afterward, the congregation surrounded him with hugs, handshakes, and words of approval and appreciation. As soon as the last church member left the building, Terry and I made our way down the aisle toward Cecil.

"Cecil, man, I just . . . wow," I started, shaking his hand as so many others had just done. "I . . . well . . . we . . ." I looked at Terry, who nodded vigorously, even more unable to find words than I was. "Cecil," I tried again, this time connecting with some of the words I was searching for, "Thank you for such an incredible and surprising sermon."

This is where something incredible happened. Shy, quiet, reserved Cecil returned. "Uh, may I please have some water?" he said, then he looked at his shoes. "I'm exhausted."

Terry looked at me, eyebrows raised, and I looked back at him, and we both busted a gut again, laughing without trying to contain it, without trying to suppress it, just letting all that pent up hilarity roll on out. Cecil, watching this, got tickled. Pretty soon, he was laughing, too, and almost as hard as we were. I was pretty sure he had no idea why, but laughter like that is definitely contagious.

As we were at long last locking up for the night, Cecil looked at me and said, "Thanks for the opportunity, Spinks. I am sure now that this is what I want to do with my life."

And he did. Cecil went on to have a long and brilliant career as a very successful preacher back in my old hometown of Shreveport, Louisiana.

• • •

As much fun as we had that summer, between working out at Toma Lodge and getting paid for it, babysitting the James kids and getting paid for it, and serving as Youth Leaders, arguably the hardest work we had ever done — and not getting paid for it at all, we were beyond eager to get our football season started.

CHAPTER 22

Sweltering in one of our first pre-season workouts, I lined up for a scrimmage play. Out of the corner of my eye I saw one of our coaches running across the football field in our direction, hollering at the top of his lungs.

None of us could make out what he was saying, but all we knew it must be important. When I could finally make out his words, my heart flip-flopped in my chest as I heard him yell, "TOMMY!!! Your wife needs you, she's going into labor!!!"

The next thing I remember, Terry and I were sprinting towards my car, while my teammates whooped and hollered and celebrated from the field. We were headed at speeds far too unsafe to mention for Lincoln General Hospital. If you are a father you will understand what I am about to describe. If you are planning on being a father, one day you will understand.

Nothing can ever prepare you for the moment when you hold your newborn child for the first time. As I carefully took the tightly wrapped bundle from the nurse, a brand new feeling of love penetrated the deepest part of my heart — a place I never even realized existed.

Becoming a father is, in a word, miraculous. The immediate responsibility you feel changes you forever. As I looked at this brand new little human who looked right back at me with my own eyes, I was instantly and forever bonded to Kimberly Reneé Spinks. From that moment on, nothing was more important to me than making sure that the lives that now depended on me would be the best they could be. And not only did my world become this baby girl in this single instant, but because she had joined our lives I was more in love with her mother than I had ever been before.

We were a real family, and suddenly everything felt different. Perfect.

• • •

"Excuse me, madam, but I just heard that the prettiest baby in the whole place was in this room," I said, entering Barbara's hospital room, flowers in hand. I still couldn't quite believe that the tiny person I had met just a few hours before was actually our baby — for keeps. I didn't dare let myself think about it for too long or I might start to get scared and that just wouldn't do.

Before I could even kiss Barbara hello and give her the flowers, the partition dividing the room moved, and I recognized the big hairy face that appeared. "Sure as hell is," my old teammate Phil Robertson said, grinning, "except that I don't think he's gonna like you calling him purty."

I laughed. "Well let's see him then," I said, sticking my head around the petition to view the newest Robertson baby. I nodded to Kay, Phil's wife. "Hey Kay!" I said. "Congratulations!" I inspected the blue-blanketed bundle Phil was thrusting my way.

"Want to hold him?" he asked. "His name's Jason."

"Oh heavens no," I said, putting both hands up, palms out. "I'm still trying to work up the nerve to hold my own!"

"Little girl, right?" Phil said.

I nodded. "Kimberly Reneé Spinks," I said. I wondered if there would ever be a day when I didn't feel obligated to say all of her names. Not today, anyway.

"Congratulations!" Kay said.

"Thanks!" I replied, and then, remembering how I left Barbara hanging, I turned back to her. "Hey Barbara, did you see baby Jason? Did you know it was Phil and Kay on the other side here?"

Barbara laughed. "No, I didn't know who was over there. I just kept falling asleep and when I would wake up, there were voices over there. I never thought it might be someone we know!"

In those days, women would stay in the hospital for a week after delivery, staying in a shared room with another mother who had just had a baby. To discover that the other in our case was Kay Robertson was an unexpected delight.

Over the course of the week, Barbara and Kay got to be good friends, and Kay, who already had one baby, gave Barbara lots of good advice about caring for a newborn. The two talked about babies, shared recipes, and talked at length about their hopes and dreams for their children and their families. I don't know if the subject of husbands came up, but I suspect they compared a few notes there, too.

"You know," Barbara mused after we said our goodbyes to the Robertsons on the day we were dismissed from the hospital, "I think if we ever have a son, we should name him Jason."

I thought for a moment. Still working on getting used to the idea of one baby, it was next to impossible for me to contemplate another one. "Jason is a nice name," I agreed, realizing even then the sweet connection that name would always hold for us. Whether they knew it or not, the Robertsons helped ease our transition into a whole new layer of life. It never ceased to amaze me that of all the babies born in that hospital, we ended up sharing a room with the Robertsons. Having those friendly and familiar faces right there with us sure made the whole thing a lot less scary.

"I'm just so thankful for them," Barbara said, as if hearing my thoughts on the way back to our house and countless times in the months and years that followed. In so many ways, the sweetness of spending that first week of motherhood with Kay and Phil set a tone for Barbara as a mother and for us as a family. Because of this serendipitous pairing, Barbara and I entered into this whole new part of our lives with all the faith and confidence in the world that being parents would be an amazing experience — all we hoped and dreamed.

• • •

The pride and excitement that "Uncle Terry" displayed any time the subject of Kimberly came up was testament to how much he enjoyed sharing and rejoicing in our joy. And, as the proud uncle he declared himself to be, he took every opportunity to hold Kimberly and show her off.

It was sometime during the first three months at home with our new baby when Barbara met me at the door when I came in from practice with a finger to her lips. I had stopped at the grocery store on the way home, so I set those bags on the kitchen counter and followed her.

Motioning me to be very, very quiet, which was next to impossible, she led me to the door of Kimberly's room where, opening the door just a crack, we could see that there in that nursery was a group of eight sweaty football players in cleats and workout gear, gathered around Terry, who was holding little Kimberly — and holding court with his buddies — as only a proud new uncle could do.

Barbara covered her mouth with both hands to suppress the inevitable giggle, but above those hands her eyes brimmed with tears, "Tommy, isn't that the sweetest thing?" she said. "Just look at them! Look at him. He's so proud of her, and so gentle."

Looking at those huge hands holding this tiny infant, it was hard not to be struck with the pure miracle of it all. I turned to Barbara, "How'd they get in there without you knowing about it?" I asked, puzzled. Eight big sweaty football players in workout gear is not a quiet thing to have tromping through your house.

"I was trying to take a nap," she whispered, "and I heard something — kind of a quiet commotion of some kind — but I was so sleepy I couldn't figure out what it was. So I came in to check on Kimberly, and there they all were. Quiet as a bunch of great big sweaty mice could be!"

We stood there, arm in arm, just watching them. Gathered around Terry in a semi-circle, they were all smiling and talking baby talk — and little Kimberly was wide-awake and cooing right back at them. Every time Terry talked to her, Kimberly would look right up at him as if she recognized his voice, and I thought maybe Terry might melt into a puddle right there on the worn beige carpet.

"That was one of the sweetest moments I have ever witnessed," Barbara said that night and countless times for years to come. She often lamented that she didn't capture this unforgettable moment on film. I didn't have to. That one scene will stay permanently etched on my mind forever.

• • •

As Kimberly grew and began to sit, crawl, and even start to walk, Terry was always right there, celebrating every milestone and delighting in making Kimberly smile and, whenever he could, laugh out loud.

One afternoon as Kimberly was coasting around furniture to get used to the idea of walking, Terry had an idea.

"Spinks," he said, "I think I might like to babysit."

Eager for a night out alone, and confident in the skills we had personally witnessed Terry acquiring, we decided to give it a try.

"Want to go to a movie?" I asked, thinking of traditional date venues.

"Let's just go to dinner," Barbara said. "That way we can stay close by just in case he needs us — and we'll just see how things go."

Makes sense, I thought. Truth be told, I'm not sure I'd want to be the only one to take care of her for much longer than that. We were getting the hang of this baby stuff, but still, it was scary to be completely in charge of a person so incredibly small.

When we returned, Terry was triumphant. "See?" he said, "Uncle Terry's got this. Next week y'all can go for dinner *and* a movie."

True to his word, during the couple of hours we were gone, Terry had fed, bathed, diapered and even put Kimberly to bed. When we looked in on her she was all tucked into her little sleep sack, sound asleep.

"Impressive," I said, punching Terry in the arm.

"Thank you, Terry," Barbara said. "You're a natural!"

With this evening under our belts, we got more and more comfortable going out for date night each week, leaving Uncle Terry in charge. In fact, we were so grateful for his help that any time he offered, we jumped at the chance for a night out.

After a couple of months, we decided to treat Terry to a home-cooked meal to thank him for all his help. We were eating dinner around our small kitchen table when Barbara excused herself to go check on Kimberly.

"Tommy, do you have any idea where I might find some more diapers?" she hollered out to us from the living room.

"I don't know, sweetie," I hollered back. "Did you try the hall closet?"

"Yes!" she said, exasperated. "There's not one diaper anywhere in this whole place! It seems like they just keep disappearing. Where could they be?" She stood in the middle of the living room, hands on hips, trying to solve this strange riddle. "We got tons of cloth diapers at our shower. Where could they be hiding?"

At that very moment, with Barbara hollering in a very frustrated tone about the diapers, I happened to glance across the table at Terry, and I immediately recognized the look on his face. Eyebrows raised high, he was stuffing mashed potatoes into his face in an attempt to erase the grin.

I narrowed my eyes at him and watched him for a second. "Okay," I whispered, looking straight at him, "where are the diapers?"

"Why would you ask *me*?" he said, not even bothering to whisper. "I'm not in charge of keeping up with your baby's stinkin' diapers."

Hearing this retort, Barbara came back into the room and, hands still on hips, focused her TV detective glare on Terry. "Terry," she began in the carefully modulated tone I knew all too well, "when you change a poopy diaper, what do you *then* do with the diaper?"

Realizing he was busted, Terry threw his napkin on the table. He leaned back in his chair, arms crossed and looked straight back at Barbara, defiant. "I BURY THEM, OKAY?" he said. Turning slightly toward the back window, he nodded his head toward the back corner. "I just *bury* those stinking, smelly suckers right out back by the fence."

"You . . . What?!?!?!" Barbara and I asked in horrified unison. That was like burying cash back there — and not in a good way.

Terry shook his head. "I'm sorry, guys. I couldn't do it. I *just* couldn't do it." He paused, looking nauseous just thinking about those poopy diapers. He pushed back his chair, looking back and forth between us as if trying to decide which of us might understand. "You don't understand," he began, stopping for a moment to regain his composure. "I would start dry heaving and . . . well . . .

there was just no possible way I could clean them out in the toilet like you told me to. It's just . . . so . . . gross."

For a moment, Barbara and I stared at Terry in utter disbelief.

Regaining his defiance, Terry glared right back at us.

Then, after a few seconds of silence, all three of us burst into fits of laughter.

Barbara put her hand to her head. "I *knew* that mound of dirt I saw by the back fence wasn't there before," she said. "I thought it was the dog getting into the flower bed!"

CHAPTER 23

"Did you know you're being given the odds-on chance of being the number one draft choice?" I asked Terry as we settled into our usual throwing routine.

"Where'd you hear that?" he asked, catching a high one and sending it back.

"Read it in the paper," I said. It made sense, but was still hard to get my mind around us being right here, entering our senior year at Tech. Even though the NFL had been knocking at our doors for over a year, none of that chatter could possibly compare to being touted as a number one draft choice. Going into our final season, Terry had already broken 17 school records and 11 conference records. I was so proud of him I thought I might burst. But of course, I was way too cool to show it. "Don't you read the newspaper?" I chided.

"Somewhere I heard you shouldn't read your own press clippings," he said, grinning at me as he threw the ball way low and to the right.

Of course I caught it and sent it right back, dead center to his solar plexus. "That's why I read them for you, ya big dork," I said. "Otherwise you might never have any idea what's going on."

"Well gee, thanks," he said. "What would I do without you?"

"I literally have no idea," I replied.

I don't know if it was having this new baby in the world or whether we were just growing up, but everything felt different as we entered that final season at Tech. Terry and I became even more focused, if that was even possible, on our goals and aspirations. We were absolutely determined to make our senior year of Tech football the most successful yet.

• • •

"So tell me what your off-season workout consisted of this year," came the now-familiar question, this time from a new cub reporter from the Ruston Daily Leader. This interview was for what would become just one of the many pre-season articles leading into our senior season.

Having walked up on this impromptu interview, I wasn't quite sure what to do with myself now. There was literally nowhere to hide. I ducked my head and cleared my throat to let them know I was there so it wouldn't look like I was eavesdropping.

"Ah! There's Mr. Dedication now!" Coach Lambright said. "Howya doin', Tommy?"

I grinned and waved at the reporters as I replied, "Just fine, sir!"

"I worked mostly on rollout passes," Bradshaw told the reporter, turning his attention back to the reporter, "and then some on my delivery and form. Tommy and I worked out every day during the week, and I also threw some to Larry Brewer, our tight end, on weekends."

"In an earlier article we ran, it said . . ." the young reporter looked down at the clipping in his hands and then read, "'Bradshaw has all the tools: size, speed — 4.7 seconds for 40 yards — a quick release, and a strong arm.'" The reporter looked up at Terry, squinting, "so how far would you say you can usually throw the ball, Terry?"

Terry grinned, then shrugged. "I guess I can consistently throw the ball about 75 yards," he replied.

"Oh, he can throw a lot farther than that," I was quick to speak up. "I personally caught a 92-yarder he once threw during practice." I was telling the truth. And besides that, I believed Terry could throw a ball to the moon if he wanted to.

• • •

"Spinks will make it as a pro — they won't be able to run him off," Coach Maxie Lambright told the crowd of reporters gathered just outside our locker room door. "They don't call him Mr. Dedication for nothing."

Coach Lambright was right, I *was* dedicated, but so was our whole team. The confidence we all felt — in our team and in ourselves individually — was evident in every game we played.

In his article that ran a few weeks later, "What makes Tommy Spinks the best pass catcher around?" O.K. "Buddy" Davis, a longtime sports editor for the Ruston Daily Leader, wrote:

> *RUSTON—"There are a lot of things, I believe," says head coach Maxie Lambright. "Basically he has outstanding hands and moves. He consistently gets open and consistently catches anything near him."*
>
> *That's pretty good for openers. It isn't the whole Spinks story though. Pretty soon his teammates and Tech's coaching staff get around to the intangible dedication. He wants to catch the ball. He works at it. He believes in himself. Because of these traits and his dedicated efforts, Spinks may be catching passes for another 10 or 12 years – as a pro.*

And once again, as difficult as it was for Terry and for me, especially in light of all the attention we were getting, we found ourselves coming out of games before we were ready. This led to endless speculation about the records we might have broken if times and players had been different. Even then we realized that while the good of the team had to come first, in all likelihood our last days on the field together were slipping by, week by week and game by game. It was excruciating not to get to play every single second we could. We could feel the end of this season — and the end of an era for us — coming faster and faster with every passing day.

And, while we of course realized that an end of one era always meant the beginning of a new one, the looming uncertainty of our next new beginning made it feel much less exciting than I ever dreamed it would. Neither faith nor confidence in our talents and work ethic could prepare us for how dread and uneasiness would wind its way through the excitement and joy of our senior year toward the edge of the uncharted waters of the NFL.

• • •

I glanced up into the press boxes when I first came onto the field for warm-up. Game time was still almost an hour away, but already they were up there, vying for a good seat, greeting one another, checking their notes, and writing on tablets and clipboards. My heart always raced a little bit to see the pro scouts filling our press boxes. It was still early in the season, and Terry was already dazzling them.

"Look up there," I said, nudging Terry with an elbow then pointing toward the press box.

"Don't point, Spinks," he said, exasperated. "Geez! Be cool!"

"Easy for you to say, Number 1," I said as we started our pre-game stretching routine. "I don't know why I'm nervous, anyway," I added, bending into a deep hamstring stretch, "they're all here for you, Bud."

"No they're not," he said, swinging his arms, "They're here for *both* of us. We're hot commodities, doncha know?"

"You know it," I said, only half-believing in my own bravado as I turned my attention to my quads. I was so excited for Terry — and relieved to see that he was finally getting the attention from the scouts he deserved. I, on the other hand, was starting to feel a little bit worried.

A few days later, another article by Buddy Davis, "Spinks Sparkles for Tech, But Play Taken for Granted. Ruston – What About Tommy Spinks?" put everything I was beginning to worry about into words:

> *RUSTON—You remember Tommy, don't you? He's caught more passes than anybody in Gulf States Conference history.*
>
> *He also happens to be the young man who does his job of playing split end for Louisiana Tech so efficiently that he is taken for granted more often than not.*
>
> *Because of this Tommy Spinks often doesn't get the publicity that would normally come with the kind of feats a receiver like him accomplishes. He simply rolls right along making outstanding plays with regularity, yet finding his name in the*

scoring summary or on top of the list of pass receivers, but not very often in the limelight.

Well, guess what? It's happened again.

Tommy Spinks, the young fellow who four years ago got a scholarship to Louisiana Tech the week before fall practice started, has carved another niche into the record books and still managed to remain a silent figure.

This time the master of moves has tied the school record for most touchdown receptions with his 20 yard scoring catch against the University of Tennessee at Chattanooga. Tommy now has 13 career TD receptions, tying Ken Liberto who graduated last year.

Tommy's latest hit of acclaim comes ironically, from the game in which he accomplished less statistically than any other all season. As is the case with his battery mate, Terry Bradshaw, Tommy has become a victim of successful circumstance this year, too.

Playing only 15 minutes while Tech was jetting away from the Moccasins 28-0, Spinks caught two passes for 32 yards.

First came the TD catch on the third scrimmage play of the game and later came a 12 yard reception for a first down on Tech's third scoring drive. Although he hasn't quite averaged three quarters of playing time so far into 1969, Spinks has still managed to maintain an excellent reception record.

Thus far he has 21 catches for 448 yards and four touchdowns. His average gain per catch is 21.3 yards. Quite likely when the 1969 season ends Spinks will again be the GSC's leading receiver-despite a nine game schedule.

In his tremendous college career, Spinks has caught 157 passes for 2,406 yards. He has already led the GSC in the recent two years and clearly become the most prodigious pass receiver in league history. Twice he has caught 15 passes for over 200 yards in a single game. No other GSC player has done it once.

All this and yet Tommy Spinks still sometimes goes unnoticed. It's actually a tribute to his ability. People simply expect him to be better than anybody else. . . .

One of my all-time football heroes was Raymond Berry, the former all-pro who played for Baltimore who reached the ultimate as a pass catcher despite a multitude of handicaps.

Comparing me to Berry, Buddy Davis went on to write in this article:

Spinks doesn't have all of those handicaps, but his speed has been questioned, just as Berry's has. However, also like Berry, Tommy keeps beating people.

He does have average speed and coupling this with the great hands and moves, there hasn't been anybody yet who could keep him from doing the job. Don't expect to find that out from any press clippings, though. It might not be there. You'll just have to watch the statistics. There's no way to keep him off that sheet.

You see, in 1969, sports writers had much more influence than most anyone can imagine now. Not only was there great power behind the printed word, every word written also reflected, in one way or another, the opinion of the person who wrote it. Fortunately for Terry and me, Buddy Davis, who was arguably one of the most well-known and deeply respected sports writers in Northern Louisiana, was always good to Terry and me.

When it came to sports, Buddy's views were pretty much taken as Gospel. He was a straight shooter who called things like he saw them — and when he spoke, wrote, or gave his opinion about players, people listened. I'll always believe that it was because of the spotlight Buddy cast on Terry and me, seen all over the country, that I wasn't overlooked by the pros in the long run.

I've never believed in coincidences. I believe that every single relationship you have in life is there for a specific reason.

Sometimes we get to discover these reasons if we are fortunate to live long enough; sometimes, for reasons we may never understand, we will not. Buddy Davis ended up becoming a close friend in my life, and I'm so grateful, not only for this friendship, but also for getting to see how it impacted my football career and my life.

• • •

Our senior season played out as expected, and our fierceness on the field won us all but two games, most of them by very large margins.

"Boys, we're heading baaaaaaaaaak to the Grantlannnnnnd Rice Bowlllllll!" Came Coach Lambright's exuberant announcement as the bid came once again to give us another chance at the Conference Championship title.

This time the bowl game would be against East Tennessee State University, to be held in Baton Rouge, Louisiana of all places. All of our dreams, all of our plans — everything was playing out just as we imagined it would, way back in those days on Shady Lane.

Everything we had worked so hard for had arrived, and we were soaking up every bit of it. To end our college careers with another shot at the Conference Championship was even more than we dared to ask for. And when it was announced that the game would be played in Baton Rouge, it seemed like this final moment of our college glory days would be ours for the taking.

"That's our home turf," Terry observed between mouthfuls of food as we ate dinner on the evening after the location for the bowl game was finalized.

"Yeah," I said, helping myself to more fried chicken. "No snow, no ice, no freezing cold wind — ain't nothin' getting in our way now!"

What did get in our way . . . was us. Before we even knew what happened, we ended up losing the biggest game of our college careers 34-14.

The newspapers said we just didn't come out enthusiastic. Some speculated that maybe having the week off before the game had somehow hurt us.

All Coach Lambright would say was, "Something was missing."

While every loss we ever experienced was painful, this one was different. Far beyond the pain of any games we had lost before, even the big games — like that championship game our senior year at Woodlawn — this one stung to the core.

I couldn't even think any of the usual post game thoughts — like what we should have done differently or could have done better. I just felt oppressively sad. And this time there was no "next year" or "next time" or "if we work more on this, we can do that better." It was over, and the final chapter of this amazing experience had ended. Badly. In a way that makes you want to throw the whole book across the room.

While we still had dreams of playing in the NFL, those dreams suddenly seemed very vague and far away. The fun, the partnership, the duo, the hard work — and the sheer joy of playing together that had gotten us to this place were over. All of it, gone with the loss to East Tennessee State University in the Grantland Rice Bowl Game, the winter of 1969.

• • •

Although we didn't win that championship in 1969, we still did what all champions do. First we felt sorry for ourselves. We whined. We complained. We lashed out. We moped. And then, just as miraculously as it was every other time it happened, we snapped out of it. We picked ourselves up, shook off any remaining shards of regret and disappointment, and then turned our focus on full blast toward the next phase of our dreams — playing in the NFL. We could almost hear the roar of the crowds as we worked out, ran patterns and continued to condition ourselves for this tough new world of play we couldn't even imagine.

As the draft approached, memories swirled, fueling my imagination and stoking my dreams: That first day when Terry and I met and began throwing the football . . . When the allure of catching that football was a brand new novelty my only goal was to save Mr. Bradshaw's squash . . . Ninth grade football as an Oak

Terrace Trojan with Coach Bruce's 18-minute talk that changed everything about what I believed I could do . . . My mom's timeless — and oddly on point — advice about tenacity in football — and life . . . Glory days as a Woodlawn High School Knight . . . and then walking on as a Tech Bulldog.

And now, I thought as I opened my eyes on the day of the draft, I have a legitimate shot to play in the NFL. It was January 27, 1970 and the day for the 1970 NFL draft arrived at last. While the draft itself was being held behind closed doors at the faraway Belmont Plaza Hotel in New York City, the only thing there was to do was wait for a phone call.

We knew objectively — far beyond our own assessments and predictions — that Terry, touted as the most successful quarterback in collegiate history at that time, was on the radar to be the number one NFL draft pick that year. However, until that call actually came — and finding out from whom — everything was hanging, just waiting for the real celebration to begin.

This was, on all accounts, Terry's day, and I couldn't have been happier about that. Not only was he an amazing talent, but also Terry had worked hard every single day to do the very most he could with all that talent. This was his dream, something he had lived and breathed into life long before he ever knew me. So while I knew for sure that Terry's draft day story was going to be a happy one, I was growing less certain of mine by the moment.

To keep my mind out of that swirly place of endless speculation and recrimination, I tried not to think about my own draft possibilities at all. Besides, it was completely out of my hands at this point, so keeping my focus on being happy for Terry was really the best thing I could do.

I also knew that I, too, had done the very best I could with everything I had to work with, just as my mother had coached us all those years ago. "Tommeh," she'd say, trying to smooth back my unruly hair, "when you do the best you can, that's doing your part. Then you gotta let the Lawd take it from there."

So that's where I knew I stood with football. I did my best, so now it was time to have faith and be patient. Even though wait-and-see has never been my favorite game plan, sometimes that's just the way it is.

When I got the news that Terry had just officially gone down in history as the 1970 Number One NFL draft pick — drafted by the Pittsburgh Steelers, no less — it was a moment I'll never forget. It was in that same moment that I think I realized for the very first time what a rare and sacred experience it is to watch someone's dream come true. And how especially sweet it is when that someone happens to be your best friend.

"I don't think I'm going to be drafted," I said to Barbara as the sun set on Draft Day. It wasn't over by any means, but I just had this feeling that it might be time for me to start thinking about doing something else with my life. But what?

"Oh, Strawberry Shortcake, why do you say things like that?" she asked, her big, blue-green eyes crinkling with concern. "It's not over!"

I laughed at her use of "Strawberry Shortcake." It was our pet name from early in our relationship that stuck for some reason neither of us could really explain, only to be pulled out now on the most special of occasions.

"No, Barbara," I said, all business, "I think we just need to accept the possibility that I'm done with football and think about what else might be out there for me. Maybe my role to play in football is over — and now I get to go do something else."

She shook her head, chin set. "I'm not listening to one word of this, Tommy Spinks," she said.

"No, you have to," I urged. "Let's face it, Barb, facts are facts. And what Buddy wrote about me is probably right. I'm not someone the NFL is going to go after as a pick. I've been hearing it from too many people."

She shook her head. What a stubborn, beautiful, infuriating woman.

I looked at Barbara then with a kind of full, vulnerable openness I rarely allowed myself to expose to anyone except her. "Please, Barb. We have to talk about this. If I get passed over in the draft, what we have to figure out then is whether I need to go do something else, or if I should try out somewhere."

"Tommy. Stop," Barbara said, reaching over to turn up the volume on the radio that sat on our kitchen counter. "Let's just be quiet now, listen to some music, and dance a little bit in our kitchen. This draft is far from over, and I'm not going to let you give up so easily."

"Yes, dear," I said, throwing in my most dimpled smile for good measure as I swept her into my arms for one of our favorite pastimes — a slow dance in the kitchen to the Weekly Top 10. I knew better than to push this discussion any further.

And all that quiet time with emotions constantly fluctuating between "Leaving on a Jet Plane" and "I'll Never Fall in Love Again," I welcomed this strange, floaty time and space. Somehow managing to step back from all the emotion I had always wrapped around my dreams of this day, I just took a good look around — at my life, my future, and what other paths might be mine if the draft didn't happen for me.

Oddly, I wasn't as devastated at the thought of not being drafted as people likely thought and predicted I would be. I had enjoyed a great run with football — and as a bonus gift had gotten to play college ball with my best friend, a guy who might indeed fulfill his own prophesy and turn out to be the greatest quarterback of all time. All things considered, life could be a whole lot worse.

But now what? The question rolled around and around in my head all that day and all night, and it was still swirling when I woke up on Sunday morning. And, based on the continued set of Barbara's chin, I knew I'd best not ask it aloud.

In the meantime, Terry was making the rounds doing media interviews, a big party was being planned in Shreveport, and Barbara and I went about our business, making small talk, as if my entire career wasn't hanging in the balance, our future being determined by someone's whim in a hotel ballroom in New York City.

After we got home from church, we ate lunch as usual, with still no talk of the draft, which we both knew was still going on. Then, while Barbara was putting Kimberly down for a nap, I began walking around our tiny house. Not pacing, exactly, but restless and wandering, needing to put my mind on something — anything — besides what was or was not happening in New York City.

"It's gonna happen for you, Spinks," Terry had said when he called the night before to share all the excitement churning around his own news. This was the moment we had dreamed of since 9th grade, and I was not about to let my own angst ruin it.

Before we hung up, Terry had repeated his predictive encouragement, "It's gonna happen! I just know it!"

"I hope you're right," I had said. "I can't wait to find out who it is!" I added with much more conviction than I felt.

Now, here I was. Standing in front of the living room window, munching on a cookie, lost in my own thoughts, I heard the phone ring. Thinking nothing of it, I walked over to the kitchen and answered it.

"Is this Tommy Spinks?" asked the voice on the other end.

I made my way to the nearby table and sat down. Hard. "Yes," I said. Where has all the air gone?

"Is everything OK, Tommy?" Barbara asked as she came into the room. The concern on her face told me a lot about the expression that was probably on mine.

I nodded, and then returned my attention to the voice on the other end of the phone line. Finally, I found some words to answer the question I was being asked, "Thank you for the opportunity," I said. "I'm humbled and honored and won't let you down."

I hung up the phone and just sat there for a moment.

"Tommy? What is it?" Barbara insisted for about the seventh time. "You're scaring me!"

"Barbara," I said, taking her hand and looking up at her as she stood next to me, "I'm going to be a Minnesota Viking."

When Barbara started screaming and jumping up and down it seemed to complete my own mental circuit and I started hollering and jumping up and down right along with her. Then I picked her up and twirled her around and we collapsed into a laughing sobbing hysterical hug that lasted long enough for my head to stop spinning.

I looked at Barbara then, uncertain of what to say next. "I did it," I said. "I didn't think it was going to happen. And it did."

"You did it, Sweetheart," she said, "and I knew it was going to happen. I KNEW it!"

I hugged her tight. Then let her go. "We have to call some people!" I said, hurrying over to the phone and grabbing our address book. With Barbara sitting beside me, and Kimberly, too, who had somehow napped through the initial commotion, but loved joining in the dancing and hollering, I think we must have called every single person we had ever known.

The first call, of course, was to Mom and Dad — and as luck would have it, Betty and Joey had just arrived at my folks' house, coming over from Monroe for a Sunday afternoon visit.

"Mom?" I said, when my announcement was met with total silence.

"Your mother is too overcome to speak right now," came my dad's voice on the line. "She just handed me the phone and is now . . . well . . . in the midst of a *moment*. What's going on over there, Son? What happened?"

I could tell my dad was assuming the worst. "I got drafted!" I blurted. "Minnesota Vikings! They just called . . . and I'm pretty much in shock, too!"

My father burst out in relieved laughter. "That's just great, Tommy!" he boomed. "I am just so, *so* proud of you, Son — and so glad those NFL boys came to their senses!"

My mother then wrestled the phone away from my father and I could hear Betty and Joey whooping and hollering in the background.

"Tommeh," my mother began, her voice still shaking. "I am just . . . so . . . thrilled. You just don't know how hard I've been prayin' about this. You deserve it, Son, and so much more . . . I just . . . Why, I don't have any words . . ."

"We'll be right over, son," Dad said, reclaiming the phone from Mom. "Betty and Joey and Mom and I want to take y'all out to dinner to celebrate!"

"Johnny Maxwell's Holiday Inn Buffet!" I heard my sister say in the background.

Johnny's Holiday Inn Buffet was one of our family's favorite local eateries, and it was always crowded with people we knew — and anyone else who wanted a good, hot, home-cooked meal without cooking it themselves. This, I was guessing, would be my family's not-that-subtle way of making this announcement to the entire town of Ruston. From the buffet line, the news would spread within hours — small town communication at its primitive and highly effective best.

The line was long, and too many friends and acquaintances to count waved and greeted us as we joined the line. Then some of them began to look my way and I could tell they were whispering, perhaps wondering how things came out with the draft. Not many things stay secret in Ruston, so I waved and nodded my casual greetings until someone finally asked the question that was apparently on everyone's mind.

"Have ya heard anything yet, Tommy?"

"Well, as a matter of fact, I did get a call this afternoon," I said, pausing "for effect."

Out of the corner of my eye I saw her smile.

"Tell us!" someone called out. "What do ya know?"

"Folks, it looks like I'm going to be playing for the Minnesota Vikings!" I said, still having a little trouble actually believing those words, even as I said them.

A big cheer went up and the room came alive with chatter, clapping, and hurrahs, then all kinds of hugs and congratulations began pouring our way. After a time, and as the line finally began moving along — probably at the insistence of the proprietors — someone started a conga-line-music-styled chant, "MIN-ne-sota Vi-KINGS, MIN-ne-sota Vi-KINGS, MIN-ne-sota Vi-KINGS . . ."

In all the years that followed, no one in my family could think, hear, or read about the Minnesota Vikings without recalling — and usually repeating — that sweet chant. Terry may have had a huge celebration in Shreveport with half the town invited, but for me, that little Holiday Inn Buffet reception with my family and a great big slice of the Ruston community was just fine with me.

Barbara and I didn't sleep at all that night — we just lay there awake in our bed, laughing and talking and dreaming out loud about what our life was about to be like. Neither of us had ever been to Minnesota, but it sounded like a mystical place, a grand adventure magically placed on our horizon. We couldn't wait to begin.

A week later a check — my signing bonus — arrived in the mail. Barbara was visiting her mother for the day in Shreveport, so I got in the car, drove to Shreveport, and without a word, walked up to where she was standing in her mother's back yard and handed her the envelope with the check in it.

"What's this?" She asked as she opened the envelope.

I still said nothing, but instead waited for her response. The check was for $3,500, and to give a little context, Barbara's *annual* salary at TL James was, at that time, about $3,000. I waited and watched for the entire moment it took for the amount of that check to fully register.

Barbara looked up at me. "Is this . . ."

"It's my signing bonus," I said.

"So . . . Just . . . This check is . . . On top of what they'll pay you?"

"Yes!" I said, grabbing her and hugging her, crumpling the check between us. As I picked Barbara up and spun her around and around, I laughed and she squealed until we were both dizzy and breathless with pure, exhilarated joy.

Of all the deals I've ever made — and of *all* the big checks I have ever received — I'll never forget how, in that single moment, it was the richest I have ever felt in every possible way. Getting that check in the mail was like winning the lottery. I'm sure they told me about it when they called, but I was so shocked that I was being drafted that all the details flew right over my head. Little did those Viking boys know, I'd probably have signed with them for nothing.

CHAPTER 24

"You are NEVER going to believe the AMAZING thing that just happened," Terry said as he burst through our front door and landed in a giant sprawl on our sofa.

Now remember, we're talking about someone who was just the number one NFL draft pick for quarterback — someone who was about to go play professional football for the Pittsburgh Steelers.

"Try me," I said, laughing, "I can't begin to imagine what it might be."

Terry sat up and looked at me with the seriousness of a sniper. He gestured toward me with both hands, as if he was guiding me down the runway. "Spinks. I am going to be on the COVER of SPORTS ILLUSTRATED!"

"No freakin' way!" I said, jumping across the room to wrap my buddy in a big bear hug. "Bradshaw, that IS amazing." I laughed, "And just when we couldn't imagine how anything could be better than the Draft!"

"I know!" he said. "This has all been like some crazy dream, and then the phone rings this morning and this guy says he needs to set up an interview and do a photo shoot with me for SI. I was, like, what?!?!?!?! You're kidding me!!! And he was, like, 'No Mr. Bradshaw, I am not kidding. You're scheduled to be on our February cover and I need to set up this photo and interview as soon as possible.'"

My best buddy — on the cover of Sports Illustrated. For those of us who grew up haunting the mailbox every single month for that thing to arrive, then reading every single word on every single page — and then going back to reread the parts we were especially interested in, being on the cover of that hallowed publication amounted to being some kind of royalty.

This was a dream neither of us had ever even articulated, one of those accomplishments just too outlandish to name. And having it come true at that particular point in time was not only beyond Terry's wildest imaginings, but it allowed me to bask in the second-hand thrill with pride as authentic as it was immense. I was best friends with the King of the World!

• • •

As the people poured in for the annual Ruston Rotary Club banquet, I began to wonder if the Tech Student Center was going to be large enough to hold everyone. There looked to be 400 or so people already, and the energy in the room was palpable. Each year the Ruston Rotary Club presented special awards to our team, recognizing players who played well in their positions.

I received the Billy Moss Memorial award, "presented to the player who best exemplifies the qualities of integrity, character, and dependability." Buster Herren, was recognized as Outstanding Offensive Back, and the Louisiana Sports Writers Association and the league coaches named Coach Maxie Lambright "Coach of the Year."

The highlight of *this* particular year's Rotary awards, however, came when Tech honored Terry. For the first time in this club's long history, Dr. Jay Taylor, President of Louisiana Tech, announced as he held up Terry's number 12 jersey that they were retiring Terry's number, meaning that never again would number 12 be worn by a Louisiana Tech Bulldog football player.

With this announcement, the room erupted into cheers and applause as everyone leapt to their feet. This was such a joyful and overwhelming sight I had to do everything humanly possible to blink back my tears. It just wouldn't be cool for me to be up there blubbering like a fool.

Terry, too, was overwhelmed beyond words. As the applause went on and on, I glanced over at him just in time to see him blinking back the tears from his own eyes.

• • •

So that's enough, right? Both of us drafted to the NFL, Terry going as number one draft choice and then landing on the cover of Sports Illustrated — and *then* having his Number 12 permanently retired by the President of the University. What could possibly surpass all the amazing things that happened during those first two months of 1970?

We got invited to the White House to meet President Nixon.

There happened to be three of us on that Tech team who were drafted by the NFL: Terry, picked by the Pittsburgh Steelers, Larry Brewer by the Atlanta Falcons and me by the Minnesota Vikings. So along with Tech President Jay Taylor, Coach Maxie Lambright, and Rep. Joe Waggoner, Terry, Larry, and I found ourselves flying on Mr. Charles Wyly's private plane to Washington, D.C.

Terry nudged me as we entered the Oval Office.

Is this really happening? My mind swirled and I somehow resisted the urge to pinch myself.

Then, during the next 20 minutes we got to meet President Nixon, and one by one, each of us shook his hand, and then we all presented him with a football that we had signed. After exchanging some back and forth conversation with our nation's President — and for the life of me I can't even remember what we talked about — we took pictures in all combinations, and then, just as strangely and miraculously as we found ourselves in the Oval Office, we were climbing back aboard Mr. Wyly's plane, headed back to Ruston. When I recall this amazing moment, I probably should admit that as giddy as we were to meet the President, we might have been just as excited to get to ride in Mr. Wyly's private plane.

• • •

"Oh my God, Tommy, are you OK?" I heard Barbara cry as I hit the water.

We had gone out for a weekend horseback ride with our friends, Fabe and Linda Mosely, and the horse I was riding decided that where I really needed to be, rather than on his back, was flying head first into a shallow pond we were galloping past.

"Yeah, I'm OK," I said, sitting up in the slimy sludge and grateful for its cushioning of my fall. About the last thing I needed to take with me to Minnesota was a broken leg. "Stupid horse," I said, sloshing to the bank. The horse, looking innocent and mildly concerned, stood just a little past the end of the pond and made no objection when I took the reins and began to lead him beside the others. "Could you just take it easy on me until we get back to the barn?" I asked him as we made our way — me walking beside him this time — back to the barn.

A few days later, I was in the hospital. Somehow, in my jaunt into the pond I had contracted an amoeba called Naegleria Fowleri that had then moved into my sinus cavity. To say this was more pain than I had ever experienced in my life up until then was the understatement of the year. And the worst part was that none of the doctors seemed to know what was causing this excruciating pain.

As I lay there, screaming and writhing and clutching my head, Barbara cried and kept trying to get the attention of the doctors and nurses. It seemed to both of us that no one in the hospital knew what they were doing — or cared that I was in terrible pain and might be dying.

I looked over at one point to see Barbara dialing the telephone in my room. Looking back at me with a tear-streaked face, she said, "I'm calling Dr. Hall."

"Barbara, I don't know what's wrong with me, but I'm pretty sure I'm not having a baby," I managed to say through gritted teeth. Dr. Hall was her obstetrician.

"Tommy, he's our friend," she said, "and he'll know what to do." The pure fright in her eyes made me stop my protest as she waited for someone to answer on the other end of the line.

"Hello?" I could hear Dr. Hall's voice coming through the receiver.

At the sound of Dr. Hall's fatherly voice, Barbara froze, just gripping the phone. Even from as far away as I was, I could see that her knuckles had gone white. Then she just began to sob into the phone. Somehow, between convulsive gasps, Barbara managed to convey the gist of what was going on to Dr. Hall.

"Barbara, Tommy is going to be okay," I heard him say. "Hand the phone to a nurse."

Barbara complied, still sobbing uncontrollably.

Within minutes, a whole new crew of people were coming into my room, taking my vitals, asking me questions, starting an IV and pumping medicine into me that, within the hour, stopped my horrific head pain. I drifted into the first sleep I had been able to have in days.

"Thank you so much for everything," I heard Barbara say. "I was just so scared — and I didn't know what else to do. I hope we're not taking too much time away from your OB patients," Barbara said, suddenly self-conscious.

I opened my eyes. There was Dr. Hall, right there in my room.

"I have another doctor taking care of them this evening," I heard Dr. Hall say. "I just wanted to come over here and make sure Tommy is doing better."

Barbara looked over at me, suddenly exhausted. Although she was not able to take any of that horrible pain away, she had been fighting it just as hard as I was, every step of the way. "He is, I think," she said, "thanks to you."

He patted her on the shoulder. "I'm glad you called me, and glad that I was able to help. If you ever need me again, you just give me a call any time." He picked up my chart that was hanging at the end of my bed. He flipped through the pages, nodded his head a few times, and then made a few notes for the nurses. "I'll not bother him now," he said to Barbara. "He needs to sleep. But I'll stick around for a little while until the labs come back and make sure of what we're dealing with."

When I was well enough to leave the hospital after nine days, I knew it was Dr. Hall who had saved my life. Climbing gingerly into the passenger side of our Ford Fairlane with the help of Barbara and a nurse, I was filled with a new appreciation for all the blessings in my life — and what a gift every day really is.

When we arrived back at our house, Terry met me at the door. After helping Barbara get me settled, he perched on the end of my bed. "You know, Spinks," he said, "I was kind of scared I might not ever get to see your big ole' ugly face again." He paused then, for a really long time, as his face grew more serious than I think I had ever seen it. "Don't scare me like that ever again, Spinks."

"Oh, ya big weirdo, I'm not goin' anywhere," I said, laughing as if the earnestness of his concern hadn't touched my heart.

We both sat there for a long quiet moment, and then Terry wiped at his eye with the heel of his hand and shifted his tone to something way more practical.

"So when can you work out?" he said.

"Doc said as soon as I feel up to it," I replied. "He said to take it easy at first, but I should be good as new in a few more days."

"Will you feel up to it tomorrow?" he pressed.

"I'm planning on it!" I said.

Standing up to leave, Terry said, "By the way, we're supposed to be at some big event next month, a convention where we're supposed to sign autographs."

"Cool," I said. And I meant it. I was going to enjoy every single minute of my life from now on, even the awkward public appearances.

"There's also going to be a big 'Terry Bradshaw' day coming up before the semester's over." He paused for a beat and grinned. "Yep, Spinks, you heard me right. Terry . . . Bradshaw . . . Day. Isn't that something?"

Without waiting for my reply, Terry exited my room — and then he poked his head back through the doorway. "Did I mention there's going to be a Terry Bradshaw Day?"

I nailed him in the face with a pillow before he could duck. If there was anyone more deserving of a day named after him, it was my buddy Terry.

• • •

With the dawning of Terry Bradshaw Day came a spectacular event the likes of which Ruston had rarely seen. In true Ruston fashion, the entire town came out to share their love for Terry.

I laughed and nudged Terry to point out the guy on stilts, but before he could make a classic Bradshaw remark, another mob of kids descended. By even the most conservative estimate, I bet he signed 5,000 autographs that day, scribbling his name on everything from bits of paper to arm casts to backs of shirts and bills of ball caps. Kids were literally everywhere we looked.

The Tech cheerleaders were there, doing all the old favorite cheers, and the whole Tech band played everyone's favorites and then some to keep the momentum going strong. Everyone there had a blast, and the excitement, love, and pure joy of this town that surrounded us bathed us like warm Louisiana rain.

For Terry, there was more going on during this day than just soaking up the adulation like I was. Because he was still negotiating his contract with the Steelers, sports writers from all over the country had appeared out of nowhere and a few of them were trying to get a rise out of Terry by asking ill-intentioned questions to provoke him into saying something that would make a good story for their papers.

This was such a different scenario than what we were used to with the press — a different kind of circus that was just beginning for him as we started to realize that not all reporters had good intentions. I stood there beside Terry as he fielded some of these ridiculous questions, and I did my best not to react to some of these mean-spirited Bozos.

It's a rare moment in life when you get to see how your unwitting early preparation is called into use by a situation that, otherwise, you'd have never been equipped to handle. In true Bradshaw fashion, Terry used his well-honed sense of humor to redirect this trouble, offering perfect humorous non-responses to every incendiary question. For Terry, the biggest lesson from Terry Bradshaw Day was a new awareness that there are people out there who don't care who they hurt or step on to get what they want.

• • •

As the school year wound to a close, things were finally getting back to normal — albeit an eerie new normal just waiting for the other shoe to drop. As Terry and I busied ourselves with our workouts and trying to learn everything we possibly could about the NFL teams we would be playing for, we tried to ignore the fact that soon we'd be leaving Tech and moving on to divergent paths for the first time since the day we met, back in the summer before ninth grade.

One sweltering summer afternoon after an especially intense workout, I was grateful to arrive home to the smell of a home-cooked meal on the table. Barbara and Kimberly were sitting at the dinner table, all dressed up, waiting for me. Barbara looked so happy — and so beautiful — and she seemed especially excited.

"What's the occasion?" I asked, washing my hands in the nearby sink and settling in to my place at the table to fill my plate with the delicious meal before me.

She smiled, "Tommy, we just have so much to be thankful for," she said. "Just think. You're going to the NFL, Terry's going to the NFL, I've got such a great job working for the James family . . ." She beamed across the table at me.

It's so sweet to see her overflowing like this with happiness, I thought as I dug into my dinner.

" . . . and we are going to have another baby."

For a moment it didn't register what she had just said. One minute I was chewing my food and smiling as she was talking, and the next I was almost choking on a full bite of black-eyed-peas as the news she had just delivered crossed paths with my need to swallow.

"Wait," I said, sputtering just a little as I reached for my iced tea. "Did you just say . . . we are going to have another *baby*?"

Barbara nodded, and then her smile faded into worry. "I know," she said. "It's so soon after having Kimberly, and you're about to go to training . . . and then we're moving to Minnesota . . . but . . ."

I stopped her right there, leaping from my chair, lifting her up from hers and twirling her around as I laughed out loud. "I don't care if it's too soon or not!" I said, adding Kimberly to our dance, her excited giggles now mixing with ours.

Just when I thought my heart couldn't hold one more bit of happiness, here was a brand new reason to be thankful for the life I was given. We danced around and around right there in the middle of the dining room until Barbara's expression let me know that a freshly expectant mom might not ought to twirl so much. I eased her back down into her chair and then continued the dance with Kimberly.

Life was good beyond anything I ever imagined. Sometimes the best dreams are the ones that arrive even before you dream them.

CHAPTER 25

"Football is not fo-evah," my mother said as she put a slice of her famous chocolate cake down on the table in front of me. We had stopped by with Kimberly for a visit and unwittingly unleashed this all too familiar diatribe, and I honestly had no idea how to make it stop.

As it became obvious to my parents that I had no intention nor desire to finish my final semester and graduate with my class, the pressure to finish my degree before I left for Minnesota began to build. The reason for all this degree hysteria was a mystery to me. I had a job, for crying' out loud — and a huge signing bonus in hand.

"Mom," I'd reason every time this came up, which was with increasing regularity as the semester, and then the summer, wore on, "I am going to play professional football. That is what I went to college for. That is what I learned how to do well enough that an NFL team has hired me. They are going to pay me a lot of money to play football for them. I did what I needed to do, and now that I'm signed I need to concentrate on getting myself ready for my new job — not getting some piece of paper to frame and hang on the wall."

"That piece of paaapah you're talkin' about is what you're gonna need to support yoah family once football is ovah," my mother would insist. "And Tommeh, you mark mah words, football is *not* fo-evah."

"Yes, mother, I know," I said, after repeating those now-infamous words under my breath right along with her. I was trying not to be short with her, but dang she was on my last nerve with this.

Usually during these discussions Dad would nod, clear his throat, and advise me to listen to my mother. *Whose side is he on, anyway?* I'd think every time this happened. He seemed completely oblivious to my imploring eyes that were begging him silently, *Reason with her, would you please?*

Barbara always managed to stay out of it when I was under fire with Grace. She usually busied herself taking care of Kimberly and left me to fend for myself.

"There's no good that can come," she'd remind me later, "from my getting crossways with my mother-in-law over a battle nobody is going to win." Then she'd kiss me and say, "I have absolute faith, Tommy Spinks, that we are going to be able to support our family no matter what you decide about finishing school — or whatever happens *after* football."

Then she'd flash that impish grin that made me fall in love with her all over again, "Because, Tommy . . .," she'd drawl in a perfect Grace impression, " . . . Football is not fo-evah," we'd say in unison before I punctuated it with a great big eye roll.

I'm not sure anyone fully understood the pressure I now felt to "get ready" for this major jump into the unknown. I needed this time for anything but sitting in a classroom taking some stupid tests and writing stupid papers for no good reason at all.

I ended up appeasing my mother with a sincere promise that I would finish school and get that degree for the wall between seasons. It was the only way I knew of to get her off my back and keep from ruining what remained of my time at home.

Graduating from college was not my dream — it was hers. And in May of 1971 I made it come true. Whether or not football was going to be my "fo-evah" career, I saw to it that Grace Spinks' son was a college graduate, and I will "fo-evah" have that framed piece of paper on my wall to prove it.

• • •

"Well, bud, I guess this is it," I heard myself say in the moment neither Terry nor I really ever fully believed was coming. It was July of 1970, and the very next morning Terry would head to Pittsburgh and I would head to Minnesota.

It was a surreal moment, and right up until we actually said good-bye, I don't think it fully dawned on either of us that we wouldn't be playing together anymore.

We attempted an awkward handshake that turned into a bear hug. "Can't believe we're really doing this," I said, trying very hard not to get choked up, but failing somewhat.

"Yeah," Terry said, "me neither. It's all we ever dreamed of, but now that it's really here I just can't quite believe it."

"You're gonna do great," I said. And I meant it. It was so cool to see Terry's dream of playing in the NFL coming true. Even though it was a contagious dream that I had somehow caught, somewhere along the way, all along this was a dream that was, first and foremost, Terry's.

"*You're* gonna do great," Terry echoed. "Just don't let anybody give you any crap about your size or speed," he added. "You've got plenty of both — and you're better than you think you are. Don't you ever forget that."

"Thanks, Bud," I said. "I'm gonna miss ya."

"Oh, don't go getting all slobbery on me, Spinks," he said, giving me a playful shove. "But I'm gonna miss your ugly face, too. Keep it real."

"Always do."

And with that we were off, each on our own path to the future we had dreamed about together for as long as we had known each other. Except ironically, from now on we'd each be continuing this dream on our own. I can still feel the sting of that moment — and a sadness I didn't anticipate and wasn't at all prepared for. For the first time, I felt alone in this dream.

• • •

One of the first things I learned when I got to Minnesota — and I later found out this feeling was the same for Terry in Pittsburgh — was that nothing can truly prepare a college player for the NFL. Everything about this experience is on a whole 'nutha' level.

"What do you mean?" Barbara would ask in our frequent phone conversations. I was missing my girls like crazy, and while we also wrote letters, every few days I just needed to hear her voice.

"All of the players are just so big, fast, quick — and angry," I said. "They're all on a personal mission to jack you up."

"Oh, surely not," Barbara would say, unable to grasp the particulars of the misery of an NFL rookie in training camp for the first time. "You've just got to get to know them, Tommy. Deep inside they're probably all guys just about like you — focused, intense, dedicated. Maybe once you get to know them better it won't feel that way."

There are some things that you ought not to even try to explain. You can only learn how to play in the NFL by *playing* in the NFL. It's the ultimate trial by fire. And until I got there, I had no idea what I was getting myself into. From day one, my only focus was survival — both in the physical sense and in not getting cut so I could actually play. Both, from the outset, were not looking so good.

For Terry, who reported living through some of these same lessons himself over in Pittsburgh, there was also an enormous amount of pressure from the expectations that came along with being the number one draft pick. And every time I talked to him during those first few months, I could tell he was feeling every bit of it.

At that time the Steelers were the worst team in the NFL — which is why they got the number one draft pick in the first place — and they believed that Terry was going to come in and singlehandedly save their team — in his first season.

"It's just so *different*," he told me in one of our many commiserating phone conversations. "These men are playing for *money*. This is their business, and they don't really mind killing somebody if that's what they need to do to keep their jobs."

This, it goes without saying, but I'll say it anyway, was a rude awakening for both of us. In this smarter, more calculated game, people were being paid to study your reflexes and instincts — and they counted on you to do the same.

For Terry, the misery of that first year seemed to be mostly rooted in his being just a rookie trying to acclimate to this new level of football with no margin of error. At first he was riding high as their darling — an instant star on their field — dazzling them silly during those first few appearances.

However, the honeymoon appeared to be short-lived. He was going out there and playing the game just as he always had, but he wasn't and couldn't be prepared for the defensive level of play he was up against.

The next thing he knew, that same crowd that was cheering and celebrating their good fortune of receiving the #1 collegiate quarterback during the draft was booing him after one interception in his very first game. Knowing Terry the way I did, and hearing the pain behind his words as he told this story, I railed against this complete unfairness. "What's wrong with these people?" I asked, again and again.

The Terry I knew so well was way too much of a people pleaser to be able to brush off that kind of rejection. He was taking it personally. As hard as I was struggling physically, he was fighting that same level of battle on the mental and emotional fronts. He honestly believed that he was failing everyone, and this continued through that whole first season with the Steelers.

Some people would grow thicker skin; for Terry, this wasn't so easy. It still breaks my heart to think back on this time for Terry. He was just a kid, toes barely wet, facing what would be some of his darkest moments as he began to actually live the dream he had worked so hard his whole life to achieve.

We all know the rest of the story and what Terry eventually was able to do for the Steelers, the game of football, the Rooney family, and the city of Pittsburgh. But no one had a crystal ball during that first year to be able to tell him what shining triumphs lay ahead.

• • •

Meanwhile, over in Minnesota I was up to my ears in great big angry guys, that same old refrain I had heard all my life playing louder and louder in my exhausted ears. "Too small" . . . "Too slow" . . . "Spindly" . . . "Skittering" . . . And, for the first time in my entire life, I was beginning to think those words just might be true.

Maybe I can't do this. Came the quiet thought, maybe for the first time in my life.

As someone who was used to being doubted by others, from Oak Terrace Junior High all the way through my gold-plated, record-breaking run at Louisiana Tech, I had never, even for a moment, doubted myself.

"You've had to fight to be recognized for your talent since we were kids," Terry told me in a now rare phone conversation when I shared my uncharacteristic angst.

It was always good to hear his voice. I had forgotten what it was like to be encouraged, to feel some connection with the guy throwing the ball. And, as goofy as this may sound, while Terry had thrown to lots of other receivers all along, I had only ever caught for Terry. That, plus the symbiosis created in all those endless hours of throwing that ball back and forth, amounted to a loss I felt acutely every time I stepped onto the field.

"Tommy, don't forget that the doubters always, eventually, saw what I've always seen in you as a player," Terry reminded me. "And remember, you've always said that there are no accidents — that everything happens for a reason. There has to be some reason for all this you're going through — and you *will* get through it!"

I wasn't so sure. Surrounded by veterans of the NFL, I was having a hard time imagining any good reason for this sudden, unexpected doubt I was feeling about the game I loved, the dream I had chased since the ninth grade, and my own ability to do what I knew how to do.

This was a cold business, I was realizing. If you don't produce, you're gone. Just like that. No one cares whether you make it or not.

"Barbara, I don't know if I can do this," I said. I was calling her one evening after practice, after the ice bath my aching body was seeming to require more and more of these days.

"Of course you can," she said. "I know it's hard, but you can do this. You've worked so hard all your life for this — and now you're here! You're doing it Tommy! You just have to have faith that God put you here — and will help you through this struggle."

I knew she was right, but she couldn't possibly know how hard this was. When you tell someone 'this is hard' they think they know what you mean. She had no idea. I was working my guts out, every minute I was out on that field, and no matter how hard I tried, it seemed that nothing I could do was good enough. This was a terrible feeling, and one I had never experienced before.

"Barb, these guys are good. And they're fast. And they don't make mistakes."

"Neither do you," she said. "You're just as good as they are or you wouldn't be there," she added. "Now you need to just settle down and be grateful for this opportunity. You're going to make it Tommy. You can do it."

It was kind of an odd, but wonderful reversal of roles. I was always the positive one, the encourager in our relationship. And now that I had somehow lost the faith in my abilities and myself that has always been the largest part of my success, Barbara had somehow managed to pick it back up, dust it off, and hand it back to me.

"I think you're doing better than you think you are," she said.

"Oh really?" I retorted. "I didn't see you out there while I was getting my brains beat out. How could you possibly know that?"

"I just know," she said.

I remembered the set of her chin when an argument was settled, and I could see it in my mind's eye. This time, however, I pressed on. "You know what they always say about me, Barb? This time I really think it might be true."

"Nonsense," she snorted. "Like what?"

"That I'm too small."

"Do I need to call your mother?"

"Oh dear God, no, please don't," I said, imagining Grace Spinks showing up here to straighten me — and those other boys — out. "Besides, I also think it's speed, Barb. I just don't think I'm fast enough."

"That's ridiculous," she said, refusing to even entertain my theories.

"It's *true*, I pressed. They keep telling me I have to get faster. And I'm trying — you just don't know how hard I'm trying — and this just might be as fast as I'll ever be."

"Which quite possibly might be fast enough," she said. "You do remember the joke about the bears and the hikers, don't you?"

"Yes, Barbara, I remember the joke about the bear and the hikers," I sighed, then quoted "I don't have to outrun the bear, I just have to outrun you."

"Exactly," she said, and then parried, "So who can't you beat? Bob Grim?"

"No, I can beat Bob Grim," I said, exasperated with this line of reasoning. "Geez, Barbara, give me some credit, willya?"

"Harrison Wood?"

"Well, yeah, I can usually beat Harrison. Most days."

"Gayle Knies?"

"Now *he's* the one I have to beat, I think, for a spot on the roster. And yes, I've beaten him a few times — in fact, more often than not."

"So who is it that you can't beat out there, Tommy?" she persisted.

"Well, Gene Washington, for one," I said triumphant that I could at last prove my point. "And John Henderson," I added. "I've *never* beaten Gene and can only beat John on a *really* good day, which I rarely have any more."

"Isn't Gene all-pro?" she asked as if she didn't even hear that last part.

What a smart aleck "Yes, he's all-pro, Barbara," I said. "So what?"

"So you're telling me, Tommy Spinks, that of the *six* receivers there, you can beat all but the all-pro and the veteran receiver? And would that also be the one who was said to be *key* to sending the number one team in the NFL last year to the Super Bowl?" I could feel her irritating positive energy crackling through the phone line. "Are you *listening* to yourself?"

"Yeah, but Barb that's just it. They can only keep *four* receivers and there are *six* of us. Two of us are going to get cut."

"Well it's not going to be you," she said, as if that settled it once and for all. "How are you catching?"

"I'm catching pretty well, actually," I said, somewhat buoyed by her calm, analytical reasoning and unshakable confidence in me as I was clinging to the last shard of my own self-confidence for dear life. "If it was just about catching the ball I don't think I'd have a worry in the world."

"If you have a worry in the world, it's because you *choose* to have a worry in the world," she said. "You've got this Tommy. Just believe it."

I hated hearing my own words ricocheting back at me and hitting me right between my own eyes.

"I'm trying, baby," I said. "Please just know how hard I'm trying." *Only God really knows how hard I'm trying.* I thought. *Or how sick to my stomach I feel when I come off the field after a crummy day.*

"I know you are," she said, her voice softening a bit to let the love creep in. "You just keep on doing what you do and being who you are, and let God take care of the rest."

That night, after my phone conversation with Barbara, was the first good night's sleep I had since I entered training camp.

There was an odd parallel, really, between Terry's and my rookie training camp experiences. The pure misery of this ugly reality we had discovered just inside the front door of our biggest dream was as shocking as it was devastating. This was *not* how living our dream was supposed to feel.

• • •

"Spinks, you'd better start catching the ball and showing me something," Lionel, the backfield coach, said to me, pausing for a moment with a meaningful glare before moving on to the next guy. We were gathered in the locker room after practice, and Lionel was going to each of the receivers, one by one, with his critique and recommendations.

I hung my head, exhausted and dejected. I had dropped a few out there that day, which was unusual for me. Except now it was starting to happen more and more often. And the more it happened, the harder it got to think of anything else.

"Every time I drop a ball in practice, all I can think about is dropping another one," I confided to Barbara in a letter. "I feel so inadequate — like a complete failure."

Another problem I was facing in practice was my lack of opportunity to up my averages. Everyone knows the best way to work through a slump is to work through it. In these daily practices I got to take part in maybe one out of every five passing drills — not enough to get the bugs out of my head about dropping that ball. In fact, the Vikings were using very few passing drills in their workouts at all.

Instead, we did mostly "skeleton drills," which test the defense with the team's own running attack. And, because it was the backfield coach who was also in charge of the receivers, there was no receiver coach I could work with or talk to or ask for more specific help.

These things, as it turned out, were all clues to the reason for the misfit I was starting to realize I was in. Minnesota was a ground attack team; they really didn't throw the ball much at all.

As training camp ebbed on, several things became painfully obvious to me: they were going to have to cut someone — two someones, actually, to get from six receivers to four. While I knew I could catch as well as any of them, the truth was my speed was an issue. But, as Barbara had wisely pointed out, I only had to beat two of them.

But then what? Even if I did somehow manage to live through training camp and actually make the final cut, would I ever get to play?

About once a week I'd get a letter from Mom and Dad, and in it would always be an article, an inspirational quote, or an encouraging message scrawled in Mom's familiar, old-fashioned handwriting. The fact that she sent these things to me meant the world. And, while I did try some of the mental toughness tips and tricks she sent — as if she knew exactly what my darkest struggle had become — nothing seemed to help very much. I was in a hole way too deep to "positive self-talk" my way out of.

• • •

"So I got in a bar fight today," I told Barbara late one evening in our phone call, which by now had become almost nightly. I was so homesick it hurt. Also every bone in my body hurt. Calling home and talking to Terry once a week or so to compare notes and commiserate were the only things that didn't hurt, so I was all too glad to do more of them.

"Tommy!" Barbara said, alarm ringing through the phone. "Are you OK? What in the world were you doing in a bar? You don't even drink . . . Do you?"

I laughed. Man, that felt good. Hadn't done much of that lately. "Well, it wasn't actually in a bar," I teased, "It was more about the bar."

Knowing me as she did, she knew it was safe now to relax. "Do tell," she urged.

I had more or less made myself a target a few days after arriving for training camp when we all went to the pizza place and I ordered a Coke instead of beer.

Later on that evening, one of the Viking veteran fullbacks, came over to the table where I was sitting with a full pitcher of beer. After he filled the other guys' mugs, he had turned to me and said, "where's yours?"

When I told him I didn't drink alcohol, he feigned a girlish faint.

Soon after that, the veterans decided what our "rookie initiation" would be. On a designated evening, all the rookie players were supposed to show up at a particular bar, and the veteran players were going to get all the rookies drunk.

Now, up until then, I had never had a drop of alcohol in my body in my whole life, and I wasn't about to change that at the whim of some big assholes trying to make a point, whatever that point might be. *Whether I end up staying with this team or not, they might as well learn right now how stubborn I can be when it comes to standing up for what I believe in,* I reasoned.

So I just didn't show up. Apparently when they realized I wasn't coming, their next idea was to come to my hotel room to get me.

I heard a loud banging on the door and some slurred hollering outside. I'm not sure what possessed me to open that door, but when I did all hell broke loose.

Funny thing about alcohol, though. When even very large individuals have enough of it in their systems, even a "scrawny, skittering, lightweight" can hold his own when provoked into a fight. The trouble was, I wasn't sure how long it was going to be before one of their drunk, meaty fists landed a punch on me somewhere that would do some damage.

Just in time, I think, a veteran named Jim Marshall appeared out of nowhere to stop the fight. Even better, because they really respected him, he told them never to bother me again. In later years Jim would turn out to be one of the most famous Vikings ever, but from that moment on he was my very favorite, for sure — a Good Samaritan for whom my unbroken bones and I thanked my lucky stars. How did he know?

"Thank you, Jim," I managed to say as I shook his hand.

He grinned. "Don't mention it," he said. He paused. "You know Spinks, I think it's very cool the way you stood up to those guys. Hell, I'm not sure you even needed me. I think you were about to get the best of them!"

I laughed. "No, I was just barely holding my own," I said. "And when the alcohol wore off they would have pounded me into jelly."

After Jim ambled away, I sat there on the ledge outside my hotel room door for a few minutes, catching my breath and looking around. Those within the sightline of this brouhaha might have thought I was pondering the outcome. Truth? I wasn't sure my shaking legs would be able to hold me up well enough to walk.

CHAPTER 26

From the moment I arrived in Mankato, Minnesota for Vikings training camp, I wondered every single day if that would be the day I would be cut from the roster. Living under that kind of pressure is something I had never experienced, could never until now have imagined, and had no idea how to cope with.

Minnesota had won the National Football League Championship the year before and had a very strong, veteran-powered team. Besides me, there was only one other rookie wide receiver signed, and he was playing on and off with the veterans.

Me? Not so much.

Even though I knew I could catch the ball as well as anyone else on the team, and my speed was pretty good and getting better, for some reason I wasn't getting much of an opportunity to show them what I could do. They weren't playing me, even in scrimmages, and this only fueled my constant worry that I was about to be cut from the team any day.

"They are supposed to cut about 10 more players on Thursday," I told reporters gathered at the gate after practice one Monday. "I might be one of them."

While I knew that Barbara, and above all my mother, were not going to like seeing that quote from me in the newspapers, I figured I might as well prepare everyone for what, to me, was pretty obvious.

We were down to the wire, and two of the six receivers were going to have to be cut — and soon.

"I'm afraid my speed is going to hurt me," I went on to explain to the eagerly scribbling sportswriters. I may have also pointed out to them that the Gulf States Conference and the National Football League have little else in common other than they both play on a field 100 yards long. So just because I was fast enough to set records back *there* didn't mean that I was in a league with these guys.

"Boy, are these guys *fast*!" I elaborated, referring mostly to Washington, but also to Henderson and Grim. "They run patterns quicker than I do, and Minnesota's posts are designed for quick moves."

While I had generally accepted that nobody could stay with Washington, I was doing pretty well staying with the others. By then my confidence had returned, and I seemed to be catching the ball as well as any of them.

The rigor of training camp had also done another couple of things for me. My weight was now up to 185, and all my speed work was starting to pay off. I was pretty sure I was faster than I ever was in college, and I knew for sure I was much quicker off the line.

As far as I could tell, Gayle Knies was still the guy I had to beat to grab that number four spot as a receiver. And, after spending the past two seasons on the Viking taxi squad, Knies knew the same thing about me.

I was still beyond homesick, but with my hard work and all the encouragement I was getting from home — and every week or so in phone calls with Terry — I was somehow emerging from the deep dark hole I had fallen into, and I was starting to make the turn back toward who I used to be. Above all, I was still hanging in there when rookies across the nation were cleaning out their lockers and heading for home.

Not just yet, Spinks, I told myself in good moments. *Just keep showing up, working hard, and keeping the faith. Let's see what happens.*

• • •

As I suited up for our first exhibition game against New Orleans I had no idea what to expect. Things had been going better in practice, and after surviving the cut for this long, a little bit of hope was starting to glimmer deep inside me that maybe, just maybe, I might make this roster after all.

To my shock and amazement, not only did I get a little playing time in that game against New Orleans, but I actually caught two passes — a sideliner for about 15 yards and a quickset for five or six yards. We ended up losing the game 14-13, but as far as I was concerned, snagging some playing time and catching two passes was about as good as it gets.

Then came the less good part.

I also saw some action on the kickoff team — also known in pro football as the "suicide squad" — and I learned firsthand that day why it had that handle. Those guys hunt you down and try to kill you. I am not kidding.

For the first time in my entire football career, I was literally afraid for my life. I'm pretty sure this state of mind did very little for my effectiveness, but I did somehow manage to get in on the tackle not once, but twice. And, if it weren't for the guy who nearly broke my jaw with his forearm, I would say that I emerged from this opportunity unscathed.

Still, did I mention that I caught two passes?

• • •

Suiting up for my second NFL exhibition game as a Minnesota Viking, the old familiar pre-game anticipation surged. And on top of the possibility of again seeing some playing time, the team we were playing was Pittsburgh, and I couldn't wait to see how Terry was faring.

It was hard to imagine that after 10 years of playing together Terry and I would be on opposite teams, but as luck would have it, in that Minnesota stadium both team benches were on the same side of the field. Every time the Steeler defense took the field I'd move to the end of our bench and Terry would come to the end of the Steeler bench and we could talk.

"You know, no one really prepares you for the sounds you hear at an NFL scrimmage line," I told him the first time we got to talk. "It sounds like a bunch of animals out there."

Terry laughed. "That it do," he said.

"First time I heard it, I was *skeered*," I said, bugging my eyes out.

"Me too," Terry said, laughing, in a conspiratorial whisper.

During these opportunities throughout the game, we caught up on news from home, where the other guys on the Tech team were and what they were doing. It was nice, easy conversation, and a mental break that did me good. Even though I'm sure he was aware things weren't going so well for me, both of us knew talking about it wasn't going to solve anything.

This, it turned out, was the most action I'd see in that game. The Steelers won, 20-13, and I have to admit to feeling a little second-hand pride when I overheard the Viking veterans marveling over how hard Terry threw the football.

After the game I hurried to get dressed and head to the Steeler locker room to see Terry before he had to go back to Pittsburgh with his team.

"You can't go in there," the guard at the locker room door said.

"But . . ." I said, spotting Terry and waving.

"TOMMY SPINKS!" Terry hollered from across the locker room.

The guard turned around to see Terry motioning me to come in, so, shrugging, he let me in.

"Guys, I want you to meet my ole' buddy Tommy Spinks," Terry drawled. I could tell by the interactions all around me that these guys really liked Terry, or "Brad" as they called him.

"Man," I told him, "you shoulda heard how the guys on my team were talking about your arm. They said they had never seen anybody throw the ball like that."

I was glad to deliver this compliment to Terry in person, in front of his new team. He seemed glad about that, too. I'm not sure he had heard many, if any, compliments like that from the people he was now surrounded by, and it didn't hurt to let them know what kind of quality they were taking for granted.

• • •

"So . . . How was Terry?" Barbara asked me in our nightly phone call the Sunday evening after the Pittsburgh game.

"Oh, he's great!" I said. "I've never seen him passing better. And all our guys — even the vets — were saying they had never seen a guy throw the ball that hard with that kind of accuracy. He really dazzled everyone."

"And his team is treating him OK?"

"Oh, yeah, Barbara, you should have seen him with them — both on the field and in the locker room — they seem to really like him. And best of all, I think they are already starting to appreciate him and what a great leader he is." I paused, remembering how they listened to him. "I'm really so glad for him, Barb. He deserves it. And having his team behind him goes a long way. Even if he still has some struggles ahead with the fans appreciating him, I really think he's really going to help that team. It may take a while for it to show up in the win-loss columns, but they have the right guy for the job." I laughed. "And they sure didn't have any trouble with us," I added.

"But you didn't get to play at all?"

"No."

"I'm sorry, Tommy. I was really hoping that after they let you play some against New Orleans they'd at least give you a little bit of playing time."

"Yeah, me too," I said, trying not to sound as disappointed as I felt. "But I guess those other rookies need a chance, too," I reasoned, thinking back to the days when Terry and I got pulled from the Tech games to give others some playing time. The optimist in me hoped that I did well enough against the guys who got to play this week, but the realist in me knew otherwise. I knew better than to voice any of this to Barbara.

"Next week," she said, as if there was no question.

"Or maybe next week I'll be back home and we can watch it on TV together," I said.

"Stop it."

"Can't. Facts are facts, baby. They have to cut someone and it's looking like it's gonna be me."

"Well, that's going to be a problem," she said, "because your parents and Kimberly and I are going to be in that Astrodome so you'd better be there, too." She paused. "Goodnight, Tommy. I love you."

The Ruston Leader summed up my role in the Houston game much better and more succinctly than I ever could: *"The*

Vikings went against the Houston Oilers on national television last week and Spinks, wearing jersey number 24, was seen pacing the sidelines."

It's a really good thing, I think, that this was back before the days when there were microphones everywhere on the sidelines. It probably wouldn't have been good for anyone to hear what I was saying as I paced along that sideline and watched everyone else play the game I loved. I knew right then I was done. Regardless of the Vikings' decision about my future with them, I had made my own.

• • •

"Coach?" I said, rapping the open door with two knuckles. "Can I talk to you for a minute?"

"Sure, Tommy," Coach Grant said. "Come on in." He looked up from the papers he was reading. "What can I do for you?"

I reached behind me and shut the door.

Coach Grant cleared his throat. "Oh," he said, as if knowing what I was about to say before I said it.

"It's just, well, Coach, with all due respect, I need to *play*." I watched his face closely for a response or an objection. Seeing neither forthcoming, I continued. "I just can't stand working this hard and knowing I'm never going to get a chance to do what I can do out there. First, because we're mostly a ground game, and second, because we have *five* good receivers. Even if we throw the ball, the chances of me getting to be the one to catch it are looking pretty slim."

I waited. Part of me was hoping for some kind of objection. None came.

"I'm just, well, I feel like I'm wasting my time — and my chance to play — by staying here." There. I said it. "I'm also afraid that if I don't move on now, I may lose my chance to play anywhere, or even worse than that, I might not ever play again." I paused, taking a deep breath to say the words I never in the world imagined I'd say. "So, Coach, I'd like to make your decision about who to cut a little bit easier."

Then I handed him my letter of resignation.

Coach looked at me, then at the paper, then back at me. I was actually relieved to see a sadness crossing his face that told me he understood — and also that he hated to see me go. "Well, son, I'm disappointed, of course," he said. "I hope you understand that I recognize and appreciate that you can catch the ball as good as anyone on this team. But you're right. We're a running team, and when we *do* throw the ball we're going to be obligated to play our established receivers first. I think, with time, you could do well here, but I do understand if you need to move on to see if you can get more playing time somewhere else."

"Thank you, Coach," I said. "I really gave it everything I had. I am deeply honored for the opportunity. I wish you and the team all the best, sir."

"Thank you, Tommy, for your honesty and for all the work you've put in here," Coach Grant said. "You're quite a talent, and wherever you go, I hope you stick to those ideals and find the right fit for what you bring to the game."

And just like that, the Vikings placed me on waivers the next morning, which meant that any team that wanted me could pick me up for $100.

I left Coach Grant's office that day feeling an odd combination of sadness and elation. It's always hard when things don't work out — even things you're not that crazy about. But sometimes it's only in letting one dream go that you can catch another one.

And, while the training camp experience with the Vikings will go down as one of the most difficult times of my life, mentally, physically, and emotionally, I wouldn't take anything for it in all the world. What doesn't kill you *does* make you stronger, and I was proud of the battle scars I had to prove it. I thought a lot of both the Viking organization and Coach Grant. He is a great coach and I respected him very much. I just didn't quite fit into their plans.

So with my weight up to 185, my speed better than it had ever been, and the fire in my belly to play pro football — if, that is, someone would have me — I opened myself up to a new opportunity. And I knew one thing for sure. If a team that needed a receiver called me that very night, I would go immediately, as long as it was a team committed to passing the ball. A lot.

"He did it with the odds stacked against him," the Ruston Leader reported in a small article titled "The Offer" that ran in its August 20, 1970 edition:

"His coaches in high school said he was too small to play regularly. He got only one college scholarship offer because coaches said he was too small and didn't have enough speed to be a successful wide receiver.

"But he made it because he had tremendous desire and they tagged him "Mr. Dedication" at Tech. He had a way of getting in the open and making the hard catches look easy and did it in a graceful manner.

"It was in that same graceful manner that Tommy Spinks bowed out Wednesday night, disappointed he didn't quite make it with the Vikings, but satisfied, too, that he gave it all he had. He went out the same way he played football — like a winner."

CHAPTER 27

"Look Barb, she has OUR dimple." Terry said when he saw our new baby girl for the very first time.

It was Christmas, and the end of 1970, when Terry just happened to be home in Shreveport when Barbara went into labor with our second child. "We're already at the hospital!" I had hollered into the phone when I called him. The baby would be here any minute, and in record time, Terry walked through the maternity ward door.

We hugged and Barbara, still laughing at his dimple remark, motioned for me to hand our baby to Terry.

"She has something else of yours, Terry," Barbara said, wiping her eyes. "I want you to meet your namesake, Teri Ann Spinks."

"Don't drop her!" I said when I saw the look of complete shock on his face.

Terry took a step back and held Teri close. Barbara and I watched the two of them in silent awe; we knew we were seeing an instant bond take shape between souls.

Terry held our little one up close to his face and kissed her tiny forehead. "Welcome to the world little Teri," he whispered.

Walking down to the hospital cafeteria to get a Coke, Terry and I had a chance to get caught up on all the football news.

"What a year, Spinks," he said as we jabbed the buttons of the vending machines and found a place to sit for a while to give Barbara a chance to rest.

"Can you believe just a year and a half ago we were still at Tech wondering what was going to happen next?" I asked.

"Seems like another lifetime," he said. "So tell me, what are you doing with yourself since you broke the Vikings' hearts?"

I laughed. "I think they got over it," I said. "Like . . . immediately." I paused. "Oh, you know," I said. "We've been getting ready for the baby. I've been working out a lot to keep myself in shape and ready to go." I took a swig of my Coke. "And I'm just about to finish school — starting my student teaching this spring."

"Really? Teaching? Spinks? What?" Terry seemed unable to speak of this new life path in more than one-word, rapid-fire sentences. This was a lot of shock to pack into one afternoon.

"You know . . . just in case," I said. "My degree will be in education so that if I don't get another chance to play football I can probably get a coaching job somewhere." I paused. "Or I may do that *aftah* football," I added, mimicking my mother's Southern drawl. "'Cause Terreh, you *know* . . . football is not fo-evah.'"

Terry laughed. "I know that's right," he said. "I've been thinking about that very thing. In the offseason I probably ought to get mine, too. Makes the parents happy, doncha know."

So there we were, sitting in a cafeteria, drinking a couple of Cokes and talking about the mundane. No football stats, trades, or speculations — and there wasn't a football in either of our hands — or within reach. Just 18 months and we were already very different men, and the dream we used to share had taken each of us onto a different path, a path that for each of us revealed the realities that tend to ride along with most dreams. In many ways, playing in the NFL, like so many faraway and magical dreams, wasn't nearly the mountaintop experience we had expected and believed it would be. Sometimes the climb up the mountain can be much more beautiful than the view from the top. Some dreams are just that way.

• • •

"So now what?" seemed to be the question on everyone's lips when I left the Vikings. Anyone who knew me very well was certain I had a plan.

The trouble was, I really didn't. I just knew that Vikings deal was the train to nowhere — and I wanted off.

The Ruston Leader was abuzz with speculation about which NFL team might pick me up, and the Steelers had been mentioned more than once. But even Terry said it was pretty doubtful that the Steelers could pick me up because they already had so many great receivers.

So all right then, I told myself. Time to move on and find a new dream. In all my life I have known three things you have to do for sure when it comes to dreams:

You have to dream big. Really big.

You have to put everything you have and everything you are into trying to achieve your dreams.

You have to know when to let go gracefully, to sit back and wait and see what God wants to do with you next — with this dream or sometimes, a whole new one. That's where the faith part comes in. And "faith" is not just some namby pamby church word. It's real. It's gritty. And sometimes, it hurts like hell.

So that's where I was. If I couldn't play football — and I mean *play* football — it must be time to do something else.

I was starting my student teaching in just a few weeks. Once that was done, I'd see which jobs opened up and wait for something — anything — to somehow put the light back on in my eyes.

Meanwhile, I'd also keep working out and hoping some football team needed a receiver who would work his guts out to put points on the board for them. My faith that this "something" was out there for me was strong. It was just hard for my ego to step aside and wait to see what that "something" was.

• • •

All the way to T.L. James I replayed my earlier conversation with Coach Chuck Knolls over and over in my head. While the words he used were a complete and soundless blur, what I *do* remember was racing to the car, and then running several lights on the way to tell Barbara, "I just got the call and we are headed to Pittsburgh!"

I was hoping to come up with something quite a bit more suave, but meanwhile, my mind churned, *What changed? What happened to the "no room at the inn" story Terry related? Did he talk Mr. Rooney into taking a chance on me? Did someone ask for a trade?*

I didn't know how or why it happened, nor did I care. I was on the way to becoming a Pittsburgh Steeler. Back in the game, back in the NFL, and best of all, back to playing football with Bradshaw. I was shaking like a leaf and giggling like a maniac as I drove through town to tell my wife who had never, not for one minute, all the way up until yesterday afternoon, stopped believing that something good was about to happen. I couldn't wait to tell her she was right.

I roared into the parking lot that stretched the whole way across the annex attached to the main building. Just inside those glass doors, I could see Barbara sitting at her desk.

Dang! I thought as I put the car in park. I should have brought flowers. Or better yet, put on that Steelers hat Terry gave me for Christmas.

I looked in the window again. No time now, she already saw me.

She waved. I waved back. *Be cool,* I told myself as I walked up the sidewalk and in through the double glass door. But no matter how hard I tried, I just couldn't manage to wipe the goofy smile off my face.

Then, just as I walked in the door, Glen Echols, Barbara's boss, and the two lab techs from down the hall who must have seen me drive up, met me in the lobby. *Well, this really wasn't how this was supposed to go*, I thought.

Mr. Echols was a great guy and a great boss. In fact, Barbara always said it was his marriage to his wife, Jonnie, and their devotion to their three girls that inspired her about how marriage and families should be. "They're all just so . . . so . . . sweet with each other," she'd say, all dreamy eyed. So in truth, I guess you could say Glen Echols inspired me, too.

The other thing about Glen Echols I especially liked was his love of football. He was a numbers guy, so he knew every stat from every year and every comparison on every player and every team — pro and college. The amount of information about football alone inside that guy's head was astounding to me. If you wanted to know someone's numbers, Mr. Echols was the guy to call. And he and his two best lab guys always loved to talk football with me for as long as I'd stand there. I felt like such a celebrity every time I entered that place, and Barbara always got a kick out of how they fussed and fawned over me. "You're gonna get the bighead if you stay around here too much," she'd say as she ushered me out the door and back toward the car.

But not today. Today I had some serious business with my wife. And just as I was pondering how to work around the sudden crowd now standing between Barbara and me those words had just popped right out of my mouth. Some things just can't stay put.

After that, everything was yet another blur that started with Barbara squealing and jumping up from her desk and into my arms, still shrieking and jumping up and down.

Mr. Echols got so excited that he wrapped his arms around both of us — and then the two lab guys joined in. It was just one big group-hug love-in, right there in the lobby of T.L. James.

"Tell me!" Barbara said as soon as she could get some air. "Tell me *everything*!"

"Well," I said, trying once again to remember exactly what Coach Knoll had said. "He wanted to know if I was interested in playing for the Steelers. Then he asked if I was available to go to a rookie training camp in May before the real one starts in July . . ." I paused, grinning ear to ear. "So then I told him that, why, yes, I believe I was available to attend both of those camps."

The next thing I knew Mr. Echols was pounding me on the back and handing Barbara her purse. "You two get out of here and go celebrate!" he said, still breathless. "And Barbara, you take the rest of the day off. I don't want to see you back in here until *tomorrow*. This is big. Really, really big. Congratulations, you two. Tommy! . . . You did it!"

I'll never forget the sight in my rearview mirror as we drove away — Mr. Echols and those two lab techs still standing in the window, watching us drive away, gesturing as they talked and laughed and speculated, I supposed, on stats to come.

Next we drove over to Mom and Dad's house so we could tell them the news in person. My mother knew something was up the moment she opened the door — I'm sure it was written all over our faces.

"Good lands!" she exclaimed after taking a good look at both of us. "Come in here, you two and tell us what's going on!"

"Mom, I made it," I said, getting choked up as it hit me, maybe for the very first time. I had been so focused on getting to Barbara, telling her, and then, after being distracted by Mr. Echols and his crew, we had sped over here to tell Mom and Dad. Suddenly, the full impact of my news came home to roost.

"Made what, sweetie?" she said, sitting down beside me on the sofa.

"Pittsburgh called," I managed to say. "They want me."

They want me. What a powerful set of words. What magic lies within them.

Almost immediately, my dad burst out into joyful laughter, mouth wide open, slapping his knee. "That's just great Son," he said between guffaws. "I always knew you had it in ya — I just didn't know how long it was goin' ta take those knuckleheads to realize it!"

As the full impact of the news settled into her brain, Mom began jumping around, hugging first Dad, then Barbara, and then, finally, me. And when she started hugging me I didn't think she was ever going to stop.

"Grace!" Dad finally said, "The boy can't breathe!"

By that time my mom was blubbering and thanking Jesus and searching through her apron pockets for a Kleenex. "My boys . . . My boys . . . My boys . . . back together," was all she could say.

Then, just as suddenly, she stopped crying and got right down to business. "Otis!" she said. "I'm gonna need a fur coat!"

Dad looked at her for a full 30 seconds before bursting out into laughter again. Wiping his own eyes, he looked at Barbara and then at me. "Don't worry, kids," he said, grabbing my mother and pulling her into something between a hug and a headlock. "We're not moving."

From that moment everything was indeed a blur. I finished my student teaching "just in case" and mostly to appease my mom, who by now was rescinding her "football is not fo-evah" edict, but nonetheless I'd have that piece of paper for my wall.

Refrains of "The boys are going to be back together!" were ricocheting through Ruston and everywhere we went people wanted to talk, to hear the story again, and to share their excitement and predictions. It was a sweet time that we never wanted to end, and even up until I left for the rookie training camp in May, we were the talk of the town.

Terry had come back to Shreveport, and we got in all the workouts we could, and by teaching me the patterns and letting me practice what he called "the real deal, Spinks," I had no worries that once I got to Pittsburgh I'd be in fine form to embrace this new opportunity.

So much would be different in Pittsburgh. I'd be catching once again for my best buddy and someone with whom throwing and catching the football was like breathing. I was wanted, appreciated, and best of all, joining a passing offense.

"Dear Barbara," I wrote after my first few days at training camp, which was located just about an hour east of the city at Saint Vincent College in Latrobe, "I cannot tell you the difference between this training camp experience and what I went through in Minnesota. For one thing, it is absolutely gorgeous here — the camp looks out over these beautiful, green, rolling hills. They say you can see all of west-central Pennsylvania from here on a clear morning. But I'm kind of partial to the foggy ones. The mist and the fog makes everything so green and . . . like there's magic in the air. I'm telling' ya, baby, I almost feel like I'm in Scotland or somewhere like that."

This was to be Coach Knoll's second season, along with Mean Joe Green and Mel Blount, both drafted the year before Terry. Even then, we could feel the excitement building, as if we could almost sense that the foundation of an NFL football dynasty was being formed.

Best of all, it would be my buddy, Terry, who would lead them — right into the center of this phenomenal era of NFL history. This team — and its future editions which would eventually welcome Jack Ham, Franco Harris and finally, in 1974, the incredible feat of selecting four future Hall of Famers in one draft year, Lynn Swann, Jack Lambert, John Stallworth, and Mike Webster — would go on to make the playoffs for eight seasons and become the only team in NFL history to win four Super Bowls in six years. We of course had no way of knowing any of this back then, but I think every single one of us lucky enough to be there in that 1971 Steelers training camp could feel that something exciting was beginning for this team.

Now don't get me wrong. The work was still hard, the guys were still tough, and there was still a seriously brutal element to it that mirrored every bit of that "whole nutha level of play" I first experienced in Minnesota.

But everything felt different, somehow. I don't know if it was because Terry was there and I was finally being given the opportunity to show what I could really do — or if I was relaxed and having fun and better able to do more of what I was capable of. Either way, I felt myself thriving in this new world, and I had to pinch myself every once in a while to believe my good fortune.

"For another thing," my first letter home to Barb went on to say, "I get a whole different vibe here. I feel like people care about me. I met Mr. Rooney one time, and already I feel like I know him and he knows me."

Was this all Terry's doing? I wondered. I'll never know — he of course denied having anything to do with my signing — but I'll always believe my time with the Steelers happened because of him.

When Barbara and the girls moved up to Pittsburgh in August, everything was still good, and we were gearing up for our pre-season opener. We settled our family in an apartment complex in Squirrel Hill that was full of Steelers and also some famous Pittsburgh Penguins hockey players.

Terry lived in the apartment directly above us, and right next door lived Carol and Dave Burrows and their son, Brett. Dave was a famous Canadian pro hockey player with the Penguins, and our families became fast friends.

Real life for us was settling in beyond any dream even I could have imagined on my wildest of days — and I thanked God and Mr. Rooney every single day for giving me this beautiful second chance to play NFL football.

• • •

"Spinks, I think you have some of the best hands I've ever seen in football," a voice from the sidelines said quietly when I came in for some water. I looked up to see Mr. Art Rooney, the owner of the Pittsburgh Steelers, looking directly at me.

"Thank you, sir," was all I could manage to say. Because of Terry's belief in me, Mr. Rooney had agreed to give me this shot at playing with the Steelers. And now, to hear those words directly from someone who would turn out to be one of the greatest men I ever met in my whole life, it was something like hearing the voice of God paying me a direct compliment.

In every single respect, that Pittsburgh summer training camp allowed Terry and me to return to the mountaintop one last time. Everything we had ever dreamed of as football players and best friends aligned perfectly from day one. We were both better, faster, and stronger than we ever were at Tech. At long last, Terry and I were back on the field together, doing what we did best.

Just as I was able to read Terry's mind on every play, he was able to trust that I would be there, as I always had been, wherever he threw that ball. We were having tremendous, out-of-our-mind practices and increasingly often, playing ahead of the veterans. Pretty soon the focus began to shift, and before we knew it, it was Bradshaw to Spinks again, just as it had been since we were kids.

In the Steelers' first exhibition game of 1971, we learned that we were going to be starters, together again as a duo on the football field — at the level of play from our boyhood dreams.

As the day of the game dawned, we knew that the sun was not the only thing that would be shining. We were on fire. Terry was throwing those bullets and I was catching them with ease. In my mind's eye, I could imagine this as a regular season game — or even a playoff, with Barbara at home watching us on television with our little girls, squealing and jumping up with excitement with every catch. A sizeable crowd of those die-hard Steelers fans had gathered to watch, eager for a first glimpse of the season to come.

In one of the final plays of the scrimmage, Terry ran back, held the ball for a second and then spotted me heading long. He unleashed the longest ball he had ever thrown, and with three opposing players on me, all reaching up at the same time, the ball landed exactly where Terry intended to put it, right into my outstretched hands.

I caught that ball, twisted myself loose, and I ran. I ran harder and faster than I had ever run in my entire life, across the goal line and for the touchdown I will never forget.

As I made a dazed half circle in the end zone with the ball still in my hand, Terry was already in the end zone. We jumped up, embraced, and pounded each other's helmets as if we had just won the Super Bowl.

At that moment we were 13 again, best friends playing backyard football in the Louisiana sunshine.

And this time, the roar from the crowd was real.

EXTRO

Returning now to that marble bench on the front lawn with Kimberly, I smile. Watching and listening to the laughter, taunts, and silliness of our family Fourth of July football games always opens my mind and heart to a world of beautiful memories.

Dreams chased, dreams caught, and new ones now budding in the hearts of everyone with my blood in their veins. I never could have imagined all this, back when football was my only dream. Other dreams are quieter. They sneak right up on you and come true before you even realize they're there. But they were in you, somewhere, all along, waiting to become your greatest blessings.

My gaze sweeps to the right, where Barbara has our youngest grandchild propped on her lap. She is still so beautiful, and even from here I can hear that laugh that I made it my business to elicit on a daily basis. Even after all these years, Barbara's laughter still fills my heart with so much love I can barely contain it.

My gratitude to God for this family, this life, this story, and all the people He placed in it is overwhelming. I am perhaps most grateful to God for making me a Dream Catcher.

EPILOGUE

Shortly after that brief moment of glory in his first pre-season game with the Steelers, Tommy Spinks suffered a career-ending knee injury during practice. After a lengthy and difficult rehab and several surgeries, he returned briefly to pro football, playing with the New York Stars in the WFL, but the damage to his knee was too great to continue.

So Tommy hung up his cleats and entered the business world with the same bravado that served him well on the gridiron as entrepreneur, publisher, and investor in the dreams of others. He weathered the many ups and downs that ride naturally along with self-made success, and in the process, touched countless lives with his unique gift for nurturing, studying, and encouraging the dreams of others.

He and Barbara had two more children, Jason and Lindsay, and later in life had fourteen grandchildren. The Spinks family dynasty kept each other close — and their own dreams alive — serving as inspiration and model for anyone who knew them. With laughter and love that always flows freely in any Spinks home, the fierceness of their devotion to one another is a force to be reckoned with. The bond Tommy so loved from his glory days on the football field is alive and well in every generation of his entire family.

• • •

Tommy Spinks left this world on August 26, 2007, surrounded by his family at his home in Arlington, Texas. With Barbara by his side and his children gathered around, holding on to one another for the strength to get through what was about to come, Tommy looked over at Barbara and tried to squeeze her hand. He looked deeply into those beautiful eyes for what would be the last time and said, "You are my forever love."

After slipping in and out of consciousness all that August afternoon, Tommy opened his eyes wide, and a faint smile crept across his face. "Mom?" he said.

Barbara, realizing that this was Tommy's final moment on earth, leaned down to touch her cheek to his. "Who do you see, Tommy?" she whispered, knowing he must have caught a glimpse of his beloved mother waiting for him on the other side.

"I see all of them," he said, still smiling.

And then he was gone.

• • •

In his four seasons at Tech he caught more passes (182) for more yards (2968) than any other college football player in Louisiana's history, including at least one interception in 29 of the 30 Bulldog games over his final three years.

Ironically, Tommy's obituary made no mention of his football career. While news clippings from The Ruston Daily Leader and Shreveport Times, along with personal interviews bore out the "Glory Days" of his football journey as Terry Bradshaw's favorite receiver, Tommy's brief time in the NFL left no footprint.

What did leave an indelible mark on the hearts of all who knew him was how these football memories he shared had very little to do with the game of football and much more to do with the game of life.

Summed up well by CNBC.com in its May 28, 2008 article, "Millionaire Blueprints: 3 Industries, 3 Fortunes, No Experience," Tommy's entrepreneurial career mirrored the tone of his football press clippings with accolades beyond all expectations:

> *"In 1978, at age 30, and with no prior knowledge of the publishing industry, Tom started a newspaper on the Steelers called The Pittsburgh Steelers Weekly with a college friend, Bennie Thornell. Within two years, they were also publishing The Denver Broncos Weekly, The New Orleans Saints Weekly,*

The University of Pittsburgh Panthers Weekly, The West Virginia Mountaineers Weekly and The University of Arkansas Razorbacks Weekly. All of these papers were eventually sold to one buyer.

In 1985, without any prior knowledge of the accounting industry, Tom started a company called National Business Accounting Associates. Within three years, he had over 2,000 accountants all over the country as clients, and he taught them how to secure new business. This business was also sold to a national firm in 1992.

In 1993, with only eight months of experience as a distributor in the multi-level marketing (MLM) industry, Tom started his own company. Within five years, he had more than 85,000 distributors in over 100 countries. That company was sold in 2002.

In 2004, following this string of successes, and with no prior experience or knowledge of the consumer magazine industry, Tom put his passion for fueling the dreams of others to work by developing and publishing Millionaire Blueprints Magazine, a publication devoted to helping aspiring entrepreneurs learn from the most successful business leaders throughout the country. After negotiating a deal with Time Warner Magazines for the launch, Tom put stories, resources and inspiration gleaned from America's top entrepreneurs into the hands of anyone with an entrepreneurial dream and a desire to make it come true. Newsgroup classified Millionaire Blueprints as one of its most successful launches in its history and the fastest growing magazine in the country at that time."

AFTERWORD

Six days before he lost his battle with cancer, Tommy asked his oldest daughter, Kimberly, "Can you help me write one more thing?"

"Sure," she replied. They had just finished writing a business book to be a spinoff from *Millionaire Blueprints*, the national magazine they had launched together three years before. Uncertain what this might be, reluctant to hear it, and yet feeling its importance hanging heavy in the air, Kimberly got a clean sheet of paper and waited for her dad to summon enough strength to speak.

Terry,

If you are reading this message it means I lost my battle with cancer, but I consider myself the lucky one. I won't have to see that big ole' ugly face of yours ever again.

I want you to know something. I am proud of you. I've been proud of you since we were kids. I've watched you lead on the field, when the odds and fans were against you. I've watched you lead your family when you were being pulled in many different directions. I've watched you lead people when opening yourself up meant taking jabs from strangers.

I am thankful for you. You were the reason I loved football. As I aged I realized that I just loved being your best friend. Your dreams became my dreams and what a blast we had working to make them come true. I don't know why things turned out the way they did for me but I don't have any regrets. Those years shaped who I became.

In those first years after my football days were over, I had to find my own way through life and it was scary at times. I appreciate that you were there to help me by using your name and your talents.

I love you, Bradshaw. My memories with you are full of so much stinkin' fun and laughter. Our childhood together was the kind of stuff that storybooks are made of. Thanks for the memories.

Take care of yourself bud.

Until we meet again,

Tommy

ABOUT THE AUTHORS

Melinda Folse is author of *Riding Through Thick & Thin*, *The Smart Woman's Guide to Midlife Horses*, *Grandmaster: A Story of Struggle, Triumph, and Taekwondo*, and Clinton Anderson's *Lessons Well Learned.* While she writes on a variety of topics and has a penchant for telling stories that inspire, motivate, and evoke connection, what uniquely qualifies Melinda to write this book is her well-honed ability to carry the voice and vision of Tom Spinks into the stories he wanted to tell. As Senior Writer for Spinks *Millionaire Blueprints* magazine, Melinda learned to capture Tom Spinks' trademark wit, wry encouragement, and gentle directness that have inspired countless entrepreneurs to follow their dreams.

Kimberly Spinks Burleson and **Teri Spinks Netterville**, shared the advantage of growing up with Tommy Spinks as their father. They also grew up knowing and loving Terry Bradshaw and hearing the many stories of the friendship now captured within the pages of *Dream Catcher*.

Teri (who was named after Terry Bradshaw) is a well-known humorist in Shreveport, Louisiana, who is often described as a "modern-day Erma Bombeck." She writes a regular column in *LOLA*, the popular Louisiana Ladies Lifestyle magazine, and co-hosts "American Mamas with Teri Netterville and Denise Arthur" on *American Ground Radio*, a nightly show on KEEL 710 AM News Radio in Shreveport, LA. Teri's book, *When I'm Dead and In My Coffin Somebody Better Love Me Enough to Tweeze My Chin*, written at the prompting of her local fan base, is now in its third printing and available in boutique stores throughout the Shreveport and Bossier City areas.

Kimberly served as her father's right-hand as Managing Editor of Time Warner's *Millionaire Blueprints* magazine, which was a later-in-life dream come true for Tom Spinks. Kimberly was also creator of *Millionaire Blueprints Teen*, *Millionaire Blueprints JR*, and the anthology she co-edited with her dad, *Prepare to Be a Millionaire*. She has made promotional appearances multiple times on MSNBC's *The Big Idea with Donny Deutch*, and other national and local talk shows.

Dream Catcher is a story the entire Spinks family is excited to share.

ACKNOWLEDGEMENTS

From Kimberly Spinks Burleson

I would like to express my gratitude to my husband, Michael, the love of my life. Thank you, Michael, for always being so encouraging and motivating. You have believed in me far more than I ever believed in myself. I can't imagine life without you and our family. To the ones I am in complete awe of, my children, Stone, Sunny, and Shane, there are simply no words to express my love and devotion to each of you. You are the greatest blessings in my life.

Thank you to my mom, Barbara Ann, sisters, Lindsay and Teri, and brother, Jason, and my aunt, Betty Carol Spinks Bales, for filling in the blanks where Dad left off.

Lastly, thank you to my dad. Thank you for watching over me and talking to me in my dreams. You were an amazing father, so amazing in fact, that I still feel your love and constant encouragement. I miss everything about you, especially hearing your laugh. I hope you are proud and happy with the way we gave Terry your message.

From Teri Spinks Netterville

I thank my husband, Kevin. You are my greatest journey. I love you. I want to thank my children, Steele, Summer, and Slade for simply being mine. You three have given me my greatest purpose in this life. I am so proud to be your mom!

I thank my mom, Barbara, for instilling in me a deep sense of devotion and loyalty to those I hold dear to my heart. I thank my younger sister, Lindsay. If ever there were a soul whom I wish I could emulate, it would be you. To my brother, Jason, you have always been very protective and fiercely loyal to our family. My sister and lifetime best friend, Kimberly, you are the absolute rock of our family.

And finally, I wish to thank my dad, Tommy Spinks. If ever there was a soul on this earth who understood what it meant to love others as yourself, it was my father. He was the one who taught me, by example, that kindness and fairness always lead to greatness; that celebrating another's success as if it were your own is one of life's sweetest joys. Ultimately, Dad taught us that we each have a grand purpose for this world.

From Melinda Folse

Even with as many words as I have at my disposal after all these years of writing for a living, none are adequate to express my gratitude to the Spinks family for the honor of helping them tell this beautiful story. As former head writer for the *Millionaire Blueprints* magazine that Tom literally dreamed into being, I had the privilege and delight of working closely with Tom, Kimberly, Teri, and Lindsay and getting to know this sweet family. I can personally attest to the dream-catching legacy of Tommy Spinks and his unique gift for inspiring others to do the same. With Tom as an employer, mentor, and friend, I experienced firsthand how putting your whole heart into something, and then doing everything within your power (and sometimes beyond), can bring even the most outlandish dreams into being. As the extended Spinks family continues to model this powerful brand of love, commitment, and tenacity, it is *my* dream that telling this story will inspire dream catching in all the lives it touches.

CPSIA information can be obtained
at www.ICGtesting.com
Printed in the USA
BVHW071732031218
534641BV00013B/880/P

9 780982 696040